The Holy Spirit in Today's World

T0204289

The Holy Spirit in Today's World

by

W. A. CRISWELL, Ph.D., D.D.
Pastor of the First Baptist Church
Dallas, Texas

ZONDERVAN
PUBLISHING HOUSE OF THE ZONDERVAN CORPORATION
GRAND RAPIDS, MICHIGAN 49506

THE HOLY SPIRIT IN TODAY'S WORLD

Copyright © 1966 by Zondervan Publishing House
All Rights Reserved
Second Edition

Printed in the United States of America

Fourteenth printing   1979
ISBN o-310-22852-2

Library of Congress Catalog Card Number: 66-29826

Dedication

to

DEACON AND MRS. JIM CANTRELL,
JEWELS OF GOD

(he a "gem" and she a "jewel")
who adorn the diadem of our Lord,
and whose encouraging philanthropies
made possible the publication of this book.

Foreword

During the eighteen years I was preaching through the Bible, it became an earnest prayer of my heart that I could study at great length the work of the Holy Spirit in the world today. The study first led to a careful examination of the inspiration and the writing of the Holy Scriptures. These messages were published by one of the faithful deacons in our church, Jim Ezell, under the title, *The Bible for Today's World*. Beyond any dream of my soul, God has greatly blessed that book and is still increasingly blessing it.

It was some time after the delivery of the messages on the Bible before I began the series on the Holy Spirit Himself. I fell into great difficulty in the study. It seems that there are as many interpretations of the work of the Holy Spirit as there are theologians. The modern charismatic movement especially bewildered me. The extravagant claims of some of these sincere people drove me to my knees in searching the Scriptures and the mind and purpose of the Lord. At long last I was ready to deliver what is, to me, the truth of God. I found rest and peace in my soul concerning these doctrines over which I had agonized so long.

Shortly after I began the preaching of the sermons, a deacon in our church, Jim Cantrell, who is also one of the leaders in our denomination, came to visit me. He emphatically said: "Pastor, these sermons must be published. You keep studying and praying and preaching, and I will provide the money for their publication." Arrangements were so made with the Zondervan Publishing House and the preparation of manuscripts began. It was agreed that the new book would be a companion volume to *The Bible for Today's World,* and would be entitled *The Holy Spirit in Today's World*. There are ten chapters in the first book. There were to be ten chapters in the second book.

However, as I continued to study and to preach, the messages that burned in my soul multiplied. They grew so extensively that they far outreached the boundaries of an ordinary book. What could I do to shorten the volume and yet present the full study? I decided to choose the messages that carried the heart of the revelation and to write them out after I preached them, presenting just the main points of the doctrine. This I have done. For each word written, a thousand other words could have been added (and in some cases in the pulpit ministry were!).

Thank you, Deacon and Mrs. Jim Cantrell, for your abounding kindnesses to me. Thank you, Miss Johnye Causbie (an associate in Mr. Cantrell's office), for your priceless help in typing the manuscripts. Thank you, Miss Olive Carter, for helping Miss Causbie check on my grammatical constructions. Thank you, dear people, who prayed and listened to these messages as though they had been spoken by an oracle of God. It takes two to make a sermon; someone has to preach but someone also has to pray and to listen.

It is our prayer that God will use this book, the fruit of so intense a study, to help the thousands of Christian people who wrestle with the doctrine of the Holy Spirit. There are so many conflicting opinions. There are so many crosscurrents and extravagant excesses. But enough of the introduction. Let us begin with the study, and may the dear Lord open our hearts to His truth as He has revealed Himself in His holy Word.

W. A. CRISWELL

Pastor's Study
First Baptist Church
Dallas, Texas
1966

Contents

Chapter 1

The History of the Doctrine of the Holy Spirit
(The Days of the Apostolic Fathers)

[handwritten: Spirit of God]

John 14

16 And I will pray the Father, and he shall give you another Comforter, that he may abide with you for ever;

17 Even the Spirit of truth; whom the world cannot receive, because it seeth him not, neither knoweth him: but ye
know him; for he dwelleth with you, and shall be in you.

If the Lord Jesus, through the promise of the Father, has
given us the Holy Paraclete that He may abide with us forever, then He is present now and has been through the centuries. This would mean that the Holy Spirit has been with
us in this earth for almost 2000 years and has a history that
can be followed through the ages. It will be pre-eminently
profitable for us to follow the story of the doctrine of the
Holy Spirit as men have sought to define His work and
presence throughout these many years.

The Trinity in Early Christian Doxologies

The history of the Holy Spirit since Pentecost is a sea of
many waves. The development of the doctrine touches every
point of theology: the Trinity, the person of Christ, the inspiration of the Scriptures, the doctrines of grace and salvation, the heavenly gifts to the believer, and every other discussion in systematic theology. When we study the history
of the doctrine of the Third Person of the Trinity, we study
the whole summary of the revelation and presence of God.

We first follow the doctrine of the Holy Spirit in the age
of the apostles and the apostolic Fathers. There never was
a time when the early Christian disciples did not confess the
deity and the saving work of all three Persons of the God-

13

[handwritten: Holy Spirit is intercessor between God and us. Doxology praise to God.]

head. Doxologies to the Father, to the Son, and to the Holy Spirit were in use everywhere in the early churches. This is clearly seen in II Corinthians 13:14: "The grace of the Lord Jesus Christ, and the love of God, and the communion of the Holy Ghost, be with you all. Amen." The naming of the Trinity is also seen in Revelation 1:4, 5: "John to the seven churches which are in Asia: Grace be unto you, and peace, from him which is, and which was, and which is to come; and from the seven Spirits which are before his throne; And from Jesus Christ, who is the faithful witness, and the first begotten of the dead."

A doxology of the triune God is also illustrated in the encyclical of the church of Smyrna recounting the martyrdom of Polycarp in about A.D. 155. The letter closes with the testimony of the martyred pastor as he speaks in his closing words of adoration: "For this, and for all things, I praise Thee. I bless Thee. I glorify Thee, with the eternal and heavenly Jesus Christ, Thy beloved Son, with whom, to Thee *and to the Holy Ghost,* be glory both now and through all ages to come."

A like doxology is found in the closing words of Julius Africanus. He was one of the most learned ecclesiastical writers of all times. Born in Libya, Africa, about A.D. 160, he settled in Emmaus, Palestine, and there gave himself to the study of the history of the Christian faith. He wrote five books recounting that study, which he entitled *The Chronology.* In the fifth and last book occurs this beautiful doxology: "We render thanks to Him who gave our Lord Jesus Christ to be a Saviour, to whom, *with the Holy Ghost,* be glory and majesty forever." The early Fathers had no occasion to debate, defend, or define the deity and the personality of the Holy Spirit. They accepted, as an elementary truth, the Godhead as it is expressed in the baptismal formula of Matthew 28:19: "Go ye therefore, and teach all nations, baptizing them in the name of the Father, and of the Son, and of the Holy Ghost . . . ."

In connection with the Third Person of the adorable Trinity, the early Fathers especially exalted the supernatural

Deity - love + god

work of the Holy Spirit in the inspiration of the Scriptures. They carried forward the spirit of the Apostle Paul when he wrote II Timothy 3:16: "All scripture is given by inspiration of God, and is profitable for doctrine, for reproof, for correction, for instruction in righteousness." The work of the Holy Spirit in inspiring the sacred Scriptures is seen in the writings of Justin Martyr. In speaking of the sacred writers, in both the Old and the New Testaments, as stringed instruments, he says: "Their task was but to surrender themselves wholly to the working of the Spirit of God, that the divine plectrum descending from heaven might make use of holy men as of a harp or a lyre, in order to reveal to us the knowledge of divine and heavenly things."

Irenaeus describes the Scriptures in these words: "They are spoken by the word of God and His Spirit; while we in the degree in which we live are inferior, and stand at the greatest distance from the Word of God and His Spirit, and are in need of the knowledge of His mysteries." And again: "The Logos has given us a fourfold gospel which is held together by one Spirit."

Reading the writings of the Greek Fathers, one cannot but be impressed with their marked peculiarity in omitting the names of the human writers of Holy Scripture and naming the Holy Spirit as the real author. The importance and the value of all parts of the Bible as the productions and the words of the Holy Spirit are constantly asserted. They so often use the introductory phrase, "As the Holy Ghost sayeth." For example, Origen writes: "We can by no means say of the writings of the Holy Ghost that there is anything superfluous or idle in them, although many a thing may appear dark to many."

The Development of the Creeds of Christendom

The apostolic doctrine of the Holy Spirit can be easily traced in the story of the creeds of Christendom. The creeds came into being because of the violent attacks of heretics against the true faith. The creed of the early churches was an attempt to say in concise and succinct form the heart of

feb 3 paw [handwritten margin note]

1st article of faith I Timothy 3-16
The Bible is our (creed) (doctrine) in the Baptist Church [handwritten]

the true doctrine of the Christian disciple. The first creed became the pattern for all the succeeding statements of belief. It is called the Apostles' Creed. Within a generation or two from the days of Peter, Paul, and John, a creed was taught the catechumens, the purpose of which was to summarize the teachings of the apostles. Some scholars think that the Apostles' Creed can be traced back to the year A.D. 100. Who composed it? No one knows, but it became the pattern of all succeeding statements of faith. The most ancient form of the Apostles' Creed reads like this:

> I believe in God the Father Almighty and in Jesus Christ, His only Son, our Lord, who was *born of the Holy Ghost* and the Virgin Mary, crucified under Pontius Pilate and buried, the third day He rose from the dead. He ascended into heaven, sitteth at the right hand of the Father, thence He shall come to judge the living and the dead.
> *And in the Holy Ghost,* the holy church, the remission of sins, the restoration of the flesh.

As time went on there developed violent attacks against the doctrine of the Trinity, a term, by the way, first used by Tertullian around A.D 200 to describe the Godhead. The heretics began to say that God is not trinitarian but unipersonal. One of the leaders in this attack against the Trinity was an able theologian named Sabellius, a contemporary of Tertullian. He was the forerunner of modern Unitarianism in his denial of the person of the Holy Spirit. It was against Sabellianism that the Church introduced the word "person" to describe the Godhead. Sabellius sought to explain the mystery of deity by a theory of modalism, a trinity of mere manifestation. Father, Son, and Holy Spirit are but different names of the unipersonal God. They are but mere modal distinctions in the Godhead. According to Sabellius, the Holy Spirit became a vague, undefined component operative through successive energies expressed in creation, in redemption, and in regeneration.

Following Sabellius, there arose the greatest heretic of all time, the gifted preacher, theologian, and song writer, Arius. He was in his prime of power and influence around A.D. 300.

He attacked the deity of the Son and the Holy Spirit. He denied their consubstantiality with the Father. He taught that the Son was created by the Father, and the Holy Spirit was created by the Son, making the Holy Spirit the creature of a creature. The violent controversy centered mostly about the deity of the Son. When the Nicaean Council was therefore convened in A.D. 325, presided over by the emperor of the Roman Empire, Constantine, the creed they wrote emphasized primarily the deity of the Son. This famous creed reads as follows:

> We believe in one *God, the Father* Almighty, maker of all things visible and invisible.
> And in *one Lord Jesus Christ,* the Son of God, begotten of the Father, only-begotten, that is, of the substance of the Father, God of God, Light of Light, very God of very God, begotten not made, of one substance with the Father, by whom all things were made, both those in heaven and those on earth; who for us men, and our salvation, came down and was made flesh, and lived as man among men, suffered, and rose the third day, ascended into Heaven, is coming to judge the quick and the dead.
> *And in the Holy Ghost.*

You will notice even in this statement of Christian faith that the Holy Spirit is referred to in just a sentence. But the period following the Council of Nicaea in A.D. 325 was filled with theological turmoil. The Council of Nicaea sought to spell out the deity of the Son of God, but it had failed to seek in words the delineation of the deity of the Holy Spirit. When the heretic, Macdemous, therefore, continued the attack against the person and deity of the Third Person of the Trinity, he drew forth a mighty array of defenders of the faith in Athanasius, Basil, Gregory, Nazianzen, and Gregory Nissen. These learned theologians led in the calling of the Council of Constantinople in A.D. 381 and there the deity of the Holy Spirit was plainly spelled out with the addition of these words to the Nicene Creed:

> We believe in the Holy Ghost, *The Lord and Giver of life, who proceedeth from the Father* (John 15:26), *who with the*

*Father and Son together, is worshipped and glorified, who
spake by the prophets.*

The Rise of Montanism

To me, one of the most remarkable of all developments in
Christian history was the rise of Montanism. The history
books avow that the miraculous, supernatural gifts of the
apostles ceased in their death (cf. *The History of the Doctrine of the Holy Spirit* by George Smeaton, pp. 256-368).
When the apostles died, the marvelous gifts bestowed upon
them also died. The history books say it was but the natural
and expected development that some Christian of piety and
zeal should claim their restoration in his own person. There
arose just such a man in Montanus, a preacher of extravagant opinion and ascetic rigor. He appeared in a village of
Phrygia about A.D. 150 as a prophet, with his two prophetesses, Maximilla and Priscilla. He claimed that the supernatural gifts of the prophets and the apostles were renewed
in him. He claimed for himself and for his two prophetesses
the same powers of the Holy Spirit which had animated the
apostles with their gifts and abilities to receive special revelation from heaven. He came forth with utterances and ecstasies which were to supersede the Holy Scriptures of the
apostles. He said that as the writings of Paul superseded
those of Moses; so his ecstasies and utterances were to supersede those of Paul. So tremendous was this Montanistic
movement that it swept away Tertullian himself in its tide.

Remember, this occurred in about A.D. 150. Polycarp, the
disciple of the Apostle John, was still alive and was pastor
at Smyrna. Papias, the disciple of John, was still alive and
pastor at Hierapolis. Even in their days, the days of the disciples of the apostles, the history books say that the phenomenal, supernatural gifts of the apostles ceased to exist.
There arose, therefore, a tremendous controversy over the
claims of Montanus. Were his utterances Scriptural? Were
his trances visions from heaven? Are the marvelous gifts of
the apostles continued in their successors? Out of the dispute of Montanism the history books say two firm conclu-

sions arose. The first concerned the finality of Scripture. The churches avowed that the Scriptures were closed. There are to be no more Scriptures. They affirmed in no uncertain terms that the ecstatic utterances of Montanus were not Scripture and certainly did not supersede the words of the apostles. They avowed that the work of the Holy Spirit is one of illumination, not a bestowing of new and further revelation. The revelation of Holy Scripture is closed in the spirit of Revelation 22:18, 19: "For I testify unto every man that heareth the words of the prophecy of this book, If any man shall add unto these things, God shall add unto him the plagues that are written in this book: And if any man shall take away from the words of the book of this prophecy, God shall take away his part out of the book of life, and out of the holy city, and from the things which are written in this book." Is the Church to expect any further revelation by prophetic visions? No, said the apostolic churches as against a Joseph Smith, or as against a Mary Baker Glover Patterson Eddy.

The second tremendous avowal that came out of the Montanistic dispute concerned the cessation of miraculous gifts bestowed upon the apostles. Montanus claimed that the early sign-gifts were to continue forever. The churches answered that miraculous gifts were never promised the church as a personal inheritance. After the closing of the canon, and after the death of the apostles, those marvelous powers such as the ability to raise the dead ceased. The work of the Holy Spirit became primarily the work of illuminating the Word of God, regenerating the soul, and forming the life and mind of Christ in the heart of the individual believer. Thus spoke the churches in the conflict that arose over Montanus.

To guide - illuminate - Holy Spirit

Chapter 2

The History of the Doctrine of the Holy Spirit
(The Controversy Concerning Apostolic Miracles)

Acts 19

11 And God wrought special miracles by the hands of Paul:
12 So that from his body were brought unto the sick handkerchiefs or aprons, and the diseases departed from them, and
the evil spirits went out of them.

Before we continue with the remainder of this brief summary of the history of the doctrine of the Holy Spirit, let
me pause to discuss a situation that has arisen over the story
of the rise of Montanism presented in the previous chapter.
Following the history of the early churches, we learned that
with the death of the apostles the churches ceased their ac-
ceptance of inspired Scripture as written by any following
authors. The churches also said that not only had the revelation from heaven, comprising the Holy Scriptures, ceased,
but also that the marvelous apostolic signs wrought by the
apostles also ceased after their death. Now, I did not say
that; the history books record that. There were many marvelous, glorious writings by devout Christian pastors and
theologians after the days of the apostles, but the history
books say that none of these were accepted as Scripture after
the days of the apostles. The ancient books record that the
supernatural phenomena that accompanied the witness of
the apostles also ceased.

What are we talking about when we refer to this ability
of the apostles to do marvelous, extraordinary wonders? We
are referring to things like this: Acts 2:8-11 is a description
of the Aramaic-speaking apostles on the day of Pentecost,
preaching the Gospel of the Son of God in every language

20

represented by those worshipers who had come from every province of the Roman Empire. It was an incomparable phenomenon. I read one time of a group of missionaries who were praying for the gift of languages in order to save them the time and effort to learn the languages of the people to whom they were going to preach the Gospel of Christ. The difference between now and then is found in the lack of answer to that supplication. If a missionary today goes to a foreign tribe he must learn the language through long and constant study. In the second chapter of the Book of Acts, these many languages were miraculously bestowed upon the disciples as they witnessed on that first day of Pentecost.

Another example of the marvelous gifts of the apostles is found in Acts 3:1-10. In this story Simon Peter takes the right hand of a man, lame from his mother's womb, and lifts him up to strength and health in the very sentence in which he names the name of Jesus Christ of Nazareth. In Acts 5:15 the very shadow of Simon Peter falling on the sick who have been placed in the streets heals their ill bodies and raises them up to health. In Acts 9:40 the power of heaven bestowed upon Simon Peter raises Dorcas from the dead. In Acts 12:1-10 the coming of an angel to deliver Simon Peter from prison strikes from his hands the chains that fetter him to the stone wall. Even the great iron door of the prison is made to open of itself and Peter walks free into the streets of the city. In Acts 19:12 handkerchiefs and aprons from the person of the Apostle Paul were taken to the sick and the sick were healed by the touch of these pieces of cloth. Even demons were cast out through the use of these woven instruments of healing. In Acts 20:2-12 Paul raises Eutychus from the dead. These are typical instances of the extraordinary, phenomenal, supernatural, miraculous powers of the apostles to do wonders in the sight of men.

The Attempt to Duplicate Apostolic Miracles

Following the history of the early churches and especially following the life of Montanus in A.D. 150, we learned that these extraordinary miracles ceased and that the Holy Scrip-

tures were ended in their writing. The churches avowed
that there were no more Scriptures to be accepted and that
there were no more apostolic wonders to be seen. They
avowed that no more authentication is needed to the Christian message and that the work of the Holy Spirit is now one
of illumination. Exception has been taken to this message
as though I said that. No, it is not I saying this. I am merely
recounting what I read in history. I am desperately trying
to find the truths of the presence and power and meaning
of the Holy Spirit, and in doing this I am trying to find the
record of the background of the doctrine and work of the
Holy Spirit through these 2000 years. Here is a typical letter
that came to me this week:

> Dear Dr. Criswell:
> I listened to you Sunday morning on television. I did not get
> to attend church due to illness. I feel impressed to write you
> this letter. I do not believe that the miracles of the apostles
> died when the apostles died. The reason I believe in the con-
> tinuation of the marvelous works of the apostles is because
> thousands of people are receiving the gifts of the Holy Spirit
> with the initial sign of speaking in tongues. I know because I
> have experienced it.

How different this is from the raising of Dorcas from the
dead! What are we talking about as we discuss the violent
controversy that arose around Montanus? Are we talking
about speaking in an unknown tongue? No, we are talking
about Acts 5:15 where the very shadow of Peter falling upon
the sick who had been laid in the streets, healed their dis-
eased bodies. We are talking about the incomparable gifts
of the apostles to raise the very dead. There is a vast difference between these miracles and speaking in an unknown
tongue.

The attempt to duplicate apostolic wonders has been made
and is being made on every hand. For example, I received
through the mail a little tract enclosing a prayer cloth. This
prayer cloth is to be laid on the bodies of the sick in order
that in prayer and in faith they might be healed. Let us

read the tract that explains the purpose and the use of the prayer cloth.

You Can Be Made Whole!

God wrought special miracles by the hands of Paul: so that from his body were brought unto the sick handkerchiefs and aprons, and the diseases departed from them, and the evil spirits went out of them. — Acts 19:11, 12.

This was, and still is, God's way of providing deliverance for those who for one reason or another cannot avail themselves of the laying on of hands . . . .

. . . Just as the woman who pressed through the mob to touch the hem of Christ's garment was made whole the moment she touched the cloth, so when you touch this bit of cloth, believing as she did, your faith shall make you whole!

Received thus in obedience and faith, the effect as you place this cloth upon your body is the same as if JESUS HIMSELF had laid His hands upon you and commanded you to be made whole, for it is by the authority which He gave to me . . . that as His agent, acting for Him in His absence —

I, . . . , NOW COMMAND, IN JESUS' NAME, EVERY AFFLICTION; EVERY INFIRMITY; EVERY UNCLEAN SPIRIT OR TORMENTING DEMON TO FLEE FROM YOU, as you place this cloth either upon your forehead or upon the afflicted part . . . .

. . . This great ministry of faith is maintained by the free will offerings of those desiring to join us in bringing deliverance to the suffering everywhere . . . .

If you have my book GOD'S GUARANTEE TO HEAL YOU, read through Chap. 12 . . . GOD'S GUARANTEE TO HEAL YOU can be obtained by sending $1.00 plus 10 cents postage and handling to . . . .

This tract reminds me of a cancer clinic in our city that was finally closed after years and years of litigation on the part of the American Medical Association. The clinic sold pills that were supposed to heal this most tragic and desperate of diseases, cancer. Letters came to me from all over America asking me about these purported cancer cures. People came to our city and many of them came to visit me, asking about this wonderful cure. When people are sick and desperate, they will turn to anything if it holds out a ray of hope. They will grasp anything if it might contain any promise of health. This clinic took advantage of the desperate illnesses of people to make uncounted thousands and thousands of dollars. I feel the same way about the apron-cure represented in this tract. The attempt to duplicate the apostolic miracle brings grief, disappointment, and frustration to so many. This raises the question of the character and the purpose of those early, marvelous miracles. What of them? What do they mean? What was their purpose? Are we to expect a like demonstration today? Are there men now who possess this great power? Is it a gift for which we can pray? Is it to be expected from God? A close study of the Holy Scriptures will bring to us a sure and certain answer.

Besides the marvelous period of the initial creation described in the first chapters of Genesis, and besides the marvelous period of the consummation described in the Revelation, there are three periods of miracles in the Bible. First, there were the days of Moses in the introduction of the law; second, the days of Elijah and Elisha in the times of the apostasy of Israel; and third, the days of Jesus and the apostles in the introduction of the new dispensation of grace. When we study closely these three miraculous periods, we discover that they have something in common. It is this: without exception the purpose of the wonder is that of authentication. God is introducing His servant with His message by His sign from heaven. Read Exodus 4:1-9. Look at the purpose of God in bestowing this miraculous power upon Moses. God says to the great lawgiver that he has the power to turn his rod into a serpent and back again into a rod, "That they may believe that the LORD God of their fathers, the God of Abraham, the God of Isaac, and the God of Jacob, hath appeared unto thee" (Exodus 4:5). The power of miracles was not bestowed upon Moses for his own glory or for the astonishment of the earth, but that he might be received as the authenticated, designated, appointed ambassador from heaven.

Read I Kings 18:36, 37. Look at the "thats" in the two verses: "And it came to pass at the time of the offering of the evening sacrifice, that Elijah the prophet came near, and said, LORD God of Abraham, Isaac, and of Israel, let it be known this day that thou art God in Israel, and that I am thy servant, and that I have done all these things at thy word. Hear me, O LORD, hear me, that this people may know that thou art the LORD God, and that thou hast turned their heart back again" (I Kings 18:36, 37). There is a distinct purpose in the marvelous miracle about to be wrought through the hands of Elijah, God's prophet.

Read Matthew 11:1-5 wherein Jesus answers the question of John the Baptist as to whether or not they were to look for another Christ. The Lord sends an answer back to the great forerunner that the marvelous miracles of raising the dead and cleansing the leper and opening the eyes of the blind are the authentications and confirmations of His Sonship from heaven. They are signs that He is the true Messiah. Jesus, Himself, appealed to those signs for that very same definite purpose of belief and authentication. In John 10:25 our Saviour says: "Jesus answered them, . . . the works that I do in my Father's name, they bear witness of me." In John 14:11 our Saviour pleads with His disciples: "Believe me that I am in the Father, and the Father in me: or else believe me for the very work's sake."

One of the phenomenal things one will find in reading the gospel of John in the original Greek is this, that John never used the word "miracle." Without exception he employs the word "sign" (*semeion*). The Apostle John not only avoids the word "miracle" and uses the word "sign," but he also writes in plain and concise language the purpose of those signs. He says: "And many other signs truly did Jesus in the presence of his disciples, which are not written in this book: But these are written, that ye might believe that Jesus is the Christ, the Son of God; and that believing ye might have life through his name" (John 20:30, 31). The purpose of the sign was authentication, a confirmation bestowed by the hands of our Saviour in order that we might know and believe that He is truly the Son of God, the Saviour of the world.

The Miracles of God Today

God is the same today as He was yesterday and will be forever. For God to do a miraculous thing, whether in the beginning of the creation or at the consummation of the age, is the same with Him. Wonders and miracles are ever seen in His sovereign grace if they are needed — if they are necessary — if they serve a purpose in His elective will. But they are not bestowed adventitiously. It is expressly stated in John 10:41 that John the Baptist did no miracle. Jesus said of this John the Baptist that of man born of woman there was not one greater than he. Yet, in all of the glory and exaltation of the mighty Baptist, there was not one miraculous work wrought by his hand.

The miracles of Jesus had in each instance a concise and distinct purpose. Read the fifth chapter of John. The story begins in the first verses of the chapter with a description of the pool of Bethesda with its five porches. We read in John 5:3: "In these lay a great multitude of impotent folk, of blind, halt, withered, waiting for the moving of the water." Out of all of this multitude who lay there at the edge of the waters of the pool of Bethesda, how many did Jesus heal? He healed just one. What of all the others? The Lord walked away and left them all sick. There must be some reason for this and that reason is easily found. It is most evident and plain. The purpose of miracles is authentication. Miracles are signs of confirmation from heaven.

Read the sermon of Jesus before His hometown people in Nazareth of Galilee. The message is presented in the fourth chapter of Luke as the Master's inaugural address upon His entrance into His Messianic ministry. In that sermon our Saviour says: "But I tell you of a truth, many widows were in Israel in the days of Elias, when the heaven was shut up three years and six months, when great famine was throughout all the land; But unto none of them was Elias sent, save unto Sarepta, a city of Sidon, unto a woman that was a widow. And many lepers were in Israel in the time of Eliseus the prophet; and none of them was cleansed, saving

Naaman the Syrian" (Luke 4:25-27). Of the many poor widows in Israel in the days of Elijah, the prophet was sent to care for only one. Out of all of those poor and starving people there was but one in whose household the barrel of meal did not waste and the cruse of oil did not fail. Of all the many lepers in the days of Elisha, there was only one delivered from his desperate affliction. There must be some reason for this sovereign choice. It lies in the purpose of heavenly authentication.

Read the twelfth chapter of Acts. Acts 12:3-11 recounts the marvelous deliverance of Simon Peter from prison. But do you remember how the chapter begins? It begins with the martyrdom of James, the son of Zebedee, the brother of John, and one of the three who belonged to the inner circle of the apostles of our Lord. Acts 12:1, 2 says: "Now about that time Herod the king stretched forth his hands to vex certain of the church. And he killed James the brother of John with the sword." In the same chapter that Peter is delivered, James is beheaded. In a previous chapter the tragic story of the stoning of Stephen is recounted. The martyrdom of Stephen and James and the deliverance of Simon Peter lie in the sovereign purpose of God. No miracle delivered either Stephen or James.

In Acts 19:12 is recounted the incomparable and marvelous story of the handkerchiefs and aprons taken from the Apostle Paul to be laid upon those who were sick, in order that they might be healed. But to the pastor of that selfsame city of Ephesus, Paul wrote in II Timothy 4:20, "Trophimus have I left at Miletum sick."

This illness is unthinkable in the light of some interpretations of the purposes of God and the Holy Scriptures. In this last journey of the Apostle from Asia to Rome, he leaves poor Trophimus sick. Why did he not place a handkerchief or an apron upon this faithful Ephesian disciple in order that he might be well? Why did he not take him by the hand and raise him up to strength and health? The reason is simple: the purpose of a miracle is for authentication and confirmation. Miracles lie in the sovereign grace and purpose of God. Even an apostle could not work a miracle at will.

God sometimes delivers with heavenly triumph. Read the mighty chapter on the heroes of the faith, Hebrews 11:1-40. Look again at verses 33-35a: "Who through faith subdued kingdoms, wrought righteousness, obtained promises, stopped the mouths of lions, Quenched the violence of fire, escaped the edge of the sword, out of weakness were made strong, waxed valiant in fight, turned to flight the armies of the aliens. Women received their dead raised to life again." What marvelous deliverance! What great miracles! What incomparable interventions from heaven! But wait, we are not through. The Holy Spirit has not finished His words. Let us continue to read verses 35b-38 of the sorrows, trials, and sufferings of other of God's people who were not delivered. How tragic their plight and how sorrowful their case. Did God not love them? Did God not take care of them? What is the answer? The answer is most plain. The purpose of miracles is authentication. It is bestowed only in the sovereign will and purpose and grace of God.

God's Will for Us

Each one of us turns to our Lord in his own life and asks: "Lord, what is God's will for me?" Is it to be life and length of days? Is it to be health and strength and success? Or is God's sovereign purpose for me to be one of suffering, agony, crucifixion and death? Read again John 21:18-22. In John 21:18, 19 Jesus prophesies the death of Simon Peter by crucifixion. He is to die by the stretching forth of the hands. He is to be nailed to a cross. Tradition says that, when Simon Peter was crucified and this prophecy fulfilled, he humbly asked that he be nailed to the tree head down because he said he was not worthy to be crucified in the same manner as his Lord. Where is the opening of the prison doors here in the crucifixion of Simon Peter? There is no deliverance as we find in Acts 12. In the story in the twelfth chapter of Acts the sovereign grace of God elects for Simon Peter the miraculous deliverance, but in the prophecy of our Saviour in the twenty-first chapter of John, there is no deliverance. There is only agony, crucifixion and death. When this tragic future is revealed to Simon, the Apostle turns around and sees his old friend and fishing partner, the beloved disciple, John. "Peter seeing him saith to Jesus, Lord, and what shall this man do?" (John 21:21). What about John? Is he to be crucified? Is he to face a final agony in the departure of this life? No, for "Jesus saith unto him, If I will that he tarry till I come, what is that to thee? follow thou me" (John 21: 22). If it is the will of heaven that John live a long, long life and die a peaceful death, then this has nothing to do with the life of Simon Peter. There is one sovereign purpose for Peter and that is agony, crucifixion and death. There is another sovereign purpose for John and that is a long life and a natural death. Both lie in the purpose and will of God.

It is thus with our lives. If there is to be for us a Gethsemane, let us pray with our Saviour, even in our agony and trial, "Thy will be done." If we are finally crucified, let us bow our heads with our Saviour and say: "Father, into Thy hands I commit my spirit." If there is for us honor and length of days, then let us receive the gift from God's hand in all humility and in grateful appreciation. The choice lies in the will and purpose of God.

Recently I spoke at a conference in a far distant state. I met there a friend from college days whom I had not seen for many years. His life had been one of indescribable sorrow. Sickness, disappointment and poverty had attended his way. Recently his wife had died. His present pastorate was difficult and increasingly disappointing. With all of the burdens that I bear as the pastor of this church, I yet could not help but think of the affluent and pleasant place in which my life and lot have been cast and of the contrast with this humble preacher who has been crushed through the years of his ministry. Why have I been chosen to be here and he chosen to be there? Is it because I am a better man than he? No, for I am not. Is it because I am more honorable than he, more given to prayer, more loving, more tender, more dedicated to the Saviour? No, for I am not. The answer lies in the sovereign purpose of God for us both. Simon Peter is chosen unto crucifixion, agony and death. John is chosen to live to a ripe old age and a translation, apart from crucifixion, unto the Lord. The answer lies for us all in the will of God. Whether we live or die, we are the Lord's. If we suffer with Him, we shall also reign with Him. If we die with Him, we shall also live with Him. Our earthly assignment is to yield our lives to the will of God in sickness, in health, in youth, in age, and in death — whatever God shall choose. "Not my will but Thine be done."

Chapter 3

The History of the Doctrine of the Holy Spirit
(The Eastern and Western Churches)

John 14

16 And I will pray the Father, and he shall give you another Comforter, that he may abide with you for ever;

17 Even the Spirit of truth; whom the world cannot receive, because it seeth him not, neither knoweth him: but ye know him; for he dwelleth with you, and shall be in you.

We continue with the history of the doctrine of the Holy Spirit after the years of the apostolic Fathers. The centuries between A.D. 500 and A.D. 1000 witnessed the increasingly tragic division between the Eastern Church, the Greek Church of the Eastern Roman Empire, and the Western Church, the Latin Church of the Western Roman Empire. The ultimate breaking up of Christendom developed over the question of the procession of the Holy Spirit: Does the Holy Spirit proceed from the Son as well as the Father? The early creeds of Nicaea in A.D. 325 and Constantinople in A.D. 381 did not expressly state that the Holy Spirit proceeds from the Son as well as the Father. However, the doctrine of the procession of the Spirit from the Son as well as the Father was largely believed throughout the Christian world. In A.D. 589 a council of all the bishops of the Western World was convened in Toledo, Spain, and at that conference they added the word *filioque* ("and the Son") to the Nicene Creed presentation of the procession of the Holy Spirit. This angered the Eastern Greek Church, which had not been consulted concerning the addition of the word. The Greek Church argued that the Spirit proceeded only from the Father, quoting John 15:26: "But when the Comforter is come, whom I will send unto you from the Father, even

31

the Spirit of truth, which proceedeth from the Father, he shall testify of me." The Latin Church argued that the Spirit also proceeded from the Son, quoting from John 16:7: "Nevertheless I tell you the truth; It is expedient for you that I go away: for if I go not away, the Comforter will not come unto you; but if I depart, I will send him unto you." The deepening schism between the Pope of Rome and the Patriarch of Constantinople continued until finally the rupture of separation was complete July 16, A.D. 1054. Upon that date the papal legate formally laid on the high altar of St. Sophia the sentence of Anathema, cursing the Patriarch and the Greek Church with this awful imprecation:

Let them be Anathema Maranatha with Simoniacs

Valerians	Pneumatomachi
Arians	Manichees
Donatists	and Nazarenes
Nicholaitans	and with all heretics;
Severians	

yea, with the devil and his angels. Amen. Amen. Amen.

The Destruction of the Eastern Christian Empire

The unbelievable division of the Christian world over this discussion of the procession of the Holy Spirit resulted not only in the separation of the Greek and Latin Churches, but it also finally worked toward the dissolution and destruction of the Eastern Roman Empire. The Greek-speaking part of the Roman Empire was constantly and increasingly threatened by a powerful advancing enemy, the Muslem Turk. It became apparent through the passing years that the Eastern Empire could not hold out against the Mohammedan advances without help from the Latin West. The Greek Church, therefore, sent an urgent appeal for help to the Council of Constance in 1414. Again they sent a like urgent appeal to the Council of Basil in 1431. To the Council of Florence, which was convened in 1439, the Emperor himself and the Patriarch of Constantinople personally made a desperate appeal. All of their cries for help were ignored. Then came the awesome and tragic year of 1453 which witnessed the siege and fall of Constantinople. Edward Gibbon's famous description of this battle, in his *Decline and Fall of the Roman Empire,* is one of the most brilliant passages in English literature. The vital issues involved gave a tragic grandeur to the event, comparable only to the destruction of Jerusalem by Titus in A.D. 70. Two able generals led the awesome war. One was Sultan Mohammed II, the Muslem Turk; the other was Constantine Palaeologus, the last Roman Emperor, a man worthy to sit on the throne of the greatest of his predecessors. When it became clear that there was no hope and that the end was swiftly approaching, there was no panic in the city. Instead, amidst the scene of sword, blood and war, there was witnessed a most solemn religious service in which the cry of a great people in its agony ascended to heaven. At length the surging host of invaders broke through the wall and poured into the city. The Emperor, refusing to survive his empire, dashed into the thick of the fight and perished in the multitude of the slain. The Sultan gave up the city to plunder. The last stronghold to fall was the great cathedral, St. Sophia itself. The barred doors soon yielded to the battle-axes of the Turks. The old were slain and the young men and women were led off in strings of captives for a worse fate. The most famous and the most beautiful of all the churches of Christendom was turned into a mosque, and the cross gave way to the star and the scimitar.

In the city of Istanbul (ancient Byzantium and Constantinople) I walked under the vast dome of St. Sophia. Larger than a baseball diamond, it is one of the architectural wonders of the world built before the days of steel trusses and iron girders. I relived again in memory the history of the tragic battle that destroyed the great church, the cathedral of the Patriarch of the east. The building had been erected by the Emperor Justinian in A.D. 500 and was dedicated to the glory of Christ as He was preached and worshiped throughout the civilized world. But look upon the vast building now — empty, undone, of interest mostly to tourists who find in it a sort of Turkish museum. What sorrowful things can overcome and overtake the Christian faith! What immeasurable tragedy can arise out of bitter dissension and division among the churches! How formalism and ritualism can empty the church of its splendor, power, and effective gospel preaching. The shell of vast, beautiful St. Sophia, now a Mohammedan mosque, is a silent witness to the destruction of the Christian church from its own inward decay. Visitation of the sword of the Muslim was but the chastening rod of the Christ of the Apocalypse, who had said to the sister Greek church at Ephesus: "Nevertheless I have somewhat against thee, because thou hast left thy first love. Remember therefore from whence thou art fallen, and repent, and do the first works; or else I will come unto thee quickly, and will remove thy candlestick out of his place, except thou repent" (Revelation 2:4, 5).

The Middle Ages and the Reformation

As we continue following the history of the doctrine of the Holy Spirit, we learn that the pre-Reformation Middle Ages were as dark spiritually as they were intellectually. There was practically no conception of the doctrine, presence, and power of the Third Person of the Trinity. Few grasped the need for personal conversion and the work of the Holy Spirit in regeneration. It was expressly denied that the Spirit could teach Christian believers through the Word of God. Earthly priests were substituted for the guiding, teaching influence of the Holy Spirit. The things of the Spirit were lost in the wilderness of sacramentalism, superstition, ignorance of the Word, humanism and scholasticism.

Then came the marvelous period of the Reformation of the 1500's. Testimony to the Holy Spirit was full and explicit as in the Apostolic Age. The Reformation was in itself a great work of the Holy Spirit. The reformers emphasized Christ's work for us and the Holy Spirit's work in us. They delineated the ministry of the Holy Spirit in the human heart, wooing, convicting, and bestowing the gift of repentance and faith. They emphasized the illuminating work of the Holy Spirit in revealing the teachings of the Word of

God. They openly advocated the reading of the Bible and translated its words into the vernacular of the people, affirming that all believers could be taught Scriptural truth by the Holy Spirit directly. This was in diametrical opposition to the Roman concept that only the priest could interpret the Word.

The post-Reformation years in the history of the doctrine of the Holy Spirit brought to birth Deism, Unitarianism, Arminianism, and other like movements which discounted the vital ministry of the Holy Spirit of God. Arminius (1560-1609) relegated the saving work of the Holy Spirit to a minor role. To this Dutch theologian, the human will altogether decided the matter of salvation, omitting the convicting work of the Spirit. Socinus (1539-1604), the direct founder of the modern Unitarian movement, boldly and directly attacked the person and deity of the Holy Spirit. Deism, born in England, spread to the continent and denied the eminence of God and any work of the Holy Spirit. In those tragic days, Deism finally covered the whole theological world of England and, in the form of rationalism and infidelism as represented by Voltaire, swept through the entire intellectual world of the continent.

It would have been a mournful and pathetic day for Christian faith — calamitous, disastrous, and fatal — had it not been for another marvelous visitation of the Holy Spirit of God. This is known in history as the time of the "Great Awakening." It was led by John Wesley (1703-1791), George Whitefield (1714-1770), and Jonathan Edwards (1703-1758). It was literally another Pentecost, another outpouring of the power of the Spirit of God upon the churches of England and America. God's people became conscious of His holy presence. Courses of lectures were prepared and delivered on the Spirit. Lost souls were convicted and converted to the Lord Jesus Christ by the uncounted thousands. World missions were born anew. Not since the Holy Spirit had said in Acts 13:2: "Separate me Barnabas and Saul for the work whereunto I have called them," had the world seen anything comparable to this marvelous and effective extension of the gospel witness. William Carey, in 1792, led in the organization at Kettering, England, of the first, modern, world-wide missionary endeavor. Bible societies were formed and the Philadelphian "age of the open door" blessed the whole world as evangelists and missionaries carried the good news of the saving grace of the Son of God.

The Modern Era of Theological Contrast

This leads us to the present era of the nineteen and twentieth centuries. Our modern period brought to the history of theology the scourge and curse of rationalism. In the nineteenth century, German rationalism and higher criticism nullified any progress of the work of the Holy Spirit. It swept away many of our great Christian institutions and blunted the missionary enterprise. It spilled over into contemporary theology with the result that the doctrine of the Trinity has become one of the first points of departure in liberalism. In modernism (liberalism) there is always the tendency to move toward Unitarianism with its denial of the deity of Christ and the deity of the Holy Spirit. This rationalism denies the supernatural and rejects the revelation of the Holy Scriptures, which Scriptures they define as being nothing but a human effort to find God in our present day. Neo-orthodoxy in America and Britain has little to say about the person and work of the Holy Spirit. Neo-orthodox theologians are almost unanimous, however, in denying His distinct personality. To this school of thought the Spirit is but a manifestation of the activity of God. The main stream of neo-orthodoxy flows toward a pseudo-Christianity governed by reason and judgment of the infallibly written Word of God.

Liberalism, with its denial of the supernatural, led to the Pentecostal reaction which came to life in the latter part of the nineteenth century. Whether or not developments in the Pentecostal movement were good or bad, it is not ours to say. But one thing can be observed with true clarity and firm persuasion; namely, the Pentecostal movement brought attention to the doctrine and the power of the Holy Spirit among the people of God. There are presently probably more than two hundred separate, religious, denominational bodies in the United States that lay heavy emphasis upon Christian perfectionism. They believe that sanctification purges the heart of inbred original sin. They believe that this sanctification is a distinct experience subsequent to salvation; hence, it is termed "the second blessing." They believe that this second blessing is bestowed instantaneously and is marvelously, supernaturally received. There are many differences of opinion concerning this reception of the Holy Spirit. Some of the groups identify the experience with signs such as speaking in tongues. This speaking in unknown tongues, which is called "glossolalia," is found in increasing evidence even among the more liturgical and conservative of the historical churches of Christendom. Its present meaning is plainly evident. It is a reaction against the dead, cold formalism of modern church worship and is an effort to recapture the joy and glory of the supernatural presence of God revealed in the Holy Scriptures and experienced by the early Christians.

Signs of the Lack of Spiritual Power

In this brief summary of the history of the doctrine of the Holy Spirit, there are lessons that we ought to learn. The first concerns our recognition of the signs of the lack and want of the Spirit's power. Let us briefly name three of these signs so much in evidence today. The first is rationalism. Rationalism, with its denial of the supernatural and its denial of the inspiration of the Holy Scripture, is impossible to the truly regenerated soul. The attitudes and approaches of liberalism have no attraction for a mind that has personally come under the regenerative operation of the Spirit of God. A regenerated mind easily accepts the divine facts, prophecies, and miracles recorded in the Bible. The second sign of impotence is ritualism. Ritualism is not a blessing but a curse to the spiritual life of any church. It is a disease that springs from a desire to substitute the sensuous for that which constitutes the true charm and glory of the Christian

faith; namely, the presence and power of the Holy Spirit.
To a mind replenished with the sweetness, wonder, and awe
of the Spirit of God, ritualistic elements have no interest or
attraction. One of the most emphatic statements I have
ever read concerning ritualism is that of Dr. George Smeaton
in his marvelous book entitled *The Doctrine of the Holy
Spirit.* On page 328 this professor of evangelical theology in
New College, Edinburgh, wrote toward the close of the last
century: "To one fact all history gives a harmonious testimony. In the ratio in which the ritualistic element ascends,
the spiritual element descends; the elevation of the one being the depression of the other." The third sign of spiritual
decline can be seen in empty activism. These spasmodic
efforts to awaken larger interests in the church by human
devices and appliances only advertise abroad the dearth of
the power of the Spirit of God. Earthly measures have
earthly results. They soon burn themselves out and are
generally followed by despondency, exhaustion and dissatis-
faction. Mechanical, man-made gadgets will never be able
to pry up from the earth the fallen house of God.

Signs of the Presence and Power of the Holy Spirit

On the other hand, the signs of the presence and power
of the Holy Spirit are plainly seen when a Pentecostal outpouring descends upon God's people and God's churches.
First, this heavenly visitation of power is made possible
when we remember our dependence upon Him. "Not by
might, nor by power, but by my spirit, saith the Lord of
hosts" (Zechariah 4:6). Church history verifies that, without full testimony to the divine personality and agency of
the Holy Spirit in bringing the power of God upon a people,
no blessing can be expected by the church. When the Spirit
is dishonored, the favor of heaven no longer descends. Second, we are to remember that the Holy Spirit is honored
by being involved in every prayer and referred to in every
sermon. Wherever religion comes in power, the presence
of the Spirit, as connecting the church on earth with Christ
in heaven, occupies a large place. A true doctrine of the

Spirit, no less than a true doctrine of justification by faith, is the article of a standing or a falling church. Third, we are to remember that our right attitude is always one of waiting for a fresh outpouring of the Spirit of God. He is in the world to help us exalt the Lord Jesus. The Spirit comes from Christ, leads to Christ, comes to glorify Christ. We ought always to pray: "Spirit of preaching, Spirit of power, Spirit of Christ, possess us anew. Consume us with Thy glory; use us in Thy work, and sanctify the witness we would dedicate unto Thee."

Chapter 4

The Pentecostal Difference

Acts 1

4 And being assembled together with them, commanded them that they should not depart from Jerusalem, but wait for the promise of the Father, which, saith he, ye have heard of me.

5 For John truly baptized with water; but ye shall be baptized with the Holy Ghost not many days hence.

There must be a tremendous difference between the work of the Holy Spirit before our Lord's Ascension into heaven and after our Lord's Ascension into heaven. There must be a vast difference concerning the Holy Spirit before Pentecost and after Pentecost. We would know this from our Lord's own words in which He speaks by way of anticipation of something entirely new. He says:

And I will pray the Father, and he shall give you another Comforter, that he may abide with you for ever; Even the Spirit of truth; whom the world cannot receive, because it seeth him not, neither knoweth him: but ye know him; for he dwelleth with you, and shall be in you. But the Comforter, which is the Holy Ghost, whom the Father will send in my name, he shall teach you all things, and bring all things to your remembrance, whatsoever I have said unto you (John 14:16, 17, 26).

But when the Comforter is come, whom I will send unto you from the Father, even the Spirit of truth, which proceedeth from the Father, he shall testify of me (John 15:26).

Nevertheless I tell you the truth; It is expedient for you that I go away: for if I go not away, the Comforter will not come unto you; but if I depart, I will send him unto you. I have yet many things to say unto you, but ye cannot bear them now. Howbeit when he, the Spirit of truth, is come, he will guide

40

you into all truth: for he shall not speak of himself; but whatsoever he shall hear, that shall he speak: and he will shew you
things to come (John 16:7, 12, 13).

And, behold, I send the promise of my Father upon you: but
tarry ye in the city of Jerusalem, until ye be endued with power
from on high (Luke 24:49).

And, being assembled together with them, commanded them
that they should not depart from Jerusalem, but wait for the
promise of the Father, which, saith he, ye have heard of me.
For John truly baptized with water; but ye shall be baptized
with the Holy Ghost not many days hence (Acts 1:4, 5).

We would know that a great difference is coming in the
world concerning the Holy Spirit by a comment of the
Apostle John which he wrote in his gospel (John 7:39).
Jesus had just said: "He that believeth on me, as the scripture hath said, out of his belly shall flow rivers of living
water" (John 7:38). The Apostle then parenthesizes with
this comment: "But this spake he of the Spirit, which they
that believe on him should receive: for the Holy Ghost was
not yet given; because that Jesus was not yet glorified"
(John 7:39). The beloved disciple plainly avows that the
Lord Jesus was speaking in John 7:38 of a future event;
namely, "of the outpouring of the Holy Spirit," which at
that time had not been given.

We would expect this vast difference concerning the Holy
Spirit before Pentecost and after Pentecost because of the
prophecies of the Old Testament. Joel says, in his great
prophetic message in Joel 2:28, 29: "And it shall come to
pass afterward, that I will pour out my spirit upon all flesh;
and your sons and your daughters shall prophesy, your old
men shall dream dreams, your young men shall see visions:
And also upon the servants and upon the handmaids in those
days will I pour out my spirit." This is the prophecy Simon
Peter refers to as he begins his tremendous sermon on the
day of Pentecost. The prophecy has a relation to Israel at
the time of the consummation of the age, but it also, according to Peter, has a relation to the inauguration of this dispensation of grace and of the Holy Spirit.

The Activity of the Holy Spirit in the Old Testament

In what way was the Holy Spirit not given when John writes of this in John 7:39? What is the difference that Pentecost made? We must remember that the Holy Spirit was in the Old Testament from the beginning. When we speak of the Spirit's coming at Pentecost, we cannot mean that He was absent from the world before that date. The Holy Spirit was active in creation.

> In the beginning God created the heaven and the earth. And the earth was without form, and void; and darkness was upon the face of the deep. And the Spirit of God moved upon the face of the waters (Genesis 1:1, 2).

He was active in the Old Testament in the revelation of the Word of God.

> Knowing this first, that no prophecy of the scripture is of any private interpretation. For the prophecy came not in old time by the will of man: but holy men of God spake as they were moved by the Holy Ghost (II Peter 1:20, 21).

The New Testament attributes many Old Testament Scriptures directly to the Spirit Himself.

> He saith unto them, How then doth David in spirit call him Lord, saying, (Matthew 22:43).
>
> For David himself said by the Holy Ghost, The Lord said to my Lord, Sit thou on my right hand, till I make thine enemies thy footstool (Mark 12:36).
>
> Men and brethren, this scripture must needs have been fulfilled, which the Holy Ghost by the mouth of David spake before concerning Judas, which was guide to them that took Jesus (Acts 1:16).
>
> Who by the mouth of thy servant David hast said, "Why did the heathen rage, and the people imagine vain things? (Acts 4:25).
>
> Wherefore (as the Holy Ghost saith, To day if you will hear his voice (Hebrews 3:7).
>
> Wherefore the Holy Ghost also is a witness to us: for after that he had said before, This is the covenant that I will make with them after those days, saith the Lord, I will put my laws into their hearts, and in their minds will I write them (Hebrews 10:15, 16).

The Holy Spirit, in the Old Testament, was active in the inspiration and in the transmission of the revelation of God in the writing down of the message of the Lord.

> All scripture is given by inspiration of God, and is profitable for doctrine, for reproof, for correction, for instruction in righteousness (II Timothy 3:16).
>
> And when they agreed not among themselves, they departed, after that Paul had spoken one word, Well spake the Holy Ghost by Esaias the prophet unto our fathers (Acts 28:25).

In the Old Testament the Holy Spirit was the great restrainer of sin.

> And the Lord said, My spirit shall not always strive with man, for that he also is flesh: yet his days shall be an hundred and twenty years (Genesis 6:3).
>
> When the enemy shall come in like a flood, the Spirit of the Lord shall lift up a standard against him (Isaiah 59:19b).

Why does not evil totally engulf this despairing world? It is because the Spirit of God sets up a standard against it, saying: "Thus far shalt thou go and no further." When in an airplane one flies over the vast Pacific, the bulwark and boundary of the seashore seems so very low and small. Why does not the sea, in its immeasurable expanse, flood over the low barrier and destroy the works of man on the land? It is because God says to the sea: "Thus far shalt thou come and no further." It is as Job says in Job 38:8: God "shuts up the sea with doors" that it can proceed no further. It is thus with evil. The Holy Spirit is the restrainer of sin. In II Thessalonians 2:7 Paul describes a time which opens the terrible Tribulation, when the Holy Spirit, the restrainer, will be taken away and iniquity will have free and unopposed access to every avenue of life.

The New Temple Which the Holy Spirit Entered at Pentecost

If the Holy Spirit, therefore, has been in the world from the beginning and has been the power of God in creation, in revelation, in inspiration, and in the restraining of sin, then what is the difference that Pentecost made when the

Holy Spirit was poured out into the world? There are three things that comprise the Pentecostal difference. First, at Pentecost the Holy Spirit of God entered into a new temple. The tabernacle, which was built according to the divine pattern shown Moses from heaven, was but an empty tent until Exodus 40:34, 35: "Then a cloud covered the tent of the congregation, and the glory of the LORD filled the tabernacle. And Moses was not able to enter into the tent of the congregation, because the cloud abode thereon, and the glory of the Lord filled the tabernacle." The temple of Solomon's glorious edifice was but an empty shell until I Kings 8:10, 11: "And it came to pass, when the priests were come out of the holy place, that the cloud filled the house of the LORD, So that the priests could not stand to minister because of the cloud: for the glory of the LORD had filled the house of the LORD." The Shekinah glory moved into His dwelling place on earth in the tabernacle and in the Solomonic temple. In the New Testament, God is choosing a new Temple. It is not one made with skins and tapestries. It is not one erected out of hewn stones and overlaid with gold. This new Temple, so Peter tells us (I Peter 2:5), is to be built on the foundation of Christ out of living stones which are the regenerated believers in the Saviour. On the day of Pentecost, the Holy Spirit came to indwell the Church of God just as the Shekinah glory of Jehovah invested the tabernacle and the temple with His glorious presence.

At Pentecost the Third Person of the Trinity took up His residence in believers. "In whom all the building fitly framed together groweth unto an holy temple in the Lord: In whom ye also are builded together for an habitation of God through the Spirit" (Ephesians 2:21, 22). "Know ye not that ye are the temple of God, and that the Spirit of God dwelleth in you? If any man defile the temple of God, him shall God destroy; for the temple of God is holy, which temple ye are" (I Corinthians 3:16, 17). Paul writes in these passages that the church is the Temple of the Holy Spirit. All the believers in a church, as a group, are corporately indwelt. The church gathered at Pentecost was but an empty shell, as empty as the tabernacle or the temple, until the Holy Spirit came to make His residence there. The members of the church were as powerless as the army Ezekiel saw in the valley of dry bones until the breath of God came upon them. The glory of the church is the glory of the presence of God, and that glory came at Pentecost.

Did you notice that when God moved into the tabernacle and into the temple all the people beheld it? It was an open, public event, marvelous, powerful and memorable. The priests themselves could not continue their ministry because of the incomparable glory. A like marvel occurred at Pentecost when the Holy Spirit of God moved into the church as His indwelling place. All the people saw the marvelous manifestation. There was a sound as of a rushing, mighty wind. There was a wondrous sight like unto cloven tongues of fire. There was a marvelous gift of tongues whereby the disciples praised God in all the languages of the Hellenistic Jews who had come to visit Jerusalem.

We name a second difference that Pentecost made. Not only did the Holy Spirit come to make His residence in the church as a corporate body but He also came at Pentecost to indwell all believers. Jesus made the promise: "[The Comforter will come.] Even the Spirit of truth; whom the world cannot receive, because it seeth him not, neither knoweth him: but ye know him; for he dwelleth with you, and shall be in you" (John 14:17). The Apostle Paul says: "What? know ye not that your body is the temple of the Holy Ghost which is in you, which ye have of God, and ye are not your own?" (I Corinthians 6:19). Each one of us is a temple individually indwelt. Every born-again child of God is a temple of the Holy Spirit of Jesus. In the Old Testament, this indwelling of the Spirit was not universal; it was not for all the people of the Lord. The experience was a special privilege; it was a gift bestowed upon the special few for special purposes. Moses was indwelt by the Holy Spirit for the purpose of administration in the government of Israel, and a like wisdom was bestowed upon the seventy who were to help him in that particular assignment. "And the LORD came down in a cloud, and spake unto him, and took of the spirit that was upon him, and gave it unto the seventy elders: and it came to pass, that, when the spirit rested upon them, they prophesied, and did cease" (Numbers 11:25). Skills to make Aaron's priestly garments were bestowed upon a chosen few. "And thou shalt speak unto all that are wise hearted, whom I have filled with the spirit of wisdom, that they may make Aaron's garments to consecrate him, that he may minister unto me in the priest's office" (Exodus 28:3). Bezaleel and Aholiab were given the Holy Spirit of God to make the tabernacle according to the divine plan. They were artisans endowed from heaven for that particular purpose.

> And the LORD spake unto Moses, saying, See I have called by name Bezaleel the son of Uri, the son of Hur, of the tribe of Judah: And I have filled him with the spirit of God, in wisdom, and in understanding, and in knowledge, and in all manner of workmanship, To devise cunning works, to work in gold, and in silver, and in brass, And in cutting of stones, to set them, and in carving of timber, to work in all manner of workmanship. And I, behold, I have given with him Aholiab, the son of Ahisamach, of the tribe of Dan: and in the hearts of all that are wise hearted I have put wisdom, that they may make all that I have commanded thee; The tabernacle of the congregation, and the ark of the testimony, and the mercy seat that is thereupon, and all the furniture of the tabernacle, And the table and his furniture, and the pure candlestick with all his furniture, and the altar of incense, And the altar of burnt offering with all his furniture, and the laver and his foot, And the cloths of service, and the holy garments for Aaron the priest, and the garments of his sons, to minister in the priest's office, And the anointing oil, and sweet incense for the holy place: according to all that I have commanded thee shall they do (Exodus 31:1-11).

In Judges 6:34 the Holy Spirit came upon Gideon as he blew the trumpet of freedom in revolt against the Midianites. "But the Spirit of the LORD came upon Gideon, and he blew a trumpet; and Abiezer was gathered after him" (Judges 6: 34). The Spirit of God came upon Daniel in his prophetic ministry. "But at the last Daniel came in . . . and in whom is the spirit of the holy gods . . ." (Daniel 4:8). ". . . the spirit of the gods is in thee, and light and understanding and excellent wisdom is found in thee" (Daniel 5:14)

In all of the vast story through the unfolding years of the ages of the Old Testament, the Holy Spirit indwelled just a few and this for a special purpose. His indwelling was not universal. This is one reason why Jesus spoke about the high privilege of the least convert in the kingdom of God in Matthew 11:11. No greater man was ever born of woman than John the Baptist, but he belonged to the Old Testament dispensation. He lived before the Pentecostal privileges of the new day in which we serve the Lord. In these marvelous days of grace, the humblest member of the Church of Jesus has a greater opportunity and privilege than John the Baptist.

After Pentecost the Holy Spirit Is Never Withdrawn From the Believer

A third Pentecostal difference lies in the fact that the gift of the Holy Spirit after the Ascension of Jesus into heaven is a personal indwelling in the believer and is never withdrawn. In the Old Testament, before Pentecost, the indwelling of the Holy Spirit was temporary and could be withdrawn. The Holy Spirit came upon Samson at times in the camp of Dan. "And the Spirit of the LORD began to move him at times in the camp of Dan between Zorah and Eshtaol" (Judges 13:25). The Holy Spirit came upon Samson as he destroyed, with his bare hands, a voracious lion.

> Then went Samson down, and his father and his mother, to Timnath, and came to the vineyards of Timnath: and, behold, a young lion roared against him. And the Spirit of the LORD came mightily upon him, and he rent him as he would have rent a kid, and he had nothing in his hand (Judges 14:5, 6).

The Holy Spirit came upon Samson as he slew a thousand Philistines with a dried bone.

> And when he came unto Lehi, the Philistines shouted against him: and the Spirit of the LORD came mightily upon him, and the cords that were upon his arms became as flax that was burnt

> with fire, and his bands loosed from off his hands. And he
> found a new jawbone of an ass, and put forth his hand, and
> took it, and slew a thousand men therewith (Judges 15:14, 15).

But in the sixteenth chapter of the Book of Judges, the sad
story is recounted of the departure of the Spirit of God from
the strongest man who ever lived.

> And he [Samson] awoke out of his sleep, and said, I will go out
> as at other times before, ... And he wist not that the LORD
> was departed from him. But the Philistines took him, and put
> out his eyes, and brought him down to Gaza, and bound him
> with fetters of brass; and he did grind in the prison house
> (Judges 16:20, 21).

What a pitiful sight did Samson make as he pulled like an
ox the grinding beam in the prison mill, his eyes put out by
the cruelty of the heathen and his hands fettered with instruments of brass. The Spirit of God had departed from
him.

A like sorrowful story is recounted in the life of Israel's
first king, giant Saul of the tribe of Benjamin. In I Samuel
10:9, 10 the descent of the Spirit of God upon Israel's new
king is gloriously described: "And it was so, that when he
[Saul] had turned his back to go from Samuel, God gave
him another heart . . . and the Spirit of God came upon him,
and he prophesied . . . ." (I Samuel 10:9, 10). After the
anointing of Samuel, God gave Saul a new heart and the
power of the Spirit of God came so mightily upon him that
he prophesied with the prophets of Israel. But what a tragic
word is written in I Samuel 16:14: "But the Spirit of the
LORD departed from Saul, and an evil spirit from the LORD
troubled him." So barren and desolate was the empty heart
of Saul when the Spirit of God left him, and so grievous
were his days when an evil spirit troubled him, that the
kingdom was searched to find a player of the harp who might
come and soothe by song and melody his troubled soul. This
accounts for the agonizing prayer of David in later years
(Psalm 51:11). King David had seen the helplessness of Saul
when the Spirit of God had departed from Israel's first king.
To soothe Saul's troubled spirit, David had played before

Israel's monarch. When the prospect of losing the Spirit of
God appeared before David himself in his grievous sin, the
sweet psalmist of Israel begged of heaven that he might
not be left thus, helpless and cursed by the departure of the
Holy Spirit. God answered that prayer of David. Not only
did God take away the sin of David, but the Holy Scriptures
say that only on David, many years earlier, had come the
Holy Spirit "from that day forward." "Then Samuel took
the horn of oil, and anointed him in the midst of his brethren: and the Spirit of the LORD came upon David from that
day forward" (I Samuel 16:13). The Holy Spirit was never
withdrawn from David as long as he lived, but his was a
unique experience. Of no one else in the Old Testament is
it so said. The earnest plea in Psalm 51:11, against the withdrawal of the Holy Spirit from his life, emphasizes the
tragic possibility in the days of the Old Testament.

But in this dispensation of the love and grace and mercy
of God, there is no such possibility of the withdrawal of the
Holy Spirit from us. We need never pray such a prayer as
David did in Psalm 51. Once saved, the Holy Spirit abides
in our souls forever. The gift is a personal one and is bestowed upon every regenerated child of God. So promised
our Lord in John 14:16. With all their faults and failures,
their sins and vices, yet Paul could write to the Corinthians
the words: "What? Know ye not that your body is the
temple of the Holy Ghost which is in you, which ye have
of God . . . ?" (I Corinthians 6:19). We may grieve the
Holy Spirit, we may hurt Him, quench Him, buffet Him, refuse His guidance, reject His wisdom, but He will never be
withdrawn from us. Once we are saved and He comes to
live in our hearts, He abides with us forever. We may be a
poor child of God, we may be a disobedient child of God,
we may be a fruitless child of God, but if we ever are a
child and have been born into the household of the Father,
we are never a disowned child. We are a child of God forever. After Pentecost, the Spirit is never withdrawn from
the life of the believer.

What a comfort this is to us who have turned to Jesus for

refuge. With all our weaknesses and sins, the Spirit is never taken away. I sometimes think of the weaknesses of Simon Peter as Paul recounts them in Galatians 2:11-14:

> But when Peter was come to Antioch, I withstood him to the face, because he was to be blamed. For before that certain came from James, he did eat with the Gentiles: but when they were come, he withdrew and separated himself, fearing them which were of the circumcision. And the other Jews dissembled likewise with him; insomuch that Barnabas also was carried away with their dissimulation. But when I saw that they walked not uprightly according to the truth of the gospel, I said unto Peter before them all, If thou, being a Jew, livest after the manner of Gentiles, and not as do the Jews, why compellest thou the Gentiles to live as do the Jews?

Openly, publicly, before the brethren, Paul rebuked Peter for his dissimulation and hypocrisy. But did God withdraw His Spirit from the first and chief Apostle? No, never, a thousand times no! Even our Lord one time said to this big fisherman: "And the Lord said, Simon, Simon, behold, Satan hath desired to have you, that he may sift you as wheat: But I have prayed for thee, that thy faith fail not: and when thou art converted, strengthen thy brethren" (Luke 22:31, 32). Satan could sift him again and again as a harvester would thresh wheat; Peter might fall again and again, as a man of his nature and temperament would fall, but the Spirit of God never left him. When he turned, he strengthened the brethren by his preaching, by his example of repentance, by his letters of exhortation, and finally by the devotion of his life when he was crucified for the faith (John 21:18, 19). It is thus with us. Weak as we may be, unworthy as we always are, prone to blunder as we sometimes do, yet the Lord loves us and for Jesus' sake forgives us. And the Spirit of God ever strives with us seeking to encourage us to conform to the mind and will of our Lord. O blessed day, that we should live in this era of grace after the outpouring of the Holy Spirit at Pentecost!

Chapter 5

The Holy Spirit—a Power or a Person

John 20

19   Then the same day at evening, being the first day of the week, when the doors were shut where the disciples were assembled for fear of the Jews, came Jesus and stood in the midst, and saith unto them, Peace be unto you.

20   And when he had so said, he shewed unto them his hands and his side. Then were the disciples glad, when they saw the Lord.

21   Then said Jesus to them again, Peace be unto you: as my Father hath sent me, even so send I you.

22   And when he had said this, he breathed on them, and saith unto them, Receive ye the Holy Ghost:

23   Whose soever sins ye remit, they are remitted unto them; and whose soever sins ye retain, they are retained.

One of the spiritually minded, Scripturally discerning members of our church came up to me last week and said: "The Holy Spirit did not come at Pentecost. He came in John 20:22." John 20:22 reads: "And when he had said this, he breathed on them, and saith unto them, Receive ye the Holy Ghost." This church member continued with these words: "Pentecost was but the baptism of power; the Holy Spirit came when Jesus breathed upon His disciples." This persuasion that the Holy Spirit came in John 20:22 is shared by many learned Bible scholars who have expressed a like opinion through the centuries. Arthur Pink, for example, in his exposition of the gospel of John, Volume III, page 287, writes: "What happened at Pentecost was the baptism of *power*, not the coming of the Spirit to indwell them."

But there are some things that trouble me concerning this position. The first thing is found in the words of our Saviour. Before His Ascension, in Luke 24:49-53, our Lord expressly

51

says that the promise of the Father is still in the future. These words were spoken after the meeting of the disciples in John 20:22. They were uttered just before our Lord's Ascension into heaven. In Acts 1:4, 5 our Lord is quoted in the same manner. The occasion for the assembling of the disciples is the Ascension of our Lord back to the heaven from whence He came. Just before His departure, our Lord tells the disciples that they are to wait for the promise of the Father in Jerusalem. As John verily baptized with water, so they shall be baptized with the Holy Spirit not many days hence. The promise of the Father, according to John 14:16, 17, is the Holy Spirit Himself. On the day of Pentecost Peter says that this is the promise of the Father (Acts 2:33). The Apostle explains that what has happened on the day of Pentecost is the coming of the Holy Spirit, which the Father had promised to His Son, the Lord Jesus. Ephesians 1:13 therefore calls the Holy Spirit "the holy Spirit of promise." It is impossible for me, therefore, to see how the Holy Spirit came in John 20:22 when upon a subsequent occasion our Saviour described the coming of the Holy Spirit as a promise to be fulfilled in the near future.

The Holy Spirit Is Not an "It"

Another thing troubles me in the attempt to identify the coming of the Holy Spirit in John 20:22. When we say "the Holy Spirit was given" in John 20:22, and "the power came at Pentecost" in Acts 2:1-4, we separate the person from the power as though they were two different things. It is easy to fall into the psychological error of looking upon the Holy Spirit as an "it," an influence, an energy, a power, a force. We think of any power as an "it." Electricity is a power and also an "it." Gravity is a power and also an "it." A mighty hurricane is a power and also an "it." It is easy, psychologically, to look upon the Holy Spirit as a power, an impersonal "it." When we separate the person from the power, we easily fall into that subconscious attitude. The Holy Spirit becomes an indefinite something or other, an enigmatic mystery.

This attitude of defining the Holy Spirit as an impersonal "it" has been furthered because of a way of translation found in the King James version of the Holy Scriptures. The original Greek language in which the New Testament was written possesses what is called "grammatical gender." Any object can be either masculine, feminine or neuter; a "he," "she" or "it." Other languages beside the Greek also possess what is called grammatical gender." German is one of those languages. The word for "girl" in German is *das madchen*, neuter gender. That sounds so strange to us in English to refer to a girl in the neuter gender, but it is a part of the formation of the German language which possesses "grammatical gender." It is not that the girl is actual neuter, but that in the spoken language the correct reference is in the neuter gender. Greek also possesses that same grammatical structure. The word for spirit, *pneuma* (our word "pneumatic" comes from it), is neuter. The translators of the King James version of the Bible were following the exact grammatical construction when they wrote in Romans 8:16: "The Spirit itself beareth witness with our spirit, that we are the children of God"; and in Romans 8:26: "Likewise the Spirit also helpeth our infirmities: for we know not what we should pray for as we ought: but the Spirit itself maketh intercession for us with groanings which cannot be uttered." But in no sense, and in no way, and at no time did the inspired apostles refer to the Holy Spirit as a "it." In writing correct Greek the Apostle Paul, in these passages in Romans, merely was following the proper construction of the language. The Holy Spirit is always a "he," a "his," or a "him." For example, look at these passages in John:

> And I will pray the Father, and he shall give you another Comforter, that he may abide with you for ever; But the Comforter, which is the Holy Ghost, whom the Father will send in my name, he shall teach you all things, and bring all things to your remembrance, whatsoever I have said unto you (John 14:16, 26).

> But when the Comforter is come, whom I will send unto you from the Father, even the Spirit of truth, which proceedeth from the Father, he shall testify of me (John 15:26).

> Nevertheless I tell you the truth; It is expedient for you that I go away: for if I go not away, the Comforter will not come unto you; but if I depart, I will send him unto you. Howbeit when he, the Spirit of truth, is come, he will guide you into all truth: for he shall not speak of himself; but whatsoever he shall hear, that shall he speak: and he will shew you things to come (John 16:7, 13).

In the Holy Scriptures the Holy Spirit is always a person and never an impersonal power.

The Holy Spirit the Breath of God

Let us turn now to the passage in John 20:22 and let us ask the wisdom of God in seeking to learn what happened upon that first Sunday evening when our Lord appeared to His disciples after He was raised from the dead. John wrote, in John 20:21, that the Lord Jesus appeared to His disciples and, after He had breathed upon them, said unto them, "Receive ye the Holy Ghost." The Greek word translated "breathe" is *enephusese*, first aorist active indicative of *emphusao*, which means "to breathe upon." The act is described as one; it is not repeated. The gift is once for all. In verse twenty-one we are introduced to the similitude of the ministry of the disciples to the ministry of our Lord. As Christ entered upon His ministry as one anointed by the Holy Spirit, so should His disciples enter upon their ministry in the presence and power of the Holy Spirit. "As . . . so . . . ." Our Lord began His public ministry when He was baptized by John the Baptist, at which time the Holy Spirit, in the form of a dove, came upon Him. In the power of the Spirit He was driven into the wilderness to be tried by the devil. In the power of the Spirit He returned to Galilee and began His marvelous Galilean ministry. In the power of the Spirit He did mighty works. By the power of the Spirit He was raised from the dead; and by the power of the Spirit He gave commandment unto the disciples before He was ascended into heaven (Acts 1:2). It is to be thus with the disciples. They were to begin their public ministry in the power and presence of the Holy Spirit, who came upon them at Pentecost.

What is the meaning of the passage in John 20:22 when the Lord thus breathed on them and said: "Receive ye the Holy Ghost"? The word *emphusao* is used nowhere else in the New Testament. It is used only here. But the word was familiar to the disciples, for in their preaching they used the Greek Septuagint translation of the Hebrew Scriptures. The word is found in Genesis 2:7. The passage reads: "And the LORD God formed man of the dust of the ground, and breathed [Greek, *emphusao*] into his nostrils the breath of life; and man became a living soul." In Genesis is recorded man's original creation. Here in John 20:22 is recorded the new creation. As Adam was quickened into a living soul, so these disciples were quickened in faith and in expectancy. Their faith and hope were the first fruits of His Resurrection. His own heavenly Spirit was imparted to them in His name. According to John 20:23: "Whose soever sins ye remit, they are remitted unto them; and whose soever sins ye retain, they are retained." They were to proclaim forgiveness and to threaten doom.

This occasion in John 20:22 was not the coming of the Paraclete, the promise of the Father. That occurred on the day of Pentecost. This occasion described by John is the symbolic account beforehand of the mighty coming of the Presence. Jesus here gave them an earnest of the gift. First, the breath, then, the mighty presence. First, the promise, then, the Pentecost. First, the stillness, then, the outpouring. This is the pattern of the Holy Word of God. First, the quietness, the softness, the stillness; then, the mighty shaking and doing and outpouring. Elijah listens to the still small voice; then the golden chariot and the whirlwind that takes him to heaven. Moses speaks with God in the quiet of the backside of the desert in the bush that burned unconsumed. Then, the confrontation with Pharaoh and the mighty demonstration of the power of God. Gideon places before the Lord the fleece and asks for the quiet gathering and distillation of the dew. Then, the blowing of the trumpets and the breaking of the pitchers. David walked in solitude and silence through the green pastures and by the still waters;

then, his bold challenge to Goliath, and the slaughter of the champion of the blaspheming Philistines. Daniel is on his knees quietly, humbly praying with his face toward Jerusalem; then, the stopping of the mouths of the lions. Nehemiah weeps silently before God; then follows the mighty building up of the walls of Jerusalem. Paul spent three years in silent communion with the Lord in the desert of Arabia; then came the mighty witness for Christ in Damascus, in Anitoch, and throughout the Mediterranean world. John was a lonely exile on the rocky island of Patmos; then, the opening of the heavens and the mighty visions of the Apocalypse. The pattern of the Holy Word of God thus follows John 20:22. First, the quiet breathing, the awesome stillness; then, the mighty outpouring at Pentecost. What happened in John 20:22 was the symbolic, mystic giving of the Holy Spirit, the reality and consummation of which is found at Pentecost.

Taking and Receiving of the Holy Spirit

The second word that we must carefully notice in this symbolic passage of John 20:22 is the word translated "receive"; "Receive ye the Holy Ghost." The word the Apostle John used is *labete*, which is the second aorist active imperative of *lambano*. It can be translated in two ways; either "take" or "receive." The exact word is thus translated in two different ways in John 10:18: "No man taketh it from me, but I lay it down of myself. I have power to lay it down, and I have power to take it again. This commandment have I received of my Father." The word is first translated "take." "I have power to take it again." The identical word is translated "receive" in "This commandment have I received of my Father." Let us, therefore, first use the word in the sense of "take." The disciples are commanded to take the Holy Spirit. It is a definite imperative. The disciples are not totally passive; they also have something to do. The identical word is used in Matthew 26:26 in connection with the institution of the Lord's Supper. After the Lord had blessed the bread and had broken and had given it to the disciples, He said,

"Take, eat." The Lord did not eat the bread for them. They ate the bread for themselves. It is thus with the Holy Spirit. The disciples were commanded to take the Holy Spirit. He is so much at our disposal. We may quench the Spirit, impede the Spirit, strangle the Spirit, grieve the Spirit, hurt the Spirit, refuse the Spirit, deny the Spirit, do violence to the Spirit. The disciples are commanded to take Him. After the faithful praying and the wide expectancy that followed the Ascension of our Lord to heaven, they were ready to "take" at Pentecost. The preceding ten days of prayer and expectancy were not lost. Those days were a part of the program of God. The Lord said to wait for the promise in Jerusalem. At the end of their days of waiting and praying they were ready to "take."

The second way the word can be translated is the one followed in the King James version of the Bible — "Receive ye the Holy Ghost." Jesus was to return to heaven to send the heavenly Gift. "Nevertheless I tell you the truth; It is expedient for you that I go away: for if I go not away, the Comforter will not come unto you; but if I depart, I will send him unto you" (John 16:7). The disciples were to remain on earth to receive the incomparable Gift. His coming is a promise of God the Father. His coming is a sovereign endowment from heaven. We receive the Holy Spirit as a mother heart receives the gentleness of love, as the olive tree receives the infusion of oil, as the green grass receives the freshness from the falling dew. We receive the Holy Spirit as a furnace receives its blast of fire, as a ship's sail receives the sweep of the wind, as a storm receives the fullness of rain, as the marsh is filled by the tides of the sea. When I was a youth, I heard a preacher at an evangelistic conference describe the raising of a ship from the bottom of the bay. The City Council advertised for bids to raise the ship from the floor of the harbor. All of the bids were astronomically high except one which was ridiculously low. They called for the low bidder and listened to his description of the method he would use in raising the hull sunken in the mud of the bay. They were astonished at his method.

He received the assignment and the work was gloriously
done. When the tide was out, he fastened wooden barges
to the sunken ship by strong cables. When the tide came in,
these steel cables tightened. The barges groaned under the
strength of the unseen but mighty power. The ship broke
loose from its floor of mud and was raised to the surface of
the waters. It is thus with us in the coming of the omnipotent power and presence of God. The Holy Spirit is given
to us from heaven for the work we are to do in the earth.
We have but to receive Him in all His might and wonder.

In 1927 the beloved assistant pastor and music leader of
this First Baptist Church copyrighted a song written by
David Ross. It is entitled *Let the Tide Come In*. The stanzas
go like this:

> We thank Thee, Lord, that power is flowing
> Joy is coming, sorrow going;
> Thy ransomed host is growing, growing.
> But may the tide come in.
> Life's precious hours are quickly flying,
> Men are dying, ever dying.
>
> Thy pleading church is crying, crying
> Now may the tide come in.
> We praise Thee for the tidings, cheering,
> Signs of conquest now appearing
> The day of victory is nearing
> Thank God! the tide comes in.

Chapter 6

The Holy Spirit as One of Us

Acts 15
28   For it seemed good to the Holy Ghost, and to us, to
lay upon you no greater burden than these necessary things.

This is an amazing text. The Scriptures state that in the
Jerusalem Conference, when the discussion centered around
the conversion of the Gentiles, the Holy Spirit came to a
conclusion concerning Gentile entrance into the Church,
and the Jewish brethren also came to a conclusion concerning the same matter. They both thought, and deliberated,
and concluded together — both the Holy Spirit and the
brethren. The Holy Spirit is numbered among those who
deliberated, who considered, and who concluded. I repeat,
it is an amazing text.

The Scriptures unfailingly represent God the Father as a
person who is conversing, fellowshiping, working, and visiting with men. Exodus 33:11 states: "And the LORD spake
unto Moses face to face, as a man speaketh unto his friend."
Jehovah God and Moses spoke to one another and discussed
things with one another as two friends considering matters
of the day. It is like the presentation of God we have in the
Garden of Eden in Genesis 3:8, 9: "And they heard the voice
of the LORD God walking in the garden in the cool of the day:
and Adam and his wife hid themselves from the presence
of the LORD God amongst the trees of the garden. And the
LORD God called unto Adam, and said unto him, Where art
thou?" The Lord God in heaven and the mortal man on
earth were friends. They were in the habit of visiting together, and talking together, and discussing things together.

59

The human nature and personality of the Second Person of the Godhead, namely, the Lord Jesus Christ, is obvious. He is both God and man. In the beautiful story of the Ascension (Luke 24:50-53), the Saviour extends His hands to bless the disciples who worship Him as God of very God. The Lord Jesus, though deity, is certainly a person.

But what of the personality of the Third Person in the Godhead? Is God the Holy Spirit a person? There is no question but that the Bible presents the deity of the Holy Spirit. He also is God of very God. The baptismal formula (Matthew 28:19) expressly says that we are to baptize "in the name of." The word "name" is singular. The full name of deity is Father, Son, and Holy Spirit. He is the Triune God. The beautiful benediction (II Corinthians 13:14) presents all three as equal. They are one in essence, in being, in attributes, in power and in glory. Whatever can be said of God can be said of the Holy Spirit. He is eternal according to Hebrews 9:14. He is omnipotent according to Genesis 1:2. He is omniscient according to I Corinthians 2:10, 11. He knows all that God knows. He is omnipresent according to Psalm 1:3; 9:7-10. He is the Spirit of Holiness (Romans 1:4). He is the Spirit of life (Romans 8:2). He is the Spirit of truth (John 14:7). He lives in the temples of our bodies (I Corinthians 6:19). He is to be worshiped, adored, loved and obeyed. We are on most holy ground thus speaking of the deity of the Holy Spirit of God. The truth involved in His person and presence is most sacred and precious.

The Personality of the Holy Spirit

Yet, even though He is deity and God of very God, He is also a fellow person. The word "person" was first used by the churches in reference to the distinctions in the Godhead when the theologians entered into controversies with Sabellius around A.D. 200. The heretic, Sabellius, defined the Holy Spirit as just one of the modal expressions and manifestations of God. He looked upon the Holy Spirit as an energy, an effluence. The best word the churches could discover to describe the Holy Spirit was the word "person." The Holy

Spirit is a person in the same sense that God the Father is a person and God the Son is a person. The Scriptures thus unfailingly present the personality of the Third Person of the Trinity. In the history of the churches, the opponents of the personality of the Holy Spirit have found it necessary to deny the inspiration and accurateness of the Scriptures in order to sustain heretical teachings, for the Bible correctly presents the Holy Spirit as a person. A denial of the personality of the Holy Spirit is a denial of the Trinity.

It is most difficult to define and describe "spirit" as such, whether in God or in us. In our own case, it is most difficult to describe our real selves in category and definition. Just what are the processes of "spirit" in our mortal bodies? Which is actually you? — the house of clay in which you live or the spirit, the personality, that inhabits your body? When you die and we look upon your still, silent face in the casket, is that you we are looking upon? Are you dust? Is a corrupting corpse you? Do we bury you in the open grave? Surely not; you are something more than dust, corruption and decay. You are spirit, personality, quickening life. But just how would you describe what happens when the spirit is separated from the body in death? If, therefore, we find it difficult to define and describe "spirit" in us, how much more is it difficult to define and describe the Holy Spirit of God!

There are some things, however, that we can say about the Holy Spirit, things which are patently obvious. In a full-orbed personality four characteristics are included: A person is someone who can think (he has mind, understanding). He can feel (he has emotions, sensibility). He can choose (he has will, purpose, volition). And he can do (he can act). All four of these characteristics of a full-orbed personality can be easily seen in the Holy Spirit of God.

First, He can think; He has mind and understanding. He is so presented in our text in Acts 15:28: "For it seemed good to the Holy Ghost, and to us, to lay upon you no greater burden than these necessary things." He has mind and intelligence as is seen in I Corinthians 2:10, 11: "But God hath revealed them unto us by his Spirit: for the Spirit searcheth all things, yea, the deep things of God. For what man knoweth the things of a man, save the spirit of man which is in him? even so the things of God knoweth no man, but the Spirit of God." He knows the deep things of God. His intelligence can be seen in Ephesians 1:17: "That the God of our Lord Jesus Christ, the Father of glory may give unto you the spirit of wisdom and revelation in the knowledge of him." Isaiah 11:2 says: "And the spirit of the LORD shall rest upon him, the spirit of wisdom and understanding, the spirit of counsel and might, the spirit of knowledge and of the fear of the LORD."

Second, He can feel. He is so presented in Ephesians 4:30. The Holy Spirit can be hurt by the disobedience and sin in our lives. Just as we can be filled with sorrow and sadness, so the Holy Spirit can be hurt and grieved.

Third, He can choose; He can will. The Holy Spirit possesses volition and purpose in I Corinthians 12:11: "But all these worketh that one and the selfsame Spirit, dividing to every man severally as he will." The Holy Spirit sovereignly bestows upon each member of the household of faith the gift that is chosen for him. The gifts of the Spirit are bestowed according to the will and purpose of the Third Person of the Trinity.

The Work of the Holy Spirit Is the Work of God

Fourth, the Holy Spirit can work; He can do; He can act. The works of the Spirit are literally the works of God.

(1) He is the author of the Scriptures. The Bible was produced over a period of fifteen hundred years, penned by over fifty different writers in sixty-six different books. Yet, there is a unity in the Holy Word of God that is undeniable. From Genesis to Revelation it follows one constant theme; namely, the redemptive purpose of God in human history. How could such a unity be attained through so many different writers, through so many different ages, over so long a period of time? The answer is obvious and is seen in II Timothy 3:16, where Paul avows that the Scriptures are "God-breathed." Accord-

ing to II Peter 1:21 the Scriptures did not originate in the mind of the writer, but holy men of God were borne along as they were moved by the Holy Spirit. This can be beautifully illustrated in II Samuel 23:1-3: "Now these be the last words of David. David the son of Jesse said, and the man who was raised up on high, the anointed of the God of Jacob, and the sweet psalmist of Israel, said, The Spirit of the LORD spake by me, and his word was in my tongue. The God of Israel said, The Rock of Israel spake to me, He that ruleth over men must be just, ruling in the fear of God." David spoke as a prophet and what he said was inspired by the Holy Spirit. Psalm 22, written by David is as exact a description of the crucifixion as if the psalmist had stood at the foot of the cross and delineated the sufferings of the Saviour. Did David the King of Israel himself ever actually experience such things as he describes in the twenty-second Psalm? No. Then, how was he able to depict such sufferings in this Messianic Psalm, describing an event fulfilled a thousand years hence? Because he was speaking by inspiration. He was borne along by the Holy Ghost.

This authorship of the Scriptures by the Holy Spirit can be seen in Ezekiel 2:2:

> And the spirit entered into me when he spake unto me, and set me upon my feet, that I heard him that spake unto me.

And, in Acts 1:16:

> Men and brethren, this scripture must needs have been fulfilled, which the Holy Ghost by the mouth of David spake before concerning Judas, which was guide to them that took Jesus.

In Hebrews 9:8:

> The Holy Ghost this signifying, that the way into the holiest of all was not yet made manifest, while as the first tabernacle was yet standing.

And, in Hebrews 10:15, 16:

> Whereof the Holy Ghost also is a witness to us: for after that he had said before, This is the covenant that I will make with

them after those days, saith the Lord, I will put my laws into
their hearts, and in their minds will I write them.

(2) The Holy Spirit is not only the author of the Scriptures; He is also the great Teacher and Illuminator. He is
presented as such in John 14:26:

But the Comforter, which is the Holy Ghost, whom the Father
will send in my name, he shall teach you all things, and bring
all things to your remembrance, whatsoever I have said unto
you.

John 16:13, 14:

Howbeit when he, the Spirit of truth, is come, he will guide
you into all truth: for he shall not speak of himself; but whatsoever he shall hear, that shall he speak: and he will shew
you things to come. He shall glorify me: for he shall receive
of mine, and shall shew it unto you.

Romans 8:14:

For as many as are led by the Spirit of God, they are the sons
of God.

The Holy Spirit is the author of the Bible and we are to
go to His words in the Holy Scriptures for truth and for
guidance. The Lord Jesus is no longer with us in the flesh
to explain to us all of the things that we need to know and
to show us all the things that we need to do. The Holy Spirit
is given to us that we might have the wisdom, the direction,
and the illumination the living presence of our Lord would
otherwise provide. Were Jesus here in the flesh, He would
walk by our side and tell us all we need to know and all we
need to do. The French critic, Renan, called the story in
Luke 24 the most beautiful in the world. There, in Luke 24,
two disciples of our Lord are described as they walked from
Jerusalem to Emmaus in despondency and despair. While
they thus walked along together, a Stranger came alongside
and walked with them. He asked them why they were so
sad. They replied that the hope of the world had died, that
the light of the earth had flickered out, that nothing remained but darkness, despondency and despair. The Stranger asked them why they thus felt so lost. The two disciples

replied that it was because the hope of Israel, Jesus of Nazareth, had been crucified. "Yea," said those disciples, "some women had come to say that He was raised from the dead, but their words were but old wives' tales; they were the victims of hallucinations and wishful thinking." It was then that the Stranger walking alongside opened their minds to the understanding of the Holy Word of God in the law of Moses, and in the Prophets of Israel, and in the holy writings — the three sections into which the ancient Hebrews divided the Word of God. Throughout the whole Book the Lord illuminated their minds that they might see that Christ must suffer and be raised from the dead, and that remission of sin must be preached in His name. After this long discussion and walking journey, they came to the little city of Emmaus and the Stranger made as though He would continue on. The two disciples urged Him to come into their humble home to spend the evening because the sun was set and the hour was late. When they broke bread together at the evening meal, the Stranger was asked to return thanks and, as He was saying grace at the table, the two disciples recognized Him. He was the Lord. What the Saviour did in walking beside and guiding the disciples into the truth of God, so the Holy Spirit does today, walking alongside to reveal to us the way, the word, and the purpose of God. He is the Paraclete, the One called "Alongside." He is our glorious Teacher and Illuminator.

(3) The Holy Spirit convicts us of sin. He is the instrument of our regeneration.

John 16:8-11:

> And when he is come, he will reprove the world of sin, and of righteousness, and of judgment: Of sin, because they believe not on me; Of righteousness, because I go to my Father, and ye see me no more; Of judgment, because the prince of this world is judged.

He regenerates the soul, John 3:5:

> Jesus answered, Verily, verily, I say unto thee, Except a man be born of water and of the Spirit, he cannot enter into the kingdom of God.

Titus 3:5, 6:

> Not by works of righteousness which we have done, but according to his mercy he saved us, by the washing of regeneration, and renewing of the Holy Ghost: Which he shed on us abundantly through Jesus Christ our Saviour.

If the preaching of the Gospel is effective, it is due to His presence and to His blessed work. Paul said to the Church at Corinth, I Corinthians 2:4:

> And my speech and my preaching was not with enticing words of man's wisdom, but in demonstration of the Spirit and of power.

He wrote to the Church at Thessalonica, I Thessalonians 1:5:

> For our gospel came not unto you in word only, but also in power, and in the Holy Ghost, and in much assurance; as ye know what manner of men we were among you for your sake.

Zechariah said, Zechariah 4:6:

> Then he answered and spake unto me, saying, This is the word of the LORD unto Zerubbabel, saying, Not by might, nor by power, but by my spirit, saith the LORD of hosts.

(4) He is the great Helper and Comforter and Sustainer in the Christian life. His comforting presence is promised in John 14:16-18:

> And I will pray the Father, and he shall give you another Comforter, that he may abide with you for ever; Even the Spirit of truth; whom the world cannot receive, because it seeth him not, neither knoweth him: but ye know him; for he dwelleth with you, and shall be in you. I will not leave you comfortless: I will come to you.

According to Romans 8:26 He helps us in our infirmities. According to Romans 8:27 He helps us in our praying. He further chooses leaders for the churches as we read in Acts 13:2. He is found checking our footsteps, guiding our paths into other fields, Acts 16:6, 7. He is speaking to the churches, Revelation 2:7. Time would fail us to speak of the work of the Holy Spirit in the lives of the saints of the Old Testament, and in the life of Christ, and in the lives of the apostles. Literally, the works of the Spirit are the works of God.

The Relationship Between the Persons in the Godhead

We turn now to discuss briefly the relationship between the Holy Spirit and the other Persons in the Godhead. There are two lines of teaching that are found in the New Testament and in the Bible as a whole.

First, the New Testament insists upon the unity of the Godhead. This is seen in I Corinthians 8:4-6: "As concerning therefore the eating of those things that are offered in sacrifice unto idols, we know that an idol is nothing in the world, and that there is none other God but one. For though there be that are called gods, whether in heaven or in earth, (as there be gods many, and lords many,) But to us there is but one God, the Father, of whom are all things, and we in him; and one Lord Jesus Christ, by whom are all things, and we by him." And in James 2:19: "Thou believest that there is one God; thou doest well . . . ."

Second, there are other passages in the New Testament, as in the Bible as a whole, which reveal distinctions in the Godhead. This is seen in the story of the baptism of Jesus (Matthew 3:16, 17), in the name of the triune God in Matthew 28:19, and in the beautiful benediction in II Corinthians 13:14. The Father sends the Son, the Son sends the Spirit, and the Spirit empowers the Son (Matthew 4:1; Luke 4:1; Mark 1:12). The Father honors the Son, the Son honors the Father, and the Spirit honors the Son. The Son reveals the Father (John 14:9), and the Spirit reveals the Son (John 16:13, 14). He is called not only the Spirit of God (Matthew 3:16), but also the Spirit of Christ (Romans 8:9), and the Spirit of Jesus (Philippians 1:19). The ministry of the Holy Spirit is performed in His own power and gives testimony to His eternal deity and glory, but His ministry is also accomplished in behalf of the Father and of the Son (John 16:13-15). The Spirit proceeds eternally from the Father and the Son. The Greek word *ekporeuetai* (proceeds) in John 15:26 is in the present tense. His procession from God the Father and God the Son is eternal and continuous. In our souls, in our lives, in our churches, He takes the place of Jesus in the flesh. Jesus has returned to heaven and the Spirit of Jesus, which is Jesus Himself, is here with us. In practical religion it is impossible to distinguish between the Spirit of Christ in the heart and Christ Himself in the heart. In I Corinthians 6:19 Paul speaks of the Holy Spirit as living in our bodies. When we possess the Holy Spirit, we possess Jesus. What is given by the Spirit in our hearts is Christ transcendent, unlimited, immeasurably, gloriously triumphant. There are not three Gods — but one. When we get to heaven we shall not see three Gods — but one. All the God there is, is one — Jehovah God. All the God we shall ever see is one, even Jesus our Lord. All the God we shall ever feel is one, the Holy Spirit. To the Three Persons in One be glory and honor and dominion forever and ever. Amen.

Chapter 7

Emblems of the Holy Spirit: The Dove

Luke 3

21 Now when all the people were baptized, it came to pass, that Jesus also being baptized, and praying, the heaven was opened,

22 And the Holy Ghost descended in a bodily shape like a dove upon him, and a voice came from heaven, which said, Thou art my beloved Son; in thee I am well pleased.

The prophet Hosea, in 12:10, quotes Jehovah God as saying, "I have also spoken by the prophets, and I have multiplied visions, and used similitudes . . . ." The Bible is a book of similitudes. It is a book of similes, metaphors, allegories, parables, types, symbols and emblems. If we are to possess any understanding of the Holy Scriptures at all, we must understand these similitudes. A simile is a figure of speech in which one thing is compared to another. Psalm 102:6 says, "I am like a pelican of the wilderness: . . . like an owl of the desert." Proverbs 25:25 reads, "As cold waters to a thirsty soul, so is good news from a far country." When Solomon wrote, in Song of Solomon 1:9, "I have compared thee, O my love, to a company of horses in Pharaoh's chariots," he was paying an exorbitant tribute to his heart's love. Horses were brought from India to Egypt at great cost; only the rich could afford them. They, therefore, brought to the king's mind the simile of costliness and preciousness.

A metaphor is a figure of speech whereby one thing is called another. When Isaiah says that the Suffering Servant is "brought as a lamb to the slaughter" (53:7), he is using a simile. When John the Baptist introduces Jesus with this exclamation, "Behold the Lamb of God . . . ." (John 1:29), he is using a metaphor. An allegory is a prolonged metaphor; a story in metaphoric language. In Judges 9:1-21 Jotham's story of the trees and the bramble bush is a tremendous allegory condemning the evil of Abimelech. A parable is a truth illustrated by a factual story, "an earthly story with a heavenly meaning." There are seven marvelous parables of the kingdom of heaven told by Jesus in Matthew 13. A type is an object or event used to prefigure another object or event. I Corinthians 5:7 says, "Christ our passover is sacrificed for us." The Paschal Lamb is a type of Christ. John 3:14 reads, "And as Moses lifted up the serpent in the wilderness, even so must the Son of man be lifted up." The Brazen Serpent is a type of Christ. An emblem is a visible sign of an idea, suggesting the idea by common qualities or recognized associations. A circle without beginning or ending is an emblem of eternity. The dove is an emblem of peace; the eagle is an emblem of power. The red, white, and blue flag is an emblem of America; the cross is an emblem of Christianity. A symbol can be an entirely arbitrary sign as witnessed in algebra, geometry, astronomy, the alphabet, the Nazi swastika, the donkey and elephant; the latter two, symbols of the Democratic and Republican parties. With these definitions in mind, we come to discuss the many figurative representations of the work and ways of the Holy Spirit of God. These emblems are so many — a dove, a seal, oil, water, fire, wind, clothing, an earnest — that we have opportunity to refer to but a few. In this message we speak of the dove as an emblem of the Spirit.

The Spirit Brooding as a Dove

Genesis 1:2 reads, "And the earth was without form, and void; and darkness was upon the face of the deep. And the Spirit of God moved upon the face of the waters." The earth had become *tohu wa bohu*, "without form and void." By what means it thus became chaotic, we do not know unless by the judgment of God upon it because of sin committed by Satan and his angels. We do know that God did not create the world *bohu*, "a waste" (Isaiah 45:18). The identical words used to describe the chaos of the creation in Genesis 1:2 are used in Isaiah 34:11 to delineate the judgment of God upon the nation's sin. The whole chapter of Isaiah 34 is a preview and a type of what Jehovah will do in the Day of the Lord, in the destruction of the Battle of Armageddon. What God did at the beginning of the creation, in His heavy judgment upon sin, God will do again at the end time. Both at the beginning in Genesis and at the ending in Revelation, the Spirit of God re-creates a destroyed universe.

"And the Spirit of God moved upon the face of the waters" (Genesis 1:2). The Hebrew word translated "moved" is *rachaph* and means "to flutter," "to hover," "to brood." In Deuteronomy 32:11 the word is translated "fluttereth." The Latin Vulgate translates the word *incubabat*, as a bird on a nest. Over the chaos, first the Spirit moves; then the fiat, "Let there be light" (Genesis 1:3). First the Spirit as a dove descends; then follows the blessedness of the power of God upon the earth.

The emblem and type of the Holy Spirit as a dove resting upon a weary world is beautifully seen in the story of the flood recounted in Genesis 8:6-12. The Bible is like a majestic mountain in which there is progressiveness in its elevation, but also oneness in its substance. The poet Shelly wrote:

> The mountains kiss high heaven,
> And the waves clasp one another.

So the Scriptures kiss high heaven in their affectionate testimony, and the Old Testament and the New Testament clasp each other in their revelation. In the Genesis story of the flood, the sending forth of the dove from the ark to the earth is a type of the sending forth of the Holy Spirit from heaven to rest upon Christ and upon us. The story is a type of the ministry of the Holy Spirit in this present age.

The Raven and the Dove Sent Out From the Ark

The raven, an unclean bird, was sent from the ark. It did not return. It sat upon the bloated, floating corpses of the dead, eating the carrion of that awesome judgment. The dove was then sent out, but it returned to the ark. The corruption of the earth was offensive to her. She found no rest for the sole of her foot. The dove that refused to feed upon the carrion of the world was ceremonially clean, acceptable for sacrifice. The raven was expressly forbidden (Leviticus 11:15). The spirit of the world (the flight of the raven) feeds upon corruption, uncleanness and iniquity. The Spirit of Christ (the dove) is gentle, harmless, loving (Matthew 10: 16).

The dove was sent out of the ark and found rest *after* the terrible judgment of God upon the corruption of the world. The pattern of God's mercy ever follows this order. First, we are introduced to the creation (Genesis 1:1), then we see the waste caused by the judgment of God upon sin (Genesis 1:2), then we behold the new re-creation (Genesis 1:3). First, we rejoice in the paradise of Eden (Genesis 2), then we despair over the waste of sin (Genesis 3), then we are blessed by the mercies and grace of God represented by the Cherubim (Genesis 3:24). First, we follow the precious presence and perfect ministry of Christ (Matthew 1 - 28), then we are terrified by the judgment of God upon a corrupt, rejecting world (Revelation 4 - 19), then we are delivered to the new heaven and the new earth (Revelation 21, 22). The first time the dove was sent forth, she found no resting place for the sole of her foot. She returned, Josephus says, with her feet "wet and muddy," attesting to man's sin and God's judgment upon it. The second time the dove was sent forth, she returned again without finding rest but this time with an olive leaf "plucked off" — a promise of coming peace. The third time the dove was sent forth she found the water abated. She found a resting place and remained. It was so with our Saviour at His baptism in our text, Luke 3:21, 22. Our Lord went through the waters of death and judgment. The representative Man, bearing the sins of the world, condemned by the law as a sinner, becoming sin for us, was slain and buried before He was raised and the Holy Spirit as a dove came upon Him. Our Saviour must go through the Jordan of God's judgment upon sin, the dark, swollen river of death, before He can send upon us the ascension gift of the Holy Spirit. He first must carry captivity captive before He can give gifts unto men. There must be death, burial, resurrection before there can be the descent of the Holy Spirit. Because Christ gave Himself up to death for our sins, He is able to bestow upon us the Holy Spirit. The Lamb of God must die for us before the Holy Spirit can live in us. If there be no Calvary of substitution, there can be no Pentecost of blessing.

The Holy Spirit Rests Upon Us

In Christ's death for us the judgment upon sin is past, the storm has exhausted itself. The Holy Spirit takes up His abode in us, even in us who are the mystical body of Christ. A passenger aboard ship came on deck one morning after the night's sleep and said to the captain: "The heavens are angry. The seas are mountainous. The sky is lowering. A great storm must be coming." "No," replied the captain, "the storm is already past. This is the aftermath. We are safe." It is thus with us who live in the finished work of the death of our Saviour, and who have received the Holy Spirit in our hearts. The storm of judgment upon our sins is past. Christ has delivered us. We now possess the abiding presence of the Holy Spirit in our lives. The dove from the ark found a resting place when the waters of judgment assuaged. John 1:32 reads, "And John bare record, saying, I saw the Spirit descending from heaven like a dove, and it abode upon him." The Greek word translated "abode" is *meno*, "to dwell." In the Old Testament the Holy Spirit went to and fro, finding no resting place. In the New Testament the dove rested upon Christ, abode upon Him, the perfect representative man, and through Him upon all of us who believe in Him.

The Holy Spirit is "with" us, *meta*. The word is used three times in the New Testament with reference to the Holy Spirit: John 14:16; II Corinthians 13:14; I Thessalonians 1:6. He is our Comforter, our Companion, and our Guardian

Helper. We most urgently need to pause and to listen to the voice of the Spirit; "Be still and know that I am God." One time John Ruskin wrote to a young friend these words: "There is no music in a rest, Katie, that I know of, but there is the making of music in it. People are always missing that part of life — melody, and scrambling on without counting . . . . People are always talking of perseverance and courage and fortitude, but patience is the finest, worthiest, and the rarest, too." An unknown poet has written the admonition most meaningfully in these lines:

In Every Life

There's a pause that is better than onward rush,
Better than hewing or mightiest doing;
'Tis the standing still at sovereign will.
There's a hush that is better than ardent speech,
Better than sighing, or wilderness crying;
'Tis the being still at sovereign will.
The pause and the hush sing a double song
In unison low, and for all time long.
O human soul, God's working plan
Goes on, nor needs the aid of man.

Stand still and see (Exodus 14:13).
Be still and know (Psalm 46:10).

The face of Moses became bright with the shining of the glory of God, not by a hurried call at heaven's gate, but by dwelling in the Lord's presence forty days and forty nights. Pentecost found a prepared company of believers when the disciples continued without interruption in prayer for ten days. Wait upon God. His coming is like a dove, soft, gentle, so easily dismissed. "Wait, I say, upon the Lord" (Psalms 27:14; 37:34).

Chapter 8

Emblems of the Holy Spirit:
The Anointing Oil

Zechariah 4

1 And the angel that talked with me came again, and waked me, as a man that is wakened out of his sleep,

2 And said unto me, What seest thou? And I said, I have looked, and behold a candlestick all of gold, with a bowl upon the top of it, and his seven lamps thereon, and seven pipes to the seven lamps, which are upon the top thereof:

3. And two olive trees by it, one upon the right side of the bowl, and the other upon the left side thereof.

4 So I answered and spake to the angel that talked with me, saying, What are these, my Lord?

5 Then the angel that talked with me answered and said unto me, Knowest thou not what these be? And I said, No, my lord.

6 Then he answered and spake unto me, saying, This is the word of the LORD unto Zerubbabel, saying, Not by might, nor by power, but by my spirit, saith the LORD of hosts.

Palestine is a land of the olive tree. As no one visits Switzerland without buying a watch (unless it be Mr. Elgin or Mr. Hamilton!), so hardly anyone visits the Holy Land without carrying away a souvenir carved in olive wood: such articles as the two covers of a Bible, carved figures of camels, or any of a thousand other things. The olive tree, to the ancient Hebrews, was a source of food, of medicine, and of oil for worship. The fruit of the olive tree played an important part in the lives of God's people in both the Old and New Testaments. Uniformly, when used typically, olive oil has reference to the Holy Spirit wherever it is presented in the Bible.

The Anointing Oil in the Mosaic Institutions

The tabernacle (Exodus 40:9-11), and all things therein, including the altar and the loaves of shewbread, were anointed with oil, setting forth the ministry of the Holy Spirit in all aspects of the work of redemption. Pure olive oil (Exodus 27:20, 21) kept the lamps burning constantly in the Holy Place, a picture of the ministry of the Holy Spirit in revelation and illumination. Apart from the oil and the light it gave, the glories of Christ portrayed in the embroidered linen, the seven-branched lampstand, the table of shewbread, the golden altar of incense, and the inner veil would have been left in complete darkness. The way into the Holy of Holies would not have been made plain. The illuminating light of the Holy Spirit falls upon Christ to make Him known to us and to lead us to Him.

The sacrifices, with their offerings of blood and anointings with oil, faithfully portray the atonement of Christ and the outpouring of the Holy Spirit. After the burnt offering described in Leviticus, chapter one, comes the meal offering described in Leviticus 2:1-11. The fine flour, beaten and ground, pictures our Lord's perfect humanity sacrificed for us. The oil mingled with the fine flour and the oil poured upon the loaves baked in the fire pictures the Holy Spirit in and upon the life of our Lord. Christ was born of the Spirit (Luke 1:35), and empowered by the Spirit for His divine work (Luke 3:22; 4:1, 14, 18). The order of these sacrifices provides a beautiful illustration of the inspiration of the Holy Scriptures. The Bible follows the typology faithfully; first, the atoning sacrifice of Christ for us, then the outpouring of the Holy Spirit upon us which the Saviour's atonement procured for us. The burnt offering is sacrificed for us before the meal offering mingled with oil is eaten by the worshipers. Our divine Isaac (Christ Jesus in type) is offered up before Eliezer (the Holy Spirit in type) is sent forth to seek a bride (the chosen and elect *ecclesia,* the church) for the beloved Son (Genesis 24). The rock is smitten (Christ must die) before the living water (the Holy Spirit, John 7:39) gushes out. The swollen Jordan (death) must be passed before Canaan (the rest provided by the Holy Spirit) can be entered. Christ must go beneath the baptismal waters (death, burial, and resurrection) before the heavens open and the Spirit descends (Matthew 3:16, 17).

The types of blood for atonement and oil for the Holy Spirit are most graphically and beautifully presented in the law of the cleansing of the leper, recounted in Leviticus 14. Two birds are brought to the priest; the first is killed over running water and the wings of the other are dipped in the blood of the first, after which the living bird is loosed to fly away in an open field. By the blood of sacrifice (Christ's atonement on the cross) and by the living water (the regenerating power of the Holy Spirit), our sins are borne away and we become new creatures in Him. The cleansed leper is then brought before the priest and the priest places blood upon his right ear, upon the thumb of his right hand, and upon the great toe of his right foot. After this, the priest anoints with oil the right ear of the cleansed leper, the thumb of his right hand, and the great toe of his right foot. First, there is blood of atonement (the death of Christ); then there is oil of consecration (the pouring out of the Spirit). Oil is placed upon the ear. "I will hear for Thee." Oil is placed upon the hand. "I will work for Thee." Oil is placed upon the foot. "I will walk for Thee." Oil is placed upon the head, "Lord, illuminate my mind, guide my thoughts that I may think for Thee." We are to know of God (I John 2:20, 27). We are to see for God (Revelation 3:18). We are to radiate the gladness of God (Psalm 45:7; Hebrews 1:9; Psalm 104:15; Isaiah 61:3). This is a heavenly language the deaf can hear and the dumb can understand.

One of the most meaningful types in the blessed Scriptures is that of the oil of anointing for service. Anointing oil (Exodus 40:12-15) was poured out upon Aaron (a type of Christ, "the Anointed One," our High Priest) and upon his sons (upon us who bear His name). The mighty works of the Saviour were done in the power of the Holy Spirit (Luke 3:22; 4:1, 14, 18; Acts 10:38; I Peter 1:12; Ephesians 3:17).

Power to preach (Luke 4:18,19) comes from the unction of the Holy Spirit. It is told that one time the devil was preaching the Gospel. When a saint vigorously objected, his fears were allayed with these words, "Have no fear; the preaching of the devil will do no good; there is no power in it." We have no power in any ministry before God without the anointing of the Holy Spirit. As upon the kings of Israel oil was poured (upon Saul, I Samuel 9:16; 10:1; upon David, I Samuel 16:13; Psalm 23:5; II Samuel 5:3), so upon us the anointing of the Holy Spirit must come (Acts 1:8). To be saved is to be called for service. To love God is to work for God. This is the very heart of the Christian faith and is so opposite to other religions. An Arab interpreter once was asked what constituted the sanctity of a certain Moslem saint. "What does he do?" The Arab interpreter replied, "He do nothing; he very holy man." This is not holiness in any Biblical sense whatsoever. There is no such thing in the Scriptures as "good for nothing." Our anointing is for service.

The Unfailing Supply of the Holy Spirit

The unfailing and continuous supply of the Holy Spirit is pictured in the marvelous vision of the prophet Zechariah, in Zechariah 4:1-6. Historically, the vision has reference to the work of Joshua and Zerubbabel, chosen priest and elected governor of the people for the rebuilding of the temple. Prophetically, the vision forecasts the work of the two witnesses as expressly stated in Revelation 11:3,4. But typically, emblematically, the vision portrays the ministry of the Spirit-anointed man in this day as well as in that day. Our strength is the strength of God. "Not by might, nor by power, but by my spirit, saith the Lord of hosts" (Zechariah 4:6). God's empowering and omnipotent Spirit is poured out upon us, not in our self-vaunted, human capacities but in our weakness, in our humble commitment to God's purpose of grace. To those who have no might, God increaseth strength (Isaiah 40:29). To Gideon's little, depleted band of three hundred, Jehovah gave victory over the Midianites.

By the Spirit of the Lord, David prevailed over Goliath. When Jehoshaphat confessed to the Almighty his abject weakness, God gave him national victory over his enemies. (II Chronicles 20:12, "O our God, wilt thou not judge them? for we have no might against this great company that cometh against us; neither know we what to do; but our eyes are upon thee.") When Daniel was shut up in the den of lions, deliverance came from heaven. When the impotent man was unable to enter the pool at the stirring of the waters (John 5:1-9), Jesus healed him. When we were yet without strength, in due time Christ died for the ungodly (Romans 5:6). When Paul was weak, God made him strong (II Corinthians 12:10). God always makes us equal, through the anointing of His Spirit, for any burden or for any assignment He places upon us. The constancy of the supply of God's Holy Spirit (John 3:34) is emphasized in Zechariah's vision by the vital contact of the lampstands with the two olive trees. The bowls of oil found their unfailing supply, not by pumps or oil drums, nor by any other man-made, mechanical device, but by the flow of pure oil from the living trees.

We are never able to deplete God's power, nor are we ever able to come to the end of God's Holy Spirit. The more we do, the more we are able to do. The more we give, the more God supplies us to give. The more we share, the more we have to share. Under the direction of God Himself the prophet Elijah said to the famished widow of Zarephath: "Fear not; go and do as thou hast said: but make me thereof a little cake first, and bring it unto me, and after make for thee and for thy son. For thus saith the LORD God of Israel, The barrel of meal shall not waste, neither shall the cruse of oil fail, until the day that the LORD sendeth rain upon the earth" (I Kings 17:13, 14). True to God's promise, the barrel of meal did not waste nor did the cruse of oil fail throughout the years of the terrible famine. In sharing what little she possessed with the man of God, she provided both for herself and for her son. This reward from the bountiful fullness of God's Spirit is beautifully versed in a poem by an unknown saint. He wrote:

OIL IN A CRUSE

Is thy cruse of comfort wasting?
Rise and share it with another,
And through all the years of famine
It shall serve thee and thy brother.
Love divine will fill thy storehouse,
Or thy handful still renew;
Scanty fare for one will often
Make a royal feast for two.
For the heart grows rich in giving,
All its wealth is living grain;
Seeds which mildew in the garner,
Scattered, fill with gold the plain.
Is thy burden hard and heavy?
Do thy steps drag wearily?
Help to bear thy brother's burden;
God will bear both it and thee.
Is thy heart a well left empty?
None but God its void can fill;
Nothing but a ceaseless fountain
Can its ceaseless longing still.
Is thy heart a living power?
Self-entwined, its strength sinks low;
It can only live in loving,
And by serving love will grow.

The Anointing Oil for the Healing of the Sick

We enter an altogether different world when we come to discuss the emblematic use of oil in anointing the sick. Is the oil medicinal and does its use refer only to its healing properties, or is the oil a type of the healing presence and power of the Holy Spirit? Mark 6:12, 13 says of the twelve apostles: "And they went out, and preached that men should repent. And they cast out many devils, and anointed with oil many that were sick, and healed them." James, the Lord's brother and the pastor of the church of Jerusalem, wrote in James 5:14, 15: "Is any sick among you? let him call for the elders of the church; and let them pray over him, anointing him with oil in the name of the Lord: And the prayer of faith shall save the sick, and the Lord shall raise him up; and if he have committed sins, they shall be forgiven him." For what purpose is this "anointing with oil"? *Ellicott's Commentary* says that its use with the sick is altogether symbolic, that it pictures the miraculous power of the Spirit of the Lord to heal. The *American Commentary* says that its use is medicinal. The *Expositor's Bible* on one page says that the anointing with oil pictures the healing presence of the Spirit, and on the next page it says that the oil is medicinal. On page 634, Volume VI of the *Expositor's Bible,* the author writes: "It is altogether beside the mark to suggest that the elders were summoned as people who were specially skilled in medicine. Of that there is not only no hint, but the context excludes the idea. If that were in the writer's mind, why does he not say at once, 'Let him call for the physicians'? The case is one in which medicine has already done all that it can, or in which it can do nothing at all." Then on the next page the author says: "What purpose was the oil intended to serve? Was it medicinal? The reason oil was selected was that it was believed to have healing properties. That oil was supposed to be efficacious as medicine is plain from numerous passages both in and outside of Holy Scripture." Now, what shall we believe? Is the oil symbolic or medicinal?

Let us believe both, but with our main emphasis upon the symbolic. As an aid to faith, the oil would have tremendous significance to the people of the New Testament. It always has been and still is easier to believe when visible means are used. Twice Christ used spittle to heal blindness in keeping with the tradition commonly held that its use was beneficial to eyesight (John 9:6; Mark 8:23). The healing properties of oil are not without mention in the Scriptures as well as in ancient history. Isaiah 1:6 reads, "From the sole of the foot even unto the head there is no soundness in it; but wounds, and bruises, and putrifying sores: they have not been closed, neither bound up, neither mollified with ointment." All of us remember the gracious goodness of the Good Samaritan who, finding the poor traveler on the Jerusalem to Jericho road, beaten and robbed, "went to him and bound up his wounds, pouring in oil and wine." The historians Dion Cassius and Strabo say that a mixture of oil and wine was used for the malady which struck the army of Aelius Gallus. Josephus writes that physicians bathed Herod the Great in oil in his last, extreme illness. Celsus recommends rubbing with oil in the case of fever and other ailments. Thus the ancient, medicinal use of oil is plainly and unequivocally demonstrated.

But in the hands of holy men of God, oil is for the most part an emblem of the Holy Spirit. It is not so much the medicinal properties of the oil that heal the sick as it is the appeal to God. James plainly avows, "The prayer of faith shall save [heal] the sick." The anointing oil, as in the Old Testament, so in the New Testament, is a type of the healing, saving presence of the Holy Spirit by whose power healing could be claimed for the sick.

Chapter 9

Other Emblems of the Holy Spirit

Hosea 12

10 I have also spoken by the prophets, and I have multiplied visions, and used similitudes, by the ministry of the prophets.

The blessings of the Holy Spirit upon us are multitudinous. To describe them, the Bible uses similitudes, similes, metaphors, types and emblems. There are five meaningful emblems of the Spirit that we shall present in this message.

The Breath of God

The first emblem is that of "wind," "breath," which in both Hebrew and Greek is the word for "Spirit." *Ruach* in Hebrew and *pneuma* in Greek literally mean "wind," "breath," but are also the words used for "Spirit." Jesus declared in John 3:8: "The wind bloweth where it listeth, and thou hearest the sound thereof, but canst not tell whence it cometh, and whither it goeth: so is every one that is born of the Spirit." The wind that blows "where it wills" is invisible in essence but no less real. The reality of the invincible world around us is made even more clear by the discoveries of modern scientific geniuses. The smallest schoolboy is conversant with the idea. Atoms, molecules, viruses are invisible to the naked eye. The air is filled with music, pictures, drama, and stories because of unseen carrier waves that penetrate the most remote recesses of the earth. Light, seen through a spectrum, is broken down into the colors of the rainbow according to their wave lengths. But there are also invisible colors: below the red, infrared; and above the violet, ultraviolet. The whole universe in the orbits of the planets is governed by gravity, the unseen, mysterious pull of matter inherent in itself. The tides of the ocean on the western side of Panama rise from twenty to thirty feet because of the gravitational pull of the moon. Think of raising the entire Pacific Ocean upward by a moon force two hundred forty thousand miles away! All of it invisible! Even so is the power of the Holy Spirit — unseen but no less real and powerful. In Acts 2:2 the outpouring of the Holy Spirit is dramatized by "a sound from heaven as of a rushing, mighty wind, and it filled all the house where they were sitting." This is an emblem of the Holy Spirit that regenerates our hearts (John 3:5-8) and empowers us for service.

The Fire of a Pentecost

Another emblem of the Spirit is that of "fire," described in Isaiah 4:4 as "the spirit of burning." The Hebrew word, *seraphim*, used by Isaiah to name the holy, heavenly creatures he saw serving before the throne of the Lord (Isaiah 6:1-8), literally means "the burning ones." They reflected the glory of the Spirit of God. The unfailing presence of Jehovah was signaled to the encampment of Israel by the burning cloud over the tabernacle (Exodus 40:34-38). His presence was overwhelmingly witnessed by the priests in the temple by the Shekinah glory that filled the sanctuary (I Kings 8:10, 11). Acts 2:3, with its story of the coming of the Holy Spirit in cloven tongues of fire, is the fulfillment of the Lord's promise that "ye [shall] be endued with power from on high" (Luke 24:49). The Holy Spirit is the fire that moves in power the whole work of God. We can illustrate our point by this little story. It is said that a factory owner walked around his new plant. It was fully complete but not a wheel moved. A man stopping by asked, "Is that your factory?" "Yes." "What does it make?" "It doesn't make anything." "Why not? Doesn't it run?" "No." "Why not?" "I do not know." "Oh," observed the visitor, "I'll tell you. Get some hooked-nosed oil cans, buy some fine oil, employ men to oil the machinery, bearings, and all the moving parts, and it will run." The owner did so, but nothing moved.

Another man came by, and after going through the same conversation, suggested that what was needed was to fresco the plant, plaster and beautify the walls, entrances and ceilings. "Set in a few stained glass windows, and paint a couple of barefooted angels with trumpets eternally ready to blow, and the factory will run." The owner did so, but nothing moved.

Another man came by and, after repeating the introductory conversation, said: "I know your trouble. Your plant has no steeple, no pipe organ, and no quartet. Get some chimes, and all the other accoutrements and embellishments of real production, and the factory will run." The man did so, but nothing moved. Another man came by and said what he needed was publicity, pictures, articles in the newspapers, stories of the work proposed, etc. But still nothing moved. The owner was greatly discouraged.

Finally, a man came by and asked, "What is the matter that the factory doesn't run?" "I do not know," replied the owner. He continued: "One man told me to oil the wheels and I did that. Another man told me to fresco the ceiling and I did that. Another man told me to hire a quartet and buy some chimes and I did that. But nothing works. Listen to the chimes sounding, and that choir chasing that anthem up and down, and look at those barefooted angels blowing trumpets, but the wheels do not move. I do not know what to do." The stranger replied, "Sir, I do not know anything about angels, or organs, or picture windows, but did you ever try putting a fire under the boiler?" "No," replied the owner, "I never thought of that." So the stranger took off his coat, rolled up his sleeves, opened the door of the furnace, shoveled in some coal, started a fire, poured in more coal, pulled back the throttle on the valves, let the steam rush into the cylinders and hit the pistons, and the great wheels began to tremble, turn, and revolve — faster and faster. Soon the whole mass of machinery was turning. Something happened, praise the Lord. The fire caused the factory to operate. Many

there are who try to run their spirtual lives with all sorts
of schemes and plans but without the fire of the Holy Spirit
in their souls. It's no wonder they can't operate as they
ought.

The Clothing of Power

Another emblem of the Holy Spirit is that of clothing.
Judges 6:34 literally says that "the Spirit of God clothed
himself with Gideon." The same expression is used again
in II Chronicles 24:20, "the Spirit of God clothed himself
with Zechariah." The figure is used by our Lord Jesus in
Luke 24:49 where the Saviour says, "Ye [shall] be endued
with power from on high." The word translated "endued"
is *enduno,* which literally means "to put on," "to be clothed."
The disciples were to be "clothed with power," the power
of the Holy Spirit covering them. The old rags of fear and
defeat were to be taken away and in their place were to be
brought the new robes of valor, courage and victory. The
old Simon Peter, cowering before the simple question of a
little maiden and hiding from the crowing of a cock, is to be
the bold, fearless preacher of Pentecost. This is the raiment
of spiritual revolution bestowed by the Holy Spirit.

The Seal of Ownership

Yet another emblem of the Holy Spirit is that of a "seal."
After we have been saved, after we have been purchased by
the blood of the Crucified One, after we have been redeemed
from our bondage to Satan, how do we know but that we
shall fall prey to the devil's pitfalls? Shall we ever make
the gates of glory? There are ten thousand blocks in the
way. Shall we arrive safely in heaven? Shall we answer to
the roll call in the sky? We most certainly shall! How do
I know? Because we are sealed by the Holy Spirit. Three
times in the New Testament the Holy Spirit is represented
as sealing the believer's redemption: II Corinthians 1:22;
Ephesians 1:13; 4:30. A seal among men is for ownership,
signifying a finished transaction (Jeremiah 32:10), and for
security proclaiming watchful care (Matthew 27:66; Revela-

tion 20:3). So, a seal before God has the same meaning. We belong to God and the Spirit seals us. God marks us as His property (II Timothy 2:19; Revelation 7:4). This is our safety and security. In Revelation 7 God sealed one hundred forty-four thousand of His saints. In Revelation 14 every one of that one hundred forty-four thousand is accounted for. Not one is lost. There are not one hundred forty-three thousand nine hundred ninety-nine with the Lamb on Mount Zion, but the full one hundred forty-four thousand. This is the work of the Holy Spirit. The Holy Spirit Himself is the seal. His presence is the sign and the signature of the ultimate fulfillment of all God's promises of grace in us.

The Earnest of Promise

Still another emblem of the Holy Spirit is that of an "earnest." An "earnest" is a pledge, a token payment that the promised remainder will be paid. Three times in the New Testament the Holy Spirit is referred to as an "earnest" that God gives to His saints. The three instances are II Corinthians 1:22; 5:5; Ephesians 1:14. The Holy Spirit Himself is the pledge and token that God will give to us all that He has promised. We shall not fail of our inheritance.

We are to recognize the Holy Spirit as the earnest of God in order that we may live in confidence and in victory. The defeated Christian is not able to make this recognition. It is possible for us in ordinary human life to be in the presence of friends and not recognize them. We are engrossed in other things. Two gentlemen were walking down the street and they passed a neighbor. One recognized him but the other did not. As the two walked on, one said to the other, "Did you see So-and-So?" "No," the other replied. "But you just passed him and looked at him." "Indeed?" replied the other. "But I did not see him." We are like that, oblivious to the victorious nearness and the comforting presence of God. A tourist asked a native, "Sir, did you see a pedestrian pass by?" "No," replied the old settler. "I have been here all day and nobody has passed by but one old man and he was walking!" We need our spiritual eyes opened and our Scriptural understanding deepened.

Of what is the Spirit an earnest? He is the down payment on our inheritance. Some of what God intends for us, we are given in this life, in this world. Most of what God purposes for us is to be ours beyond the grave in the world that is to come. Look at the assurance with which Peter writes in I Peter 1:3-5: "Blessed be the God and Father of our Lord Jesus Christ, which according to his abundant mercy hath begotten us again unto a lively hope by the resurrection of Jesus Christ from the dead, To an inheritance incorruptible, and undefiled, and that fadeth not away, reserved in heaven for you, Who are kept by the power of God through faith unto salvation ready to be revealed in the last time." No less full of conviction is Paul in I Corinthians 2:9,10: "But as it is written, Eye hath not seen, nor ear heard, neither have entered into the heart of man, the things which God hath prepared for them that love him. But God hath revealed them unto us by his Spirit: for the Spirit searcheth all things, yea, the deep things of God."

But beyond our inheritance in glory, the Holy Spirit is the earnest for our identity of place with Christ our Lord. What our Lord is, we shall be. We are one with Him. This is an astonishing thought, but in the earnest of the Spirit it is true for the saints of God. The Saviour said in John 17:11, "And now I am no more in the world, but these are in the world, and I come to thee, Holy Father, keep through thine own name those whom thou hast given me, that they may be one, as we are." Paul wrote in Philippians 1:6 this precious promise, "Being confident of this very thing, that he which hath begun a good work in you will perform it until the day of Jesus Christ." He had already avowed a like promise in his second letter to Thessalonica, II Thessalonians 2:13,14, "But we are bound to give thanks alway to God for you, brethren beloved of the Lord, because God hath from the beginning chosen you to salvation through sanctification of the Spirit and belief of the truth: Whereunto he called you by our gospel, to the obtaining of the glory of our Lord Jesus

Christ." Cheer up, my brother! The Holy Spirit of God will see us through. He will not let us down. Having Him, we have all. He is the earnest in our hearts of all that God is and of all that God purposes for us throughout eternity. Praise His name forever!

Chapter 10

The Outpouring of the Spirit

Joel 2

28 And it shall come to pass afterward, that I will pour out my spirit upon all flesh; and your sons and your daughters shall prophesy, your old men shall dream dreams, your young men shall see visions:

29 And also upon the servants and upon the handmaids in those days will I pour out my spirit.

30 And I will shew wonders in the heavens and in the earth, blood, and fire, and pillars of smoke.

31 The sun shall be turned into darkness, and the moon into blood, before the great and terrible day of the LORD come.

32 And it shall come to pass, that whosoever shall call on the name of the LORD shall be delivered: for in mount Zion and in Jerusalem shall be deliverance, as the LORD hath said, and in the remnant whom the LORD shall call.

The prophecy of Joel concerning the outpouring of the Holy Spirit and its quotation by Simon Peter in his Pentecostal sermon (Acts 2) is one of the most significant utterances in all the Word of God. The prophecy is twofold throughout its references. Regarding "the last days," it relates to Israel (Isaiah 2:2-4; Micah 4:1-7) and also to the Church (Hebrews 1:1, 2, the days that began with Christ; I Timothy 4:1; II Timothy 3:1). Regarding the fulfillment of the prophecy, it relates to this age of grace (Joel 2:28, 29, 32), and also to the consummation of the age at the return of Christ (Joel 2:30, 31). Regarding the results of the prophecy, it reveals the marvelous, glorious enrichment of the gift of the Spirit during this Christian dispensation (Joel 2:28, 30), and also the terrible judgment awaiting those who reject the Witness (Joel 2:31). The sin never forgiven is the sin against the testimony of the Holy Spirit. An airplane can be a carrier of life. It can also be a carrier of death. Atomic fission has an infinite capacity to bless life. It also has an equal capacity to destroy life. Either life unto life or death unto death is merited in our response to the appeal of the Holy Spirit.

The Marvelous Visitation From Heaven

God means the gift for good, infinitely so. The outpouring of the Spirit is to be none other than a marvelous visitation from heaven. The promised outpouring reflects the whole Biblical message that there is a great day coming. This battered old earth has known glorious days in times past, but they are as nothing compared with the grandeur of the days that are yet to be. The first page of the Bible, and the second; the first book of the Bible, and the second; the middle page of the Bible, and the last triumphantly announce, "There is a greater day coming." There is progress, outreach, development in the kingdom of God. The Lord never recedes. He continuously, necessarily advances. His creation is followed by redemption. His redemption is followed by sanctification. His sanctification is followed by glorification. This is the reason the elect of God are not to be troubled (II Thessalonians 1:7). Convulsions of nature, disruptions of social order, the desolations of war are not to discourage the Lord's people (Daniel 9; Matthew 24). These sorrows are to be. But God's sovereign purposes move inexorably on — unchanging, unwavering. The saints shall inherit the earth.

The divine government under which we live has set all the dates that govern the redemptive course of history. The date for the coming of the Holy Spirit was written in heaven and was spoken of by Joel in this prophecy (Joel 2:28-32). This is in keeping with the elective purposes of God in all our lives and is sovereignly illustrated in the life of our Lord. A date was set in heaven for the incarnation (Daniel 9:25). The very place He was to be born was chosen (Micah 5:2), and the manner of His birth was outlined (Isaiah 7:14).

The date for the sacrifice of Christ our Passover was known to God (Exodus 12; Matthew 16:21; I Corinthians 5:7). The way He was to die was vividly described hundreds of years before His death (Psalm 22; Isaiah 53). The emblems of bread and wine by which we are to remember His atonement were presented in type by Melchizedek two thousand years before He came into the world (Genesis 14:18). The date for the resurrection of Christ was chosen in glory and revealed in type through Moses (Leviticus 23; Sunday, the first day after the Sabbath). The date for the return of Christ to this troubled earth is known to God (Matthew 24:36); and the times of that coming were revealed in the Apocalypse to the Apostle John. Pentecost is no accident. The coming of the Holy Spirit was a fulfillment of the Word of the Lord through His prophet Joel, and the outpouring was at a time chosen by God before the foundation of the world.

The New Abode of the Holy Spirit

The prophecy of Joel in its Pentecostal reality and fulfillment means so much to us. For one thing, the Third Person of the Godhead is to have a new abode. He is to dwell in the Church, the congregation of the Lord (Ephesians 2:19-22), and He is to dwell in the individual believer (I Corinthians 6:19). As in the old days the Spirit was known by His presence in the tabernacle (Exodus 40:34-38), and in the temple (I Kings 8:10, 11), so in these new days the Spirit proclaims His presence in the saints of the Lord, in the congregation of the redeemed. There was a time when Christ did not have a body. In the ages of the ages before Bethlehem, He was pure Spirit, reigning as the Crown Prince of glory. But now, after the incarnation, our Saviour lives forever in a body, the *man* Christ Jesus (Revelation 1:13-16; I Timothy 2:5). So the Spirit of Jesus is incarnate in His Church and in His individual saints. He dwells in our hearts, and lives with us in our church gatherings. As Christ is at the right hand of God (though omnipresent), so the Holy Spirit is now abiding in this world, in His people (though omnipresent).

The quickening power and the living presence of the Holy

Spirit is most gloriously seen in the continuing building of the Church. After the Lord God formed Adam of the dust of the ground, He breathed into his nostrils the breath of life "and man became a living soul." It is thus that God has done with His Church, the temple of the Holy Spirit. John the Baptist gathered the material. (The qualifications for an apostle in Acts 1:21, 22 were that he had to be baptized by John the Baptist, had to be taught by the Lord Jesus, and had to be a personal witness of His Resurrection.) Jesus was the Builder of the Church (Matthew 16:18). He gave it the two ordinances of baptism and the Lord's Supper, and assigned its world-wide task in the Great Commission (Matthew 28:18-20). He even outlined its discipline and procedures of love and brotherhood (Matthew 18:15-20). But the Church, formed and organized under the hands of Christ, was like the body of Adam formed of the dust of the ground. The quickening breath must come if Adam is to live. The Spirit must come if the Church is to be the tabernacle of God. The prophecy of Joel spoke of that outpouring, and the day of Pentecost (Acts 2) recounts the fulfillment of the prophecy. The quickening Spirit of God fell upon the Church formed by the Lord Jesus (compare Ezekiel 37) and it became a living organism. "The Lord added to the church daily such as should be saved" (Acts 2:47), and the long history of that Christian era of grace and salvation began.

The Universality of the Outpoured Gift

The prophecy of Joel speaks of the universality of the outpoured gift of the Spirit. "And it shall come to pass . . . that I will pour out my Spirit upon all flesh; . . . your sons and your daughters . . . your old men . . . your young men . . ." (Joel 2:28). All alike may possess the fullness of the Spirit. In ancient times, in the Old Testament, the Spirit of God came upon a select few at intervals and at certain seasons (Judges 13:25). But in the new day the gift will not be just upon a Samson, or a Samuel, or a Saul, but upon the whole congregation of the Lord. The pew is to be as inspired as the pulpit. If there is to be an inspired ministry, there is also to be an inspired Church. Constantly, daily, hourly the child of God in the new day is privileged to equal the most favored among God's ancient people. The humblest among us may rise to the same spiritual attainments, or even to higher than those achieved by a Samuel or an Isaiah. And that glory may come without distinction in sex, age, rank or condition. The Greek words used in Acts 2:18, quoting the prophecy from Joel, are *doulous* and *doulas,* which translated mean "men-slaves" and "women-slaves." "And on my servants and on my handmaidens I will pour out in those days of my Spirit," the King James translates.

This new day opened the way for the Richmond slave, John Jasper, to become one of the most effective preachers of all time. I have heard the Cherokee Indian preacher, Jim Pickup, translate, without stopping, an entire sermon I had preached in English, into his native Cherokee. When I think of the fervent preachers of the Gospel I have heard in Africa and in China, or when I think of the marvelous trophies of grace among the savage Aucas and other tribes of the Amazon jungle, I cannot but comment when I read Joel's prophecy, "Surely, the half has not been told." The gift of God's Spirit is without measure (John 3:34), and without distinction among believers. In the household of faith, all may prophesy (I Corinthians 14:31), the old, the young, the rich, the poor, the learned, the unlearned. The Church is to be an old folks' church; it is to be a young people's church. It is to be a rich man's church; it is to be a poor man's church. It is to be a children's church; it is to be a grandparents' church. The blessedness of the gift is upon all.

The Marvelous Effects of the Outpouring of the Spirit

The marvelous effects and results of the outpouring of the Holy Spirit are vividly recounted by the prophet Joel. He says, "And your sons and your daughters will prophesy." The word *propheteuo* (to prophesy) means to forthtell, to witness of divine things in power and in heavenly unction. The meaning "to foretell" is secondary and incidental. The prophet is saying that even the young and the inexperienced will be marvelous witnesses of God's saving grace. Any Spirit-filled youth night service will underscore the power of this testimony. But there is more. The prophet says, "Your old men shall dream dreams." Some of us may be old in years but we need not be in spirit. Our faces may wrinkle but not our hearts. It is the soul that must not gray. The inner man is to be renewed day by day (II Corinthians 4:16), forever young. "Winter is on my head," wrote Victor Hugo, "but spring is in my heart." The difference in men is not in their years but in their spirit. The dissolute Lord Byron wrote on his thirty-sixth birthday:

> My days are in the yellow leaf,
>   The flowers and fruits of love are gone;
> The worm, the canker, and the grief
>   Are mine alone.

How different the triumphant words of the Christian poet, Robert Browning, when he said:

> Grow old along with me!
> The best is yet to be,
> The last of life, for which the first was made
> Our times are in His hand
> Who saith, "A whole I planned
> Youth shows but half: trust God: see all, nor be afraid!"

But not only shall the old men dream dreams. The prophet says more. He adds, "And your young men shall see visions." Woe to the Church when the young men shall see no visions and when the old men shall dream no dreams, when the people are dull, ox-like, uninspired. Remember Proverbs 29:18, "Where there is no vision, the people perish." It is a glory in the Church to see the soul quickened by fire, filled with the burning of the Holy Spirit, attempting great things *for* God, and believing great things *from* God. The New Testament records the expanding, extending vision of the Spirit-filled men who at Pentecost, upon the fulfillment of Joel's prophecy, faced the whole, unbelieving world with assurance of victory. We are to be like that. Forever we are to be on the way upward, onward, outward, forward. The best song is yet to be sung. The best poem is yet to be written. The best picture is yet to be painted. The best sermon is yet to be preached. The best Sunday school is yet to be built.

We do not glorify God in the defeatism evidenced by empty chairs, vacant pews, and apologetic services. We do not glorify God with our streets filled with forgotten, lost, neglected children, living in the circle of pagan, heathen homes. Sound the trumpet! In the power of the Spirit, three thousand were added to God's household of faith in Acts 2:4! The members had grown to five thousand *men* (Greek, *andron*) in Acts 4:4. God meant for Pentecost to be the little end of the horn. "Greater works than these shall ye do," said the Lord Jesus, "because I go unto my Father." "Herein is my Father glorified," He added, "that ye bear much fruit; so shall ye be my disciples." The Holy Spirit is with us for power, victory, conquest, evangelization. The other day I picked up a book and the very chapter headings reflected this spirit of world redemption. They read: "Revival in Los Angeles," "Revival Spreads in Canada," "Miracles in France," "Latter Rain Falling in India," "The Outpouring in China," "A Great Work in Egypt," "God's Visitation in Venezuela," "The Isles of the Sea." This is God's will for us, winning souls everywhere in the power of the Holy Spirit.

Chapter 11

The Greatness of the Promises

Luke 24

49 And, behold, I send the promise of my Father upon you: but tarry ye in the city of Jerusalem, until ye be endued with power from on high.

Acts 1

4 And, being assembled together with them, commanded them that they should not depart from Jerusalem, but wait for the promise of the Father, which, saith he, ye have heard of me.

Someone has said that there are over three thousand promises in the Bible but only one is called "*the* promise of the Father." The words, "the promise of the Father," in Luke 24:49 and Acts 1:4 refer to the Upper Room address of our Lord to His disciples the night in which He was betrayed, recorded in John 14 - 16. Jesus specifically and plainly said that night:

And I will pray the Father, and he shall give you another Comforter, that he may abide with you for ever; Even the Spirit of truth; whom the world cannot receive, because it seeth him not, neither knoweth him: but ye know him; for he dwelleth with you, and shall be in you (John 14:16, 17).

But the Comforter, which is the Holy Ghost, whom the Father will send in my name, he shall teach you all things, and bring all things to your remembrance, whatsoever I have said unto you (John 14:26).

But when the Comforter is come, whom I will send unto you from the Father, even the Spirit of truth, which proceedeth from the Father, he shall testify of me: And ye also shall bear witness, because ye have been with me from the beginning (John 15:26, 27).

We can only surmise how incomparably comforting were these words of the Saviour to the sorrowing disciples. If the promise of the coming Messiah was the hope of the human race in the Garden of Eden (Genesis 3:15), and the hope of Israel in Egypt (Genesis 49:10), and the brightness of Judah in the dark days of apostasy (Isaiah 7:14; 9:6); and if the coming of the Lord the second time is our assurance of ultimate victory (John 14:3; Jude 14; Revelation 1:7), then the promise of the coming of the Holy Spirit is truly the earnest of God the Father in heaven that we shall not fail in our inheritance of these glorious good things He has prepared for us who love Him (I Corinthians 2:9, 10; Ephesians 1:14). In all the Word of God the two most meaningful promises are that a Saviour is coming and that the Holy Spirit is to be poured out (Joel 2:28, 29; John 14, 16).

The Promise of the Spirit Is for Power and Encouragement

The coming of the Holy Spirit, "the promise of the Father," is for comfort and encouragement, so much so that the very name chosen for the Third Person of the Godhead in John 14, 15, and 16 is "Paraclete," which means "Comforter," "Encourager." It was a sad night for the twelve apostles, that night of the Last Supper. They were in the depths of despair. Jesus knew that the effect of His words would be one of overwhelming sorrow. "Because I have said these things unto you, sorrow hath filled your heart" (John 16:6). But there is more. Jesus continued: "Nevertheless I tell you the truth; It is expedient for you that I go away: for if I go not away, the Comforter will not come unto you; but if I depart, I will send him unto you" (John 16:7). He said again, "I will not leave you comfortless [Greek, *orphanes*, 'orphans']: I will come to you" (John 14:18). The coming of our Saviour in the person of His Holy Spirit (called the Spirit of Christ in Romans 8:9; I Peter 1:11) was not only the strength and consolation of the apostles in their day of sorrow, but is also our assurance for victory today. Wherever we are gathered in Christ's name, there also is the blessed Spirit of Jesus with us. "For where two or three are gathered together in my name, there am I in the midst of them" (Matthew 18:20). And upon whatever mission the Saviour has sent us, there also is the guiding Spirit of Jesus to sustain us. His Great Commission closed with the sublime promise, "Lo, I am with you alway, even unto the end of the world" (Matthew 28:20).

One time I heard a missionary describe a night he had spent in the top of a tall tree in an African jungle with the forest below him filled with savage cannibals searching for his life. He had escaped from their carnivorous hands through a miracle of God. With lighted torches they were probing the jungle and any minute might discover him. But he said, "I never felt Jesus so near as I did that night in the top of that tree." Then he added, "I would go back and into that perilous hour if only I could feel again the presence of God with me as I did that dark night." On one of the islands of Hong Kong harbor a missionary pointed out to me the place where he was interned during World War II. He said that when he was marched into the concentration camp between two brutal Japanese soldiers, he felt the divine presence of God as he had never known Him before. When David Livingstone stood undecided at the headwaters of the Zambezi River, warned against proceeding further because of the terrible danger, he prayed, opened the Bible for a sign from God, and found the Holy Book had opened at Matthew 28:20, "Lo, I am with you alway." Accepting the promise, Livingstone followed on his way to discover the Victoria Falls and the eastern outlet from the heart of the dark continent. The Holy Spirit is Jesus with us in the place of His bodily presence. For awhile (for forty days) the resurrected Lord was with them here, there, in an upper room, on the seashore, on an appointed mountain, on the road to Emmaus, speaking to them, encouraging them, comforting them, teaching them, directing them. Then, as they grew in faith and in assurance, they needed not these visible epiphanies to know that the Saviour was with them. By

His Spirit working with them, they knew Him to be as close as breath, as near as hands and feet.

The Promise of the Spirit Is for Power

The promise of the Spirit is also for power. This is the age, the dispensation of the Holy Spirit. The Gospel itself is called, in II Corinthians 3:8, 9, "the ministration of the Spirit" in opposition to the dispensation of the law, which is called "the ministration of condemnation," "for," writes the Apostle in verse 6, "the letter killeth, but the Spirit giveth life." In this discussion in II Corinthians 3:16-18 Paul avows that the heart of the Gospel is found in the Spirit of quickening life that accompanies it, not in the deadness of the letter by which a Word of God might be written, even in stone. Take away the Spirit from the Gospel and we render it a dead letter. The Scriptures are but words of sound and syllable apart from the convicting Spirit. Separate the Spirit from the Word and we destroy it. Isaiah 59:21 solemnly proclaims that God's Word and God's Spirit shall go together. Separate the spirit of a man from the body of the man, and he becomes a corpse. Death, spiritual death, no less ensues when the Spirit of God is separated from the Word of God. "The letter killeth; the Spirit giveth life."

The effectual ministry of the Word and the communication of the grace of Christ can only be achieved through the power of the Holy Spirit. Without the presence of the Spirit there is no conviction, no regeneration, no sanctification, no cleansing, no acceptable works. We can pray without Him, but our prayers do not reach beyond the sound of our voices. We can preach without Him, but our sermons fall to the ground. We can sing without Him, but our melodies are hollow and meaningless. We can perform duties without Him, but our service is dull and mechanical. Life is in the quickening Spirit. In a protracted series of meetings, in which no souls were being saved, the pastor of the church called me into his study for prayer. He closed the door, fell on his knees, and poured out his heart to God in burdened intercession. As he sat in the pulpit that night, even during the song service and the announcements, he could not keep back the tears, so great was his burden of heart. This opened the floodgates of heaven.

> God came down our souls to greet
> And glory filled the mercy seat.

Our power lies in the Spirit of the Lord.

The Promise of the Spirit Is for Truth

The promise of the Spirit is for truth. Our only source of ultimate truth lies in the self-revelation of God. We are not able to discover it in ourselves. We are so limited, so finite, before the infinitude of God. We see but through a glass darkly. We are confused even in what little we do perceive. The world has been, still is, and ever shall be, a maze of false religions, false cults, false ideologies, false philosophies, false science, false direction. What is truth? Who speaks the truth? Where can we find the truth? The false prophet, purporting to deliver the ultimate word, but actuated by an unclean and lying spirit, has ever been the curse of the world. In the Bible the false prophets were of two kinds. The first were such as professedly served false gods, as in I Kings 18:26 where in the days of the terrible apostasy they cried unto Baal. Paul says in I Corinthians 10:20: "But I say, that the things which the Gentiles sacrifice, they sacrifice to devils and not to God: and I would not that ye should have fellowship with devils." The Apostle calls Satan the god of this world and the one who blinds the minds of those who believe not (II Corinthians 4:4). The descriptions of those who speak false doctrines under the inspiration of lying spirits veil the truth from uncounted thousands of sincere but deluded worshipers of pagan gods.

The other kind of false prophets in the Bible were those who spoke in the name of the true God but who were instigated by the devil to fill men with vain hopes and carnal security. This did Satan in the beginning with Adam and Eve when he brazenly said of their proposed transgressions,

"Thou shalt not surely die." With these false emissaries of Satan, Jeremiah (against Hananiah, Jeremiah 28:1-17; against Shemaiah, Jeremiah 29:24-32) and Ezekiel (cf. Ezekiel 13:1-4), and most of the true prophets had to contend. No more dramatic story could be read in all literature, secular or sacred, than the contest between God's prophet Micaiah and the false prophet Zedekiah over the life and death of King Ahab in his campaign against Ramoth-Gilead (I Kings 22:1-38).

The record of deception and distortion regarding the truth of God is no less tragically seen in the New Testament and in the history of Christendom. The deceits and abuses which have abounded in the church under the pretense of the inspiration and direction of the Holy Spirit are legion in number. Christ spoke of it in these words: "For there shall arise false Christs, and false prophets, and shall shew great signs and wonders; insomuch that, if it were possible, they shall deceive the very elect" (Matthew 24:24). Peter warned of it in these words:

> But there were false prophets also among the people, even as there shall be false teachers among you, who privily shall bring in damnable heresies, even denying the Lord that bought them, and bring upon themselves swift destruction. And many shall follow their pernicious ways; by reason of whom the way of truth shall be evil spoken of (II Peter 2:1, 2).

John spoke of it in these words:

> Beloved, believe not every spirit, but try the spirits whether they are of God: because many false prophets are gone out into the world. Hereby know ye the Spirit of God: Every spirit that confesseth that Jesus Christ is come in the flesh is of God: And every spirit that confesseth not that Jesus Christ is come in the flesh is not of God: and this is that spirit of antichrist, whereof ye have heard that it should come; and even now already is it in the world (I John 4:1-3).

Thus Paul wrote in his last epistle:

> This know also, that in the last days perilous times shall come. For men shall be lovers of their own selves, covetous, boasters, proud, blasphemers, disobedient to parents, unthankful, un-

holy, Without natural affection, trucebreakers, false accusers, incontinent, fierce, despisers of those that are good, Traitors, heady, highminded, lovers of pleasures more than lovers of God; Having a form of godliness, but denying the power thereof: from such turn away (II Timothy 3:1-5).

How are we to know the truth? In order that we know the truth without error and with heavenly assurance, Jesus promised us "the Spirit of truth." Our Lord emphatically said: "Howbeit when he, the Spirit of truth, is come, he will guide you into all truth: For he shall not speak of himself; but whatsoever he shall hear, that shall he speak: and he will shew you things to come" (John 16:13).

The Spirit will guide us "into *all* truth." If we possess the will to know and to do His will, we shall surely know the doctrine (the teaching, the way) thereof (John 7:17). God will not lead us astray. Even before the days of the completed New Testament, God made provision for the infant church to know what to believe and what to do. Paul wrote in I Corinthians 14:29-32:

> Let the prophets speak two or three, and let the other judge. If any thing be revealed to another that sitteth by, let the first hold his peace. For ye may all prophesy one by one, that all may learn, and all may be comforted. And the spirits of the prophets are subject to the prophets.

The word from the Lord brought by the prophet to the church was to be judged by the prophets who listened to it. "The spirits of the prophets are subject to the prophets." The gift of "discerning of spirits" was preciously and meaningfully held by many members of the church (I Corinthians 12:10). The Holy Spirit is not forgetful of us who live in a world of false doctrines and easy delusion. He will guide into all truth those who look with yielded hearts and minds to Him.

The Promise of the Spirit Is for Salvation

The promise of the Holy Spirit is for salvation. It is He who convicts us of sin; it is He who leads us to Jesus; it is He who regenerates our souls; it is He who sanctifies us; it is He who will attend our way from earth to heaven. To

deny the witness of the Holy Spirit is to suffer an eternal
exclusion from the glories of heaven. To blaspheme the
Holy Spirit is to incur eternal death, a judgment that has
not forgiveness either in this world or in the world to come.
Such awesome and frightful words are said of this eternal
sin in the pages of the Holy Scriptures. Mark 3:28, 29 reads:

> Verily I say unto you, All sins shall be forgiven unto the sons
> of men, and blasphemies wherewith soever they shall blas-
> pheme: But he that shall blaspheme against the Holy Ghost
> hath never forgiveness, but is in danger of eternal damnation.

Matthew 12:31, 32 reads:

> Wherefore I say unto you, All manner of sin and blasphemy
> shall be forgiven unto men: but the blasphemy against the Holy
> Ghost shall not be forgiven unto men. And whosoever speaketh
> a word against the Son of man, it shall be forgiven him: but
> whosoever speaketh against the Holy Ghost, it shall not be for-
> given him, neither in this world, neither in the world to come.

Hebrews 10:26-29 reads:

> For if we sin wilfully after that we have received the knowl-
> edge of the truth, there remaineth no more sacrifice for sins,
> But a certain fearful looking for of judgment and fiery indig-
> nation, which shall devour the adversaries. He that despised
> Moses' law died without mercy under two or three witnesses:
> Of how much sorer punishment, suppose ye, shall he be
> thought worthy, who hath trodden under foot the Son of God,
> and hath counted the blood of the covenant, wherewith he was
> sanctified, an unholy thing, and hath done despite unto the
> Spirit of grace?

I John 5:16 says:

> If any man see his brother sin a sin which is not unto death,
> he shall ask, and he shall give him life for them that sin not
> unto death. There is a sin unto death: I do not say that he
> shall pray for it.

These words strike terror to the soul. If we refuse the pleading and the wooing of the Holy Spirit of grace, there remains
no other way to be saved. God has not another Son to offer
for the sacrifice of sin. God has not another Spirit to make

the sacrifice effectual for us. We listen to the testimony of the Holy Spirit and are saved, or we refuse the witness and die. God grant that we look and live, that we believe and be saved, that we turn and find eternal life.

Chapter 12

When the Spirit Is Come

John 16

7 Nevertheless I tell you the truth; It is expedient for you that I go away: for if I go not away, the Comforter will not come unto you; but if I depart, I will send him unto you.

8 And when he is come, he will reprove the world of sin, and of righteousness, and of judgment:

9 Of sin, because they believe not on me;

10 Of righteousness, because I go to my Father, and ye see me no more;

11 Of judgment, because the prince of this world is judged.

Language can hardly describe the Spirit of God. The reality of the presence of the Almighty is too much for syllable and sentence to bear. The words, therefore, used in the Holy Scriptures to present the Holy Third Person of the Trinity are but picture approximations of the awesome majesty from heaven. The Hebrew Old Testament and the Greek New Testament use the word "breath," "wind," to depict the Spirit of God. It is *ruach* in Hebrew, *pneuma* in Greek, both words meaning the same thing, "breath," "wind." John 4:24 reads in Greek, *pneuma ho theos,* "God is breath, wind, Spirit." The word presents a picture of illimitable, infinite power. Witness the awesome might of a tornado or hurricane. Heavy rolling freight trains are controlled by brakes using air. The manager of a granite quarry in North Carolina said: "We supplied the granite for the municipal building in New York City. We can lift an acre of solid granite ten feet thick to almost any height we desire for the purpose of moving it. We do it with air. We can do it as easily as I can lift a piece of paper." Air! Air — this invisible envelopment in which we live and move, this substance so immaterial that we can move our hands through it as though it had no reality at all. But the power it possesses! How great, how terrible!

And yet, with all its infinite properties and capacities, how gentle, how soft, even like breath is this *pneuma,* this *ruach.* It is like a softly spoken word. I remember the story of Elijah in I Kings 19:11, 12 when God said to the discouraged prophet, "Go forth and stand upon the mount before the Lord." Elijah went forth out of his cave, "And, behold, the Lord passed by and a great and strong wind rent the mountains, and brake in pieces the rocks before the Lord but the Lord was not in the wind: and after the wind an earthquake; but the Lord was not in the earthquake: And after the earthquake a fire; but the Lord was not in the fire: and after the fire a still small voice." "A still small voice" — the breath of God. The Holy Spirit is so gentle He is likened to a dove, easily dismissed, sent away. He is like a sublime sunset that can be shut out by closing the eyes — the soft, gentle breath of God. "And [Jesus] breathed on them, and saith unto them, Receive ye the Holy Ghost" (John 20:22).

Our passage here in the sixteenth chapter of John uses another word to describe the Holy Spirit. The Greek word is *parakletos,* transliterated into English, "Paraclete." It comes from two Greek words, *para,* meaning alongside (like our English word "parallel"), and *kaleo,* meaning "to call." "Paraclete," therefore, means "one called alongside," "pleader," "exhorter," "helper," "intercessor," "advocate," "comforter." It is a word most difficult to translate into the English language with all its real meaning in the Greek. What Jesus was to the grief-stricken two disciples, walking beside them on the way to Emmaus (Luke 24), the Holy Spirit is to us today, walking with us, comforting us.

The Convicting Work of the Holy Spirit

But not only is the Holy Spirit the "Paraclete," the "Comforter," but He is also "the Convictor," the "Reprover." The Saviour says in John 16:8, "And when he is come, he will reprove [Greek, *elegcho,* 'convict'] the world of sin, and of righteousness, and of judgment." Jesus continues to speak in the next verse of the nature of the conviction: "Of sin, because they believe not on me." *The* sin is lack of faith in Christ. This is the sin that is mother to all the rest. What good does it do to plead against this sin, that sin, the other sin, when the soul is not right with God? No sooner do we patch up the life here than it breaks out in a new place yonder. Small and meager is the result when we minister to the pimples on the skin while the disease is in the bloodstream that courses through the heart.

Never shall I forget the first time I ever heard that word "penicillin." A little girl in my congregation was facing death from a series of abscesses. No sooner was one outbreak healed than another followed in a different place. The infection was in the bloodstream. At last the little girl seemed sentenced to die when an abscess gathered in a vital part of her body. I went to the hospital to console the sorrowing family, and as I spoke to the grief-stricken father he replied to me: "But, Pastor, there is hope. A drug has just been discovered that can save her life. It is a precious drug called 'penicillin' (my first time to hear the word). There is just a small, small amount of it in the world thus far, and what little supply is available is in the office of the Surgeon General of the United States in Washington. We have made appeal to the Surgeon General for some of the miracle drug. Maybe they will grant our request." The request was honored; the little girl was saved; she is a beautiful woman today, a mother in a gracious home. But the healing had to come from within. The bloodstream had to be purified.

All sins are but manifestations of *the sin*, the black drop, in our lives. The Holy Spirit convicts "of sin because they believe not on Christ." As long as there is rejection of Christ in the life, the healing of all other sins is impossible. The sin of theft, robbery, is due to a lack of faith in God and committal to Christ. The thief does not believe God will take care of him, so he steals. He does not ask God to give him this day his daily bread, so he takes it by violence. The angry man of vengeance does not trust God for settlement. "Vengeance is mine, I will repay, saith the Lord" (Romans 12:19). But he takes matters into his own hands and seeks in anger to administer the recompense of God. Young people so often are fearful of following Christ because they do not trust Him for a good time. They are afraid that all pleasure and fun will be bereft of life if they love Jesus. Thus it continues on and on through every category of sin. There is but one sin, mother to all the rest, and that sin is lack of faith in the blessed Lord Jesus.

Herein is found the convicting, pleading word of the Paraclete. He woos the heart toward the Saviour. He pleads for faith in Christ Jesus. For joy and peace, He points the soul to Him. For salvation, He directs our steps toward Him. In sorrow and in bereavement, He brings us nigh to the heart of the sympathizing Jesus. In youth, in old age, in death, He opens the way to everlasting life in the Son of God. This is the office-work of the divine Paraclete.

The Holy Spirit Is Jesus With Us

Our Lord continues to speak in the text (John 16:8, 10), ". . . he will reprove the world . . . . Of righteousness because I go to my Father, and ye see me no more." Our Saviour herein says that His representative on earth for righteousness is the divine Paraclete. As long as Jesus was here in the earth He could show us the way of truth and righteousness. But when our Lord goes away and returns to heaven, what then? Who is to be our guide? Jesus answers in John 16:13, 14: "Howbeit when he, the Spirit of truth, is come, he will guide you into all truth; for he shall not speak of himself; but whatsoever he shall hear, that shall he speak . . . . He shall glorify me: for he shall receive of mine, and shall shew it unto you." The Holy Spirit is Christ's representative in our hearts, Christ's other self, yea, Christ Himself. He points the way for us to go. As in Sheldon's famous book, *In His Steps,* or *What Would Jesus Do?*, the divine Comforter answers for Christ in every situation we face.

When we do wrong, we do despite unto the Spirit of Jesus.

This is Paul's appeal in Ephesians 4:30, "And grieve not the holy Spirit of God, whereby ye are sealed unto the day of redemption." It is a terrible hurt to crush the leadership of the Paraclete in our lives. The first King of Israel, Saul, did that. I Samuel 16:14 reads, "But the Spirit of the Lord departed from Saul, and an evil spirit from the LORD troubled him." Ananias and Sapphira did that. Acts 5:3 describes the withdrawal of the supporting presence of the Holy Spirit in their lives and they died frightfully. The whole nation of Israel did that in the wilderness. Isaiah 63:10 recounts the tragic story, "But they rebelled, and vexed his holy Spirit: therefore he was turned to be their enemy, and he fought against them." Except for two men, Joshua and Caleb, they all died outside the Promised Land. Oh, how fraught with disaster is the grieving of the Holy Spirit, Christ's representative for righteousness in the earth! The threat in Genesis 6:3 was not an idle warning when God said, "My spirit shall not always strive with man . . . ." When we refuse His leadership chaos awaits us.

But when we yield to the leadership of the Paraclete in our lives and do right, we honor our Lord; and, what is more, we ourselves become invincible. Stephen's face shone "as it had been the face of an angel" (Acts 6:15). When was Stephen thus so glorified? When he stood before the apostles and the church in Jerusalem? No, rather, when he stood before his enemies who took his life. God was with him and the glory of the Holy Spirit shone in his face. Even if we fall into death, the same power of the Spirit of God that raised up Jesus from the dead (Romans 1:4) will raise us up to everlasting life. The Holy Spirit in the life of the believer is Christ Himself among us. When we follow the leadership of the Spirit, we follow the representative of our Lord into a righteousness that cannot fail. This is the road to victory, triumph, and glory in the Christian life. It was the pure-hearted Sir Galahad who found the Holy Grail in the story of King Arthur and the Knights of the Round Table. Remember Alfred Lord Tennyson's portrayal of him as the warrior speaks in the first stanza of the poem:

My good blade carves the casques of men,
  My tough lance thrusteth sure,
My strength is as the strength of ten,
  Because my heart is pure.

The Pronounced Doom of Satan

Our Saviour now speaks in the text (John 16:8, 11) of the third great work of the Paraclete. "When he is come," Jesus says, "he will reprove [convict] the world . . . of judgment, because the prince of this world is judged." The prince of this world, Satan, is judged already. He is already sentenced. He represents a lost cause. He is as a sinking ship. He reigns over a doomed dominion. And the ultimate tragedy of a lost soul is this: those who elect to follow Satan will share in his condemnation and destruction. I have stood in the city square where the followers of Hitler, by the thousands, cheered their leader in Munich, Germany. I have also stood in the desolate area of East Berlin where he committed suicide. Did he fall alone? He brought down with him the millions of dupes who followed him. It is thus with the followers of Satan.

The devil cannot win. He is judged already. The doom of Satan is sure and certain. He is already defeated. The King James version in Luke 10:18 quotes our Lord as saying, "I beheld Satan as lightning fall from heaven." The Greek text reads, "fallen." Our adversary has already been cast down, his powers despoiled, his kingdom finished. It is but a matter of time, now, until there will be a new heaven and a new earth wherein dwelleth righteousness. Any hour of any day the Lord may come to "gather out of his kingdom all things that offend, and them which do iniquity." Evildoers and Christ-rejecting men face the judgment when those who spurn the overtures of mercy are sent into everlasting fire, prepared for the devil and his angels" (Matthew 25:41). When we give our lives to Satan, we shall inevitably share his fate. Love of money, of the world, of sin, of lust, of pleasure, damn us with the devil when we substitute them for the love of God.

The Holy Spirit reveals that condemnation to us with terrible emphasis. When we leave Christ out of our lives and bring the world into our lives, the judgment is swift and merciless. An affluent family gave themselves to the pleasures of the world. In their social ambition they had no time for God, no time for the church, no time for prayer or the reading of the Bible. They had a little boy who became critically ill and finally lay at death's portals. The little lad had never been to Sunday school or church. He had never been told of Jesus or of the heavenly home beyond the skies. Death to him was a frightful and lonely despair. He began to plead with his parents, "O Daddy, O Mother, do not take me to the cemetery to bury me. It is so far away. Please, Daddy, please, Mother, bury me by the door so I can be close to you." To the little boy there was nothing beyond the world he knew in a worldly home. Oh, the judgment upon the pleasure-minded! They give themselves to a lost cause, an empty, vain and fleeting dream.

How sweet and how precious the heavenly rewards of those who follow the leadership of the Holy Spirit to love the Lord Jesus! In preaching through the Book of Revelation, I had completed a sermon on the open door into heaven, a vision described in Revelation 4:1-11. After the message a mother came to me and said: "Our little boy has leukemia. We have been crushed, waiting in the valley of the shadow of death. But now I see the door opened into heaven. Our little lad will soon be with Jesus who loves him even more than do we." This is the reward of the Holy Spirit to those who will heed His pleading. He warns of judgment to come. He pleads for Christ, for heaven, for the joys and the blessings of a salvation that can never fail or pass.

Chapter 13

The Baptism of the Holy Spirit

Matthew 3

11 I indeed baptize you with water unto repentance: but he that cometh after me is mightier than I, whose shoes I am not worthy to bear: he shall baptize you with the Holy Ghost, and with fire.

The study of the New Testament presentation of the baptism of the Holy Spirit has brought astonishing, amazing discoveries to me. The truth is nothing as I would have expected. For one thing, the term as such is not found in Scripture. The term "the baptism of the Holy Spirit" is so much used and so greatly abused, but it is not in the Word of God. Only in reference to the prophecy of John the Baptist, concerning the ministry of Christ, is any mention made in the gospels or in the Acts to a baptism by the Holy Spirit. After reading Matthew 3:11 one would expect page after page in the four gospels to describe this marvelous experience. It is never referred to by name; it is never mentioned as such. After reading Acts 1:5 and Acts 11:16, one would expect to read in the Acts page after page of discussion concerning that baptism by the Holy Spirit. Again, it is never referred to by name; it is never mentioned as such. In fact, the word "baptize," with reference to the Spirit, is never used in recounting the story of Pentecost, of Samaria, of Caesarea, of Ephesus, or of anywhere else. This is amazing!

But what is more astonishing, we are never told, commanded, or urged to seek the baptism of the Holy Spirit. The idea is alien to the Scriptures. Some seek, pray, wait for such an experience. They are persuaded that God has reserved for a chosen few that unusual baptism. They expectantly, prayerfully, and sometimes agonizingly wait before the Lord for this heavenly gift. Some even build whole systems of theology upon it, presenting it in their teaching as a second work of grace. First, they say, we are regenerated (saved); then we are baptized by the Holy Spirit in a further, deepening consecration to God.

The Baptism by the Spirit in the Gospels and the Epistles

When we seek the Scriptural truth concerning any such baptism of the Holy Spirit, we cannot find it in the gospels. There such an experience is not referred to save in John's prophecy (Matthew 3:11). Nor is the doctrine discussed in the Book of Acts. There, again, the subject is not referred to save in John's prophecy (Acts 1:5; 11:16). It is in the epistles that the doctrine is unfolded. This is not an accident. It is according to the studied purpose of God.

As we turn to the epistles, a multitude of questions crowd into our minds. What is the baptism of the Holy Spirit? When did it happen? When does it happen today? Who is the baptizer? Into what does He baptize? What are the results? Are there any signs accompanying such an experience? Let us begin our inquiry in the middle of the doctrine (some would say "controversy") and work out from there.

Who is the baptizer and with what does He baptize? In Matthew 3:11; Acts 1:5; 11:16, the three passages presenting the prophecy of John the Baptist, Jesus is unmistakably the baptizer and it could be that the Holy Spirit is the sphere into which He baptizes. But in the epistles, in I Corinthians 12:13, the Holy Spirit is the baptizer and the body of Christ is the sphere into which He baptizes. (I Corinthians 12:13: "For by one Spirit are we all baptized into one body.") Are there, then, two different baptisms, one by the Lord Jesus and one by the Holy Spirit? We might think so but for the fact that the same Greek phrase is used to describe both baptisms, *en pneumati*. Can we build two separate doctrines of the baptism of the Holy Spirit on the same Greek phrase, on the same Greek preposition? Many do so! These dualists interpret the Greek preposition *en* used in Acts 1:5 in a location sense, meaning a baptism into the sphere of the Holy Spirit. Then they interpret the same Greek preposition *en* used in I Corinthians 12:13 in an instrumental sense, meaning a baptism into the sphere of the body of Christ. The *en* employed in I Corinthians 12:13 is clearly and only instrumental. The baptizer is the Holy Spirit; it is *He* who does the baptizing.

But what of the prophecy of John the Baptist in Matthew 3:11 where Jesus is clearly presented as the baptizer? In what sense is *He* the baptizer? In answering this question, we shall find the answer as to why the Spirit baptism is not discussed in the gospels. The gospels present pre-ascension events (John 7:39). Before there can be a Spirit baptism, there must be an atonement made on earth for our sins and a justification declared in heaven for our souls. Before the Spirit can be poured out, Christ must be put to death, raised from the grave, and must ascend into heaven. Water baptism is that in picture; Spirit baptism is that in fact and reality. (Romans 6:3-5; Colossians 2:12, we are dead with Christ, buried with Christ, and raised with Christ.) The result of the death, burial, Resurrection, and Ascension of Christ will be the ascension gift, the promise of the Father, the outpouring of the Spirit. There is no outpouring of the Spirit, there is no ascension gift until Christ has died, been buried, been raised, and has ascended into heaven. *After* the gospels, *after* the Ascension, *then* the gift (John 16:7; Ephesians 4:8). The coming of the Holy Spirit at Pentecost is the ascension gift of our Lord to His church.

In this sense, and only in this sense, is Christ the baptizer. He was the Giver of the original ascension gift. He sent the Paraclete to take His place. Through and by Him the Spirit is poured out. But after the Spirit's advent, the Spirit and not Christ is spoken of as the baptizer. The agent and the instrument in the baptism is the Holy Spirit (I Corinthians 12:13). In all instances and in all experiences, Christ is the ultimate source or agent in the baptism by the Spirit, as

Matthew 3:11 prophesies. Christ sent the Spirit. But as Christ is the primary agent, so after Pentecost the Holy Spirit is the immediate agent. The Spirit does the actual baptizing, joining believers in Christ to His body, the church.

The Time of the Baptism by the Spirit

We turn now to the question, when did and when does the baptism occur? John the Baptist, in Matthew 3:11, announced the reality as something beyond himself and his ministry. Jesus in the flesh (John 14:16, 26) spoke of it as a future event. In Acts 1:5; Jesus, raised from the dead but not ascended, referred to the gift as immediately coming. Acts 11:16 speaks of the baptism as having already taken place. The fulfillment of the promise clearly occurred at Pentecost and continued thereafter, joining both Jews and Gentiles to the body of Christ. This baptism of the Holy Spirit is the new departure at Pentecost. It inaugurated the present day of grace which was unknown in the days of the Old Testament. The baptism of the Spirit places believers in the body of Christ, the church. The church is built upon the death, burial and Resurrection of Christ and is an institution that had no breath of the Spirit (John 20:22) until the ministry of our Lord Jesus was complete. The church, including both Jews and Gentiles, was unknown to the prophets. The institution was a secret hid in the heart of God (Ephesians 3) and is distinctive of this present age.

The pouring out of the Spirit, the baptism of the Spirit, occurred at a set date, by divine promise. It is an ascension gift. The gift was not bestowed as a reward for praying or for human merit. Christ was born at a set time, He was crucified at a set time, He was raised from the dead at a set time, He ascended into heaven at a set time, and He sent the Holy Spirit in accordance with the promise of the Father at a set time.

In Luke 24:49 the Lord told the disciples to tarry in the city of Jerusalem until the promise of the Father should be sent upon them. The Greek word translated "tarry" is *kathizo*, which means "to sit down," "to stay," "to remain."

The disciples were not to attempt any work of witnessing (Acts 1:8) until the Holy Spirit came upon them. While they waited, they prayed, had fellowship, elected an apostle, spoke of Judas, and did other things; but all that was unconnected with the coming of the Holy Spirit. He came at a divinely scheduled time (Acts 2:1), at a divinely designated place (Joel 2:32. Had they been tarrying in another place except Jerusalem they would have missed the blessing), and in accordance with Old Testament types (Leviticus 23:15-22).

The Spirit of Pentecost Is With Us Forever

The Holy Spirit, having come, is to be with the believer forever. John 14:16 promises, "And I will pray the Father, and he shall give you another Comforter, that he may abide with you for ever." There is to be no second Pentecost in the sense of an ascension gift inaugurating a new age. In the economy of God a second Pentecost would be as impossible as a second incarnation. The Holy Spirit is here without measure and with the followers of the Lord forever.

The blessed Spirit of Jesus is here with us now: "And I will pray the Father, and he shall give you another Comforter, that he may abide with you for ever; even the Spirit of truth; whom the world cannot receive, because it seeth him not, neither knoweth him: but ye know him; for he dwelleth with you, and shall be in you" (John 14:16, 17). Never again do we have to wait ten days or ten seconds. He indwells *now* every believer. The waiting now is on the part of the Holy Spirit to empower us, to fill us to the utmost. It is but for us to yield our souls, hearts, minds, bodies to the indwelling presence. Pentecost is with us all the time, every day and hour. We are to live every minute in the fullness of God. This accounts for the agony of our prayers: not that the Holy Spirit is reluctant to come (He is already here), but that we are reluctant to yield our members to Him. He possesses so little of us. Our sins blot Him out, as said the prophet Isaiah: "Behold, the LORD's hand is not shortened, that it cannot save; neither his ear heavy, that it cannot hear: But your iniquities have separated between you and your God, and your sins have hid his face from you, that he will not hear" (Isaiah 59:1, 2). Sometimes we must wrestle through the night of despair as Jacob did at Peniel until broken and yielded we also cry, "I will not let thee go, except thou bless me" (Genesis 32:26). God grant to us this yieldedness of our lives that we might possess the fullness of the Spirit.

Chapter 14

The Results of the Baptism of the Holy Spirit

I Corinthians 12

13 For by one Spirit are we all baptized into one body,
whether we be Jews or Gentiles, whether we be bond or free;
and have been all made to drink into one Spirit.

In this message we come to the heart and center of the
doctrine of the Holy Spirit. The Scriptures are very plain
in their teaching concerning the work of the presence of
God in our lives. It is *we* who misunderstand, misappropri-
ate, misuse, and misapply what the Bible has lucidly set before us. Following the Word of the Lord, we shall consider
first what the baptism by the Holy Spirit is not; then we
shall present what the baptism by the Holy Spirit is.

The Baptism of the Spirit Is Not Regeneration

Spirit baptism is not regeneration; it is not salvation.
There is a vast difference between the two. The disciples
were saved before Pentecost. The marvelous transforma-
tion that came into their lives at Pentecost was nothing
short of miraculous but it was not salvation. They knew
the Lord in His saving, forgiving grace before they gave
themselves in prayer and to waiting for the promise of the
Father. Regeneration is not baptism. In regeneration the
believer accepting Christ is saved. Christ comes into his
heart. He becomes a Christian through the committal of his
life by faith to the Lord Jesus. Revelation 3:20 beautifully
outlines what happens when a sinner opens the door of his
heart and lets Jesus come in. "Behold, I stand at the door,
and knock: if any man hear my voice, and open the door, I
will come in to him, and will sup with him, and he with me"

119

(Revelation 3:20). The appeal of the gospel song reflects the precious invitation of our Lord:

> If you are tired of the load of your sin,
> Let Jesus come into your heart;
> If you desire a new life to begin,
> Let Jesus come into your heart.
>
> Just now your doubtings give o'er
> Just now reject Him no more;
> Just now throw open the door,
> Let Jesus come into your heart.

That is salvation, letting Jesus come into your heart. But by Spirit baptism, the believer is placed "in Christ." Galatians 3:27 reads: "For as many of you as have been baptized into Christ have put on Christ." The Greek word translated "have put on Christ" is *enduno,* which literally means in this verse "to clothe one's self with." We are in Christ as we are in our clothes. We are clothed in Christ. Spirit baptism places us there. This difference between regeneration by the Spirit and baptism by the Spirit is seen in John 14:20, "At that day ye shall know that I am in my Father, and ye in me, and I in you." "I in you" is regeneration. "Ye in me" is the baptizing work of the Holy Spirit.

In regeneration the soul is quickened from death to life. Paul writes in Ephesians 2:1, "And you hath he quickened, who were dead in trespasses and sins." In salvation the Spirit imparts life. In Spirit baptism the believer is taken out of the old creation of death in Adam and placed eternally in the new creation of life in Christ. This is marvelously illustrated in the picture of baptism in Romans 6:3-5.

> Know ye not, that so many of us as were baptized into Jesus Christ were baptized into his death? Therefore we are buried with him by baptism into death: that like as Christ was raised up from the dead by the glory of the Father, even so we also should walk in newness of life. For if we have been planted together in the likeness of his death, we shall be also in the likeness of his resurrection.

This new creation into which the believer is introduced is also seen in II Corinthians 5:17:

> Therefore if any man be in Christ, he is a new creature: old
> things are passed away; behold, all things are become new.

In regeneration the believer is made a child of God (John
1:12; Galatians 3:26). He is made a joint-heir with Christ
(Romans 8:16,17). In Spirit baptism the child of God is
made an organic part of the body of Christ.

> For by one Spirit are we all baptized into one body, whether
> we be Jews or Gentiles, whether we be bond or free; and have
> been all made to drink into one Spirit (I Corinthians 12:13).

The Baptism by the Spirit Is Not the Anointing

Spirit baptism is not the anointing. It is most common for
Bible teachers to say that Jesus was baptized with the Holy
Spirit following His water baptism in the Jordan River. One
great preacher writes, "Jesus never entered His public ministry until He was baptized with the Holy Spirit." No, Jesus
was anointed by the Holy Spirit as He stood before John in
the Jordan. He was divinely filled without measure (John
3:34). Spirit baptism is a result of Christ's finished work
of redemption. It is an ascension gift. The purpose of the
Spirit baptism (I Corinthians 12:13) is to join us to Christ
as Christ is joined to the Father. Christ needed no such baptism. He needed not to be joined to the Father. He was already one with the Father. What happened, then, at Jesus'
baptism when "the Holy Spirit descended in a bodily shape
like a dove upon him . . ."? (Luke 3:22; cf. Matthew 3:16).
The answer is plain. Jesus was anointed for His holy, Messianic office upon which He was now entering. The coming
of the Holy Spirit upon Him was His consecration to the
priesthood as He prepared to offer the sacrifice which will
wash our sins away. The Levitical law required all priests
to be consecrated when they began to be about thirty years
of age (Numbers 4:3; Luke 3:23). The Levitical consecration for the priesthood was twofold: there was first a wash-
ing in water; then there was the anointing with oil (Exodus
29:4, 7; Leviticus 8:6, 12). In His water baptism Jesus identi-
fied Himself with sinners. He was baptized — washed with
water. He was then anointed with the Holy Spirit. He was

consecrated — set apart — for the holy office to which He had committed His life.

Spirit baptism is not the sealing whereby Christ stamps us as His own for eternity. It is not the indwelling whereby Christ grants us His continuing presence. It is not the filling. There is one baptism; there are many fillings. There is no command, ever, to be baptized by the Holy Spirit. There is distinct injunction for every believer to be filled with the Spirit. Because in two instances (at Pentecost and at Caesarea) the baptism by the Holy Spirit and the filling of the Holy Spirit occurred at the same time, Bible teachers have made the two the same. This is a tragic error. The baptism is not the filling.

By the Baptism We Are Joined to the Body of Christ

What, then, is baptism by the Spirit? The all-important answer to this question is found in these Scriptures: I Corinthians 12:13; Romans 6:3-5; Galatians 3:27; Ephesians 4:5; Colossians 2:12; I Peter 3:21. According to I Corinthians 12:13 the baptizing work of the Holy Spirit has to do with the Church, the body of Christ. We repeat, the baptizing has to do with *the Church*. By the Spirit baptizing we are joined to the body of Christ. We are baptized into the Church. Never is it said in Scripture that anyone is baptized into the Holy Spirit. We are never baptized, placed, immersed in the Spirit. The Spirit is the baptizer. He is the instrument, the agent, who places the believer into the body of Christ. The creation of this one body, the Church, was a mystery hid through the ages in the heart of God (Ephesians 3:3, 5, 6, 9, 10). The prophets of the Old Testament never saw it. It was hid from their eyes. That Gentiles were to be saved was no mystery (secret kept in the heart of God). Moses (Deuteronomy 32:21), Isaiah (42:6, 7; 65:1), Hosea (2:23), Joel (2:28-32), and others had told of Israel's blindness and the subsequent mercy to the Gentiles. But that there was to be a Church, a body into which both Jews and Gentiles were to be baptized, was a mystery (secret) hidden in the counsels of the Almighty. The creation of that one body is the result of the baptizing work of the Holy Spirit.

In the creation of one unity with many believers, three figures are used. One figure is that of a bride (Revelation 21:9, 10). An angel said to John the Seer, "Come hither, I will show thee the bride, the Lamb's wife." And when John was carried away in the Spirit to a great and high mountain, and saw that fabulous bride, what he saw was the Holy City, "descending out of heaven from God" (Revelation 21: 10). All the saved in Christ Jesus, the bride with her friends and companions and guests, live in the beautiful city. Together they comprise the New Jerusalem. Another figure representing this unity in Christ, the result of the baptizing work of the Holy Spirit, is that of a building. Christ is the foundation (I Corinthians 3:11), and we are living stones built upon the foundation to make up the holy Temple of God (I Peter 2:4-7). A third figure presenting this baptizing work of the Holy Spirit is that of a body. Christ is the head (Ephesians 1:22), and we are different members of that one body (Ephesians 5:23; I Corinthians 6:18; 12:13-27). At the moment of our salvation the baptizing work of the Holy Spirit joins us as a living member to the body of Christ.

This creative, uniting work of the blessed Spirit is wrought by a "separation from" and a "joining to." Romans 5 and 6 present a contrast between the sinner "in Adam" and the saint "in Christ." The sinner in the old Adam's nature is under the condemnation of death. The saint in the new nature is not only saved, justified, delivered from death into everlasting life, but is "in Christ," joined to the living body of our Lord. Thus we read in I Peter 3:20, 21 that baptism is a type of deliverance out of death into life. The waters of the flood separated the eight from the perishing world. They, the saved, were in the ark, "in Christ." Our being "in Christ," the result of the baptizing work of the Holy Spirit, is all significant, eternally important. Noticeable in the list of the things that unite the body into one organic structure (Ephesians 4:3-6) is the "one baptism." There is one baptism, the operation of God's Spirit, which places the believer in Christ, in His mystical body, of which the one water baptism is a symbol. We are saved, regenerated, born again; then we are baptized, added to the Church, the body of Christ.

The Baptism by the Spirit Is Universal Among All Believers

The baptism by the Holy Spirit is experienced among all believers. Galatians 3:26, 27 says: "For ye are all the children of God by faith in Christ Jesus. For as many of you as have been baptized into Christ have put on Christ." I Corinthians 12:13 reads: "For by one Spirit are we all baptized into one body, whether we be Jews or Gentiles, whether we be bond or free; and have been all made to drink into one Spirit." The Scriptures expressly state that all born-again believers have been baptized into the one body of Christ. Paul did not exhort the Christian believers to be baptized in order to be more spiritual. He simply states that *all* had been baptized (Greek *ebaptisthemen,* aorist tense). Notice to whom Paul is addressing these words. He is writing to a troubled, disordered, carnal church. They were divided over personalities, comparing one preacher, as Apollos, to another, as Paul. They were divided over doctrine, some holding to the truth, others to rank heresy. They were divided over practices, some even desecrating the Lord's table. They were divided over discipline, some even condoning gross incest. They were divided over legal matters, some carrying others into court. Yet, the Apostle states that they had *all* been baptized by the Holy Spirit.

This explains why there is an amazing absence of exhortation in the Scriptures that we get baptized by the Holy Spirit. The baptism is already a universal gift of God to all believers. We need not seek it, pray for it, try to achieve it, or receive it. We already have it. It is but now for us to take possession of our possession, to act upon the promises. We are but to yield to the heavenly power, to seek the fullness, to obey God's Word, to do God's will, to exercise prevailing prayer. The baptism of the Spirit is come. We have it and we have *Him.*

There was a time when the Holy Spirit as a heavenly fire was a mysterious force, flashing like lightning in the skies; we knew not why nor whither. He came now upon a Moses and again upon an Elijah. Sometimes the celestial force would strike out in Israel's camp in the destroying flame of God's anger. Sometimes the fire would fall upon a Mount Carmel in awesome majesty, consuming the altar along with the sacrifice. Sometimes the fire would appear in the burning bush at Horeb, sometimes as the blessed Shekinah glory in the temple, the strange, mysterious symbol of Jehovah's presence. But since Christ's Ascension, the Holy Spirit is poured out upon us all (Joel 2:28). He is with us and within us forever. For power, for conquest, for glory, we have received the baptism by the Holy Spirit. According to our faith and our yieldedness, we are able to do great and mighty things for Him.

Chapter 15

The Baptism and the Filling

Acts 2

1 And when the day of Pentecost was fully come, they were all with one accord in one place.

2 And suddenly there came a sound from heaven as of a rushing mighty wind, and it filled all the house where they were sitting.

3 And there appeared unto them cloven tongues like as of fire, and it sat upon each of them.

4 And they were all filled with the Holy Ghost, and began to speak with other tongues, as the Spirit gave them utterance.

Studying the Scriptures closely, intently, has changed not only my understanding of the work of the Holy Spirit in our hearts, but also the very language and nomenclature of that work. Much of the description I have used heretofore concerning the baptism of the Holy Spirit has been incorrect; many of the doctrinal statements I have followed are not Scriptural. When we let the Bible say what it says, an amazing overhauling of our systematic theology comes to pass.

Incorrect Interpretations of Scripture

Having committed myself to the presentation of the work of the Holy Spirit as the doctrine is revealed in the Scriptures, I can now easily see the twisting of interpretation on the part of preachers and theologians toward preconceived, self-chosen ends. The results of this willful misconstruction of the Word of God are seen in the vast confusion and spiritual helplessness all around us. As an example of plain, unadulterated, false exegesis of the inspired Word presented in defense of a false doctrine, let me quote from a page in

126

a book written by a world-famed English scholar-preacher.
He writes: "In I Corinthians 12:13 Paul says, 'For by one
Spirit are we all baptized into one body . . . .' Here the King
James version uses the preposition 'by' — 'by one Spirit are
we all baptized.' However, the preposition used in the original Greek is the preposition *en* — 'in one Spirit are we all
baptized.' Unfortunately, the accident that the King James
translators used the phrase 'by one Spirit' has given rise to
some strange doctrines which suggest that the Holy Spirit
Himself is the agent who does the baptizing. Had the authors of these strange doctrines paused long enough to con-
sult the original Greek text, they would have found no basis
or suggestion of any such doctrine. In fact, the whole teaching of the entire New Testament in this connection agrees
in this fact, clearly and emphatically stated: Jesus Christ
Himself alone — and no other — is the One who baptizes in
the Holy Spirit." "The theologian who writes the above
words supposes we have not looked at the original Greek
text. That is the point. We have. And it is the looking at
that Greek text that has changed our ideas of the baptism
and the filling of the Holy Spirit.

The Greek preposition translated by the King James version in I Corinthians 12:13 with the English word "by" ("by
one Spirit") is the Greek word *en*. Thayer's *Greek Lexicon
of the New Testament* lists forty-four different uses of the
preposition *en* besides page after page of other shades of
meaning. The word *en* can be translated "in," "upon,"
"among," "before," "by," "during," "with," according to its
context. Is there an instrumental use of the preposition *en*
whereby it is translated "by"? Yes, indeed, and this most
exclusively and emphatically. Look at Matthew 12:27, 28;
21:23, 24; 23:16-22; Acts 4:12; Romans 5:9, 10; 12:21; Revelation 13:10. In each instance (and these are but a few chosen
from a legion of passages) the word *en* can mean only the
instrumental "by." For one passage typical of them all, take
the last one cited, Revelation 13:10: "He that killeth *en* [the
Greek word] the sword must be killed *en* [the Greek word]
the sword." The preposition is solely instrumental. It can-

not mean "in." The verdict of the scholastic world would no less certainly translate the Greek word *en* in I Corinthians 12:13 with the English instrumental word "by" ("by one Spirit are we all baptized . . ."). The baptizing is done by the Holy Spirit. He is the agent and He baptizes us into the body of Christ.

The tremendous emphasis of the Scriptures is not upon the baptizing work of the Holy Spirit but upon the filling. Notice again the text in Acts 2:4, "And they were all filled with the Holy Spirit . . . ." The passage does not read here or anywhere else, "And they were all baptized with the Holy Spirit. . . ." There is no such language in the Bible. But what is said here is repeated again and again, "And they were all filled with the Holy Spirit." From the prophecy in Matthew 3:11 and Acts 1:5, one would suppose that exhortation after exhortation, plea after plea, would have been made that we be baptized with the Holy Spirit, that we constantly seek this baptism. The subject is never mentioned. It is never referred to, not by even a syllable of one word in any sentence. But the injunction that we be filled with the Holy Spirit is plainly stated (Ephesians 5:18). And the record that the disciples were repeatedly filled with the Holy Spirit is the recurring theme in the story of the early church.

The Difference Between the Baptism and the Filling

In order that we might plainly and accurately see the difference between the baptism by the Holy Spirit and the filling of the Holy Spirit, let us list five major differences between the two. First, there is no command, ever, for anyone to be baptized with the Holy Spirit. But every believer is under commandment to be filled with the Spirit. The verb in Ephesians 5:18 (Greek, *plerousthe*) is in the imperative mood and present tense. It refers in Greek to continuous, repeated action. We are constantly being filled by the Holy Spirit.

Second, the baptizing work of the Holy Spirit is a once-for-all operation. It happens at the time of conversion. We are baptized once when we are saved; thereafter, we are never baptized again. The Greek verb used in I Corinthians 12:13 (*ebaptisthemen*) is in the aorist tense, the Greek way of expressing a once-for-all experience. On the other hand, the filling of the Holy Spirit is again and again. The present tense is used in Ephesians 5:18, denoting continuous, repeated action. There is one baptism; there are many fillings. The once-for-all baptism of the Holy Spirit places us in the body of Christ (I Corinthians 12:13). If this could be repeated, it would mean that a person could be placed in the body of Christ; then removed from that body; then reinstated by a second baptism. Such a fanciful idea is foreign to Scripture. It is not the plan of life that we cut off a hand, or a foot, or an arm, or a leg, and that we replace the member. The member is given to us one time to stay. It is thus with us who are added as members to the body of Christ. It is not the purpose or even the contemplation of Scripture that we be cut off, then added back again. There is one Lord, one faith, one baptism (Ephesians 4:5). Having been baptized one time, the baptism is never repeated. We are born into the family of God. We cannot unborn ourselves. That new birth is never repeated. But the great work of the Spirit in filling us, and the mighty personal experience of being filled may happen again and again. We never reach some elevated plain where God has nothing more for us. Through the power of the blessed Spirit I may have reached a glorious height yesterday, but there are even more celestial heights for me to reach today.

A third difference between the baptism and the filling lies in its positional, experiential aspect. The baptism of the Holy Spirit is positional, like writing our names in the Book of Life up in heaven. It is something God does for us in establishing our relationship with Christ and with the fellow members of Christ's body. The filling of the Holy Spirit, however, is experiential. The experience has to do with divine empowerment. It radically affects Christian life and service. The filling of the Holy Spirit is truly Pentecostal as Acts 2:4 graphically avows.

A fourth observation concerning the baptism and the fill-

ing is self-evident when we see the results of the two. The
baptism places us in the body of Christ and, as such, places
us in a position to receive power, but it does not in itself
bestow or guarantee that power. The Corinthians had been
baptized by the Spirit (I Corinthians 12:13) but they were
grossly carnal (I Corinthians 3:1, 2; 5:1; 6:1). The Galatians
had been baptized by the Spirit, they had put on Christ
(Galatians 3:27), but they were in the very act of apostatiz-
ing (Galatians 1:6; 4:9). There is nothing in the baptism,
as such, that gives power. But the filling is just the opposite.
The filling is power itself. It is victory, conquest, march,
missions, everything the Christian needs to do valiant service for the Master. Compare Peter the Coward in Matthew
26:69-75 with Peter the Bold in Acts 2:4, 14, 23, 37; 4:8. (If
I were a teenager following the story of the crowing of the
rooster, I would say, "Compare Peter the Chicken in Matthew 26 with Peter the Lion in Acts 2"!) The tremendous,
miraculous difference seen in Peter is explained by the filling recorded in Acts 2:4 at Pentecost. We have a like record
of victorious power in the story of the deacons in Acts 6:
3-8, 15; again in the story of Stephen in Acts 6:5; 7:55; again
in the summary of the life of Barnabas in the beautiful verse
of Acts 11:24; again in the life of Paul in Acts 9:17-22; 13:9.
These fillings brought unusual power in witnessing and in
missionary conquest.

A fifth and a last difference between the baptism of the
Spirit and the filling of the Spirit can be most effectively
demonstrated in the Pentecostal second chapter of the Book
of Acts. What happened at Pentecost? What did the disciples experience on that fiftieth day? In answer, can we
trust the Word of God for what came to pass? Or shall we
place man's word in God's mouth? Let God say what He
says. It is when we do this that we see with amazing clarity
that the word "baptize" is never used at Pentecost (nor in
any other like situation). What is the word used? It is the
word "filled" (Acts 2:4 as in Acts 4:8, 31; 7:55; 8:17; 9:17;
10:44; 11:15; 19:6). The fulfillment of Matthew 3:11 and
Acts 1:5 was found in the ascension gift of Christ upon His

return to heaven wherein He poured out the Holy Spirit in keeping with the promise of the Father. Thereafter the work of the Holy Spirit is one of creating the new and divine institution, the Church which is the body of Christ. The Third Person of the Trinity regenerates the new members in Spirit conversion and adds them to the body in Spirit baptism. He has been doing that since Pentecost added three thousand converts to the household of faith. This is the baptism of the Holy Spirit fulfilling Matthew 3:11 and Acts 1:5.

But something else happened at Pentecost. What was it? It was the glorious experience recorded in the Pentecostal chapter, verse four: "And they were all filled with the Holy Spirit." The baptism added to the body, but the filling wrought wonders in the church. As a result of the filling, Acts 2:4 states that the disciples witnessed in foreign languages; Acts 2:11 describes their praising the wonderful works of God; Acts 2:14 presents their intrepid boldness in preaching; Acts 2:42 outlines their steadfastness in doctrine; Acts 2:44, 45 delineates their unselfishness of heart, and Acts 2:46 speaks of their glorious gladness of ecstatic worship. Oh, the glory of the fullness of the Spirit! O God, do it again and again and yet again! Do it now! Fill us with the power and presence of the blessed Spirit!

Chapter 16

The Command to Be Filled With the Spirit

Ephesians 5

18 And be not drunk with wine, wherein is excess; but be filled with the Spirit.

The Greek words used in this pointed command are *plerousthe en pneumati,* "to be filled with the Spirit." Aside from the fact that through inspired writers God employed the Greek language to create His New Testament, the words in the original language are most interesting and meaningful in themselves. Let us look at the mandate closely.

There Are Several Different Kinds of "Fillings"

There are several Greek words that can mean "fill." One is *kortazo,* which is always used with reference to hunger. Look at Matthew 5:6; 14:20; Luke 16:21; John 6:26; James 2:16; Revelation 19:21. Another word is *pletho* (from *pimplemi*), which is a factual word to describe the filling of anything with something else. In Luke 4:28 the city of Nazareth was "filled" with anger. In Luke 5:7 both ships were "filled" with the large catch of fish. In John 19:29 (Matthew 27:48) the sponge was "filled" with vinegar. In Acts 19:29 the whole city of Ephesus was "filled" with confusion. The word is used to record the factual filling by the Holy Spirit in such passages as Luke 1:15, 41; Acts 2:4; 4:8, 31; 9:17; 13:9.

A kindred word to the above *pletho* is the verb *pleroo.* It is the verb used in this command in our text, Ephesians 5:18. Thayer's *Greek Lexicon of the New Testament* has a long, involved discussion of the usages of this Greek word. Of prophecies and promises, it means "to bring to pass," "to accomplish" (Matthew 1:22; 2:15; Acts 1:16). Of a ministry, it means "to complete it," "to fulfill it" (Acts 12:25; 14:26; Colossians 4:17; Revelation 3:2). Of God, it means "to pervade," "to fill with His presence, power and activity." In Ephesians 1:23; 4:10 the exalted Christ, the head of the Church, "fills" the universe. In Ephesians 3:19 the Lord takes possession of the heart, soul and life, "filling" the whole personality. It is thus the verb is used in Ephesians 5:18. To be filled with the Holy Spirit means for us to be so controlled and motivated with the presence and power of the Spirit until our whole being is one perpetual psalm of praise and service to God (Ephesians 5:19-32).

God Commands That We Be Filled With the Spirit

Notice that the word *plerousthe* is in the imperative mood. It is a mandate. There is never a command that we be baptized by the Spirit, or that we be sealed or indwelt by the Spirit. These are positional; they refer to something God does for us, as writing our names in the Book of Life. The command that we be filled with the Spirit relates not to our position before God but to our daily service and walk. For, you see, a believer can be a carnal, worldly, unfruitful Christian. The New Testament looks upon a man as a trichotomy. He is made up of three parts. There is the *somatikos* man, the body man (from *soma,* "body") (I Timothy 4:8). There is the *psukikos* man, the sensuous, volitional man (from *psuche,* the self as the seat of the affections and will) (I Corinthians 2:14). There is the *pneumatikos* man, the spiritual man (from *pneuma,* "breath," "spirit") (I Corinthians 2:15). But the Christian believer, this *pneumatikos* man, can be also a *sarkikos* man, a fleshly, carnal man (from *sarx,* "flesh") (I Corinthians 3:4). The carnal man lives by the power and dictates of the flesh. The truly spiritual man lives by the power and dictates of the Spirit of God (Galatians 5:16,17).

The Filling a Repeated Experience

Notice that the verb *plerousthe* is in the present tense. "Tense" to us in the English language means "time." We cannot say anything in English without placing it in some "tense," in some time, as past, present, future. But what we call "tense" in Greek verbs is not "tense" at all. Greek verbs express kinds of action, as a point (aorist), continuous as going on (present), having been completed and remaining completed (perfect), etc. This verb *plerousthe*, therefore, being in what is called the present tense, refers to enduring, continuous action. The translation literally would be, "Be ye being continuously filled with the Holy Spirit." The experience is repeated again and again. A Christian living a normal life of moment by moment yieldedness to God experiences a moment by moment fullness of the Spirit. Some men experience a spectacular, miraculous, unique fullness that stands out over all other fillings like a mountain peak in a lofty range, like the lone grandeur of a Kilimanjaro in Africa or a Fujiyama in Japan. Such men of marvelous witness and testimony are John Wesley, Charles G. Finney, Dwight L. Moody, and R. A. Torrey. They had one great filling of the Spirit that stood out above all others. (Some of them, as R. A. Torrey, wrongly call it "the baptism of the Holy Spirit.") But most of us experience the filling of the Spirit in repeated succession like a mountain chain of many equal peaks. Each day's work brings its measure of endowment and inspiration.

Notice that the verb *plerousthe* is plural in number. The command is addressed not only to the pastor, the preacher, the deacon, the Sunday school teacher, but to every Christian and to every church member. The Ephesian letter from which this text is taken is a circular letter. When Paul wrote it, he most likely left the salutation blank whereby the name of the church could be later inserted. In some ancient manuscripts the word "Ephesus" is omitted. In other ancient manuscripts the name "Laodicea" is written in, most certainly in keeping with the Laodicean letter referred to in Colossians 4:16. All of this gives emphasis to the fact that the injunction that we be filled with the Spirit is addressed to all churches, all leaders, all Christians everywhere through all times and generations.

The Man Under the Influence of the Spirit

Notice, lastly, that the verb *plerousthe* is in the passive voice. The subject is acted upon (as in English grammar, the passive voice is illustrated in the sentence, "He is carried," "He is swept away"). It is we who are acted upon by the Holy Spirit. In the complete text, "And be not drunk with wine, wherein is excess; but be filled with the Spirit," Paul is using an illustration of a man who is acted upon, dominated, controlled by something other than himself. The comparison is between the man under the influence of alcohol and the man under the influence of the Holy Spirit. Paul describes the man under the domination of alcohol as "asotia," translated "excess" but a word which really refers to "a course of abandonment" (cf. Titus 1:6; I Peter 1:4). When the man is drunk with wine and is given over to the influence of liquor, he is a changed person. Sometimes a most neatly groomed and dressed individual becomes disheveled, untidy, and downright dirty. Sometimes a shy, reticent man now talks loud and laughs unroariously. Sometimes a fellow who would never sing in his life now sings at the top of his voice. Sometimes a poor creature so inhibited that he is afraid of his own shadow now becomes as bold as a lion with courage to attempt anything. I heard about two inebriates, one of whom leaped out the window to fly around the block. In the hospital, when the other one came to see him, the much bandaged and broken up patient said to his friend, "Why did you let me do it?" His friend replied, "I thought you could!" Under the domination of the Holy Spirit, we also are changed persons. We are doing what we never thought of doing. We are saying what we never thought of saying. We are attempting what we never thought of attempting. In God we are different, changed people.

At Pentecost the ascended Saviour poured out the Holy Spirit upon the world without measure (John 3:34). He is here in all His heavenly presence and miracle-working power. Having come, the Spirit jealously desires the whole of us. James, the Lord's brother and the pastor of the Church at Jerusalem, wrote a tremendously strong statement in James 4:5, "The spirit that dwelleth in us lusteth to envy." The Greek verb translated "lusteth" is *epipotheo* which means "to desire earnestly," "to long for." In 1611, when the King James version of the Scriptures was made, the word "lusteth" was an exact translation of *epipotheo*. But "lust" to us today has come to have another and unspiritual meaning. James meant that the Holy Spirit so desires to possess us that He envied other loves and interests that command our affection. Think of it! The Holy Spirit of God envying anything that we love more than Him! The verse is enough to make us weep for contrition in our very souls.

For the Spirit to have us, we must yield ourselves to Him. We must be emptied of self to be filled with all of His fullness. Our hands cannot be filled with other things if they are to know the fullness of God. Our hearts cannot be filled with worldly affection and ambition if we are to possess the Spirit without measure. Our souls must be emptied of self when we bring them to the fountains of heaven for the blessing. It seems that Paul's motto was "not I but Christ" (Galatians 2:20). Oh, that we could surrender ourselves to a like commitment! As we grow in grace, maybe at first it was all of self and none of Thee. Then, it was some of self and some of Thee. Then it was less of self and more of Thee. But now, God grant it, it is none of self and all of Thee. "Filled with the Spirit."

Chapter 17

The Second Blessing

Acts 8

4 Therefore they that were scattered abroad went every where preaching the word.

5 Then Philip went down to the city of Samaria, and preached Christ unto them.

6 And the people with one accord gave heed unto those things which Philip spake, hearing and seeing the miracles which he did.

7 For unclean spirits, crying with loud voice, came out of many that were possessed with them: and many taken with palsies, and that were lame, were healed.

8 And there was great joy in that city.

14 Now when the apostles which were at Jerusalem heard that Samaria had received the word of God, they sent unto them Peter and John:

15 Who, when they were come down, prayed for them, that they might receive the Holy Ghost:

16 (For as yet he was fallen upon none of them: only they were baptized in the name of the Lord Jesus.)

17 Then laid they their hands on them, and they received the Holy Ghost.

The success of Philip the Evangelist (one of the seven men of God ordained in the Jerusalem church) in Samaria was nothing short of phenomenal. The whole city where he was preaching turned to Jesus and there was joy and gladness on every hand. It was real revival. Preparation for the wonderful harvest of souls had been made by the Saviour in His visit to Sychar (John 4:1-42). John 4:25 presents the Samaritan expectation of a coming Messiah, an expectation as deep and as vivid as that entertained by the Jewish nation itself. When Acts 8:12 carefully notes that "they were baptized, both men and women," I could hope that included in this great company of believers was the woman Jesus talked to by the well. With the Lord's blessing upon them all, no wonder "there was great rejoicing in that city."

Note the divine change in the preaching of the Gospel found in the Samaritan revival. In Matthew 10:5 Samaria, as well as the Gentiles was expressly forbidden to the ministering apostles. The Lord said, "Go not into the way of the Gentiles, and into any city of the Samaritans enter ye not." That exclusion has now passed away. After the death, burial, Resurrection, and Ascension of Christ, the Gospel is to be progressively delivered to the whole earth. Beyond Jerusalem it is to be preached in Judaea; beyond Judaea in Samaria; beyond Samaria "unto the uttermost part of the earth." This emphatically reminds us that we must interpret any passage of Scripture in its context, in the day and way and purpose for which it was written. To note this dispensational change in preaching the Gospel to the Samaritans is most vital here as we shall see later on.

When news of this marvelous Samaritan revival came to the ears of the apostles at Jerusalem, they sent two of their number, Peter and John, to look up the results personally. This is doubly interesting in view of the fact that John, with his brother James, wanted Jesus to call down fire from heaven to consume a Samaritan village that refused to receive the Saviour (Luke 9:52-56). But it is a new day now. When Peter and John arrived and had witnessed for themselves the grace of God upon the new converts, they prayed for them that they might receive the Holy Spirit (for as yet He had fallen upon none of them). "Then laid they their hands on them, and they received the Holy Ghost" (Acts 8:15-17).

The Differing Interpretations of the Samaritan Revival

The interpretations of this coming of the Holy Spirit upon the Samaritans are literally legion in number. The passage is used to bolster a thousand differing doctrines. Some ap-

peal to the text to demonstrate the superiority of the bishop
to the pastor (the Jerusalem apostles over the local Samaritan leadership). Some see in the story an illustration and
confirmation of apostolic succession in ordination to the ministry. Recently, I attended a Cathedral Whitsunday service
(commemorating the descent of the Holy Spirit at Pentecost) and listened to the bishop's sermon. He used this chapter in Acts to "prove" that only through the laying on of
hands by the apostles and their successors could there be
any valid ordination. Some appeal to this passage for the
Biblical basis of the rites of confirmation. Actually and
historically, this is the doctrinal starting point for what
afterward developed into the ritual known as "confirmation."
In modern usage it becomes the confirming of the promises
made by the parents for the infant when the child was
christened. Some see in the text "the second blessing" —
saved then sanctified. The first work of grace, they say, is
seen in the conversion of the Samaritans. The second work
of grace, they avow, is seen in the coming of the Holy Spirit
upon them. Some use the text as a defense for speaking in
unknown tongues. To these interpreters, speaking in tongues
is a sign of the descent of the Spirit upon the individual life.
Tongues are not mentioned here, but these doctrinarians are
most positive that there could be no other sign that the new
converts had received the Spirit other than their speaking
in unknown tongues. And thus on and on the discussions
continue. It all reminds me of a Hindu fable called "The
Blind Men and the Elephant" that the poet John Godfrey
Saxe wrote down in verse. The story goes like this, a story
which the author applied to theological differences:

THE BLIND MEN AND THE ELEPHANT

It was six men of Indostan
To learning much inclined,
Who went to see the Elephant,
(Though all of them were blind)
That each by observation
Might satisfy his mind.

The *First* approached the Elephant,
And happening to fall
Against his broad and sturdy side,
At once began to bawl:
"God bless me! but the Elephant
Is very like a wall!"

The *Second*, feeling of the tusk,
Cried, "Ho! what have we here
So very round and smooth and sharp?
To me 'tis mighty clear
This wonder of an Elephant
Is very like a spear!"

The *Third* approached the animal,
And happening to take
The squirming trunk within his hands,
Thus boldly up and spake:
"I see," quoth he, "the Elephant
Is very like a snake!"

The *Fourth* reached out an eager hand,
And felt about the knee.
"What most this wondrous beast is like
Is mighty plain," quoth he;
" 'Tis clear enough the Elephant
Is very like a tree!"

The *Fifth* who chanced to touch the ear,
Said: "E'en the blindest man
Can tell what this resembles most;
Deny the fact who can,
This marvel of an Elephant
Is very like a fan!"

The *Sixth* no sooner had begun
About the beast to grope,
Than, seizing on the swinging tail
That fell within his scope,
"I see," quoth he, "the Elephant
Is very like a rope!"

And so these men of Indostan
Disputed loud and long,
Each in his own opinion
Exceeding stiff and strong
Though each was partly in the right,
And all were in the wrong!

The Moral:
So oft in theologic wars,
The disputants, I ween,
Rail on in utter ignorance
Of what each other mean,
And prate about an Elephant
Not one of them has seen!

God's Choice of Peter and the Apostles

Although I run the risk of being the *Seventh* Blind Man
to examine the elephant, I have a very definite persuasion
concerning the meaning of this story in Acts 8. Looking at
the narrative in its context, as a part of a greater whole, I
can see that it follows in its order the sovereign choice of
God for us and our lives. It is the Father's will that we have
the greatest of all gifts, the ascension gift of Christ, which is
the Holy Spirit in our hearts. This purpose of God for us is
promised again and again (Matthew 3:11; Luke 11:9-13; 24:
49; John 20:22; Acts 1:4,5). But God chose a sovereign pro-
cedure by which the gift is to be communicated to the world
and to us. The Lord made the solemn promise to Peter and
to the apostles that the keys of the kingdom to open the door
of salvation to the hosts of the earth would be placed in their
hands. The promise was made to all the apostles in Matthew
18:18, and emphatically and especially to Simon Peter in
Matthew 16:18, 19: "And I say also unto thee, That thou art
Peter, and upon this rock I will build my church; and the
gates of hell shall not prevail against it. And I will give
unto thee the keys of the kingdom of heaven: and whatsoever thou shalt bind on earth shall be bound in heaven: and
whatsoever thou shalt loose on earth shall be loosed in
heaven." The holy promise was not made to Philip or to
any of the seven. It was most distinctly made to Peter and
to the apostles.

In each instance, as the gospel message proceeded outward in accordance with the commission recorded in Acts
1:8 (Jerusalem, Judaea, Samaria, uttermost part of the
earth), God sovereignly used Peter and the apostles as instruments through whom the Holy Spirit was introduced to

the believers. In Acts 2:14 Peter, in his Pentecostal sermon, addresses his audience with these words, "Ye men of Judaea, and all ye that dwell at Jerusalem . . ." The keys of the kingdom were used herein to announce the opening of the door of salvation and the coming of the Spirit of grace to the Jewish nation. In Acts 10:28, 44-48 a like marvelous gift was extended through Peter to the Gentiles. So vivid was Peter's vision concerning the Gentiles and so mightily did God open the door to them in the descent of the Holy Spirit, that Peter not only ably defended his visit to the pagans in Acts 11, but he refers to God's sovereign choice of him as the heavenly instrument for this blessing in his address at the Jerusalem Conference in Acts 15:7: "And when there had been much disputing, Peter rose up, and said unto them, Men and brethren, ye know how that a good while ago God made choice among us, that the Gentiles by my mouth should hear the word of the gospel, and believe." It is Peter and the apostles whom God used throughout this expansion of the gospel ministry, according to His holy promise in Matthew 16:19 and Matthew 18:18.

Following the order stated in Acts 1:8, and true to His promises in Matthew 16:19; 18:18, God bestowed the Holy Spirit upon the Samaritans through Peter and his fellow Apostle, John. God did not give the Holy Spirit through Philip. God did not do it through any of the seven. According to the outline in Acts 1:8, God did not open the door through any other leader or prophet or evangelist. God had said He would do it through Peter and the apostles; and here in Samaria, to the Samaritans; as at Jerusalem, to the Jews; as at Caesarea, to the Gentiles; God is keeping His promise. The keys of the kingdom, the opening of the door of salvation, and the gift of the Spirit of grace to the nations is through the Apostle Peter. God chose him (Acts 15:7). The record here in Acts 8 confirms that choice. We must always remember that the Book of Acts is a transitional Book. The history recounts the transition from Judaism to Christianity, from Jew to Gentile, from law to grace, from Jerusalem to Antioch, from Judaea to all the world. Acts 8 is a part of that transitional experience. After the transition is made and the door of salvation is opened and the spirit of grace has come, Peter is not mentioned again in the record of Acts after chapter twelve, save for his defense of what he had done in welcoming the Gentiles in Acts 15. But in the transition period, of which Acts 8 is a part, Peter and not Philip was the sovereign choice of God through whom the gift of the Spirit was made.

The Repeated Blessings of the Holy Spirit

As we reread the story, therefore, in Acts 8, of the revival under Philip, and the coming of the Holy Spirit under Peter and John, are we to conclude that there are two distinct experiences of grace for the believer, a first and a second blessing? Is there an experience of salvation and also an experience of sanctification? Is there a gift for believers when they accept Christ, then a special gift for a special few which second blessing is received later in Christian experience? Having been saved, are we also to seek a second gift of the Spirit?

Many use the verse in Acts 19:2 to confirm the reality of such a second experience. "He said unto them, Have ye received the Holy Ghost since ye believed? And they said unto him, We have not so much as heard whether there be any Holy Ghost." Recently, I received a tract with the title printed in bold letters on the front page: "Have Ye Received the Holy Ghost *Since* Ye Believed? HAVE YOU?" The title is most arresting and is designed to startle almost any Christian believer. Unfortunately for the author of the tract, however, the New Testament was not written in the Elizabethan English of 1611 but in the Koine Greek of the first century. The Greek verb Paul used in his question to the twelve Ephesian disciples of John is *pisteusantes*, an aorist participle meaning "having believed." Paul asked, "Back there when you believed, did you receive the Holy Spirit?" There is no hint or approximation of the meaning *"since ye believed"* in the text at all. Paul wanted to know if they were truly converted or not, and to him the sign of a genuine conversion is the reception of the Holy Spirit in the believer's heart.

We are to have the Holy Spirit, "having believed," according to Paul's query in this passage in Acts 19:2. His presence is the sign of our salvation. Receiving the Holy Spirit is associated with repentance, faith and salvation. This is distinctly stated in Acts 2:38, in I Corinthians 12:13, and here in Acts 19:2. The gift of the Holy Spirit is not related as such to our progressive, experimental sanctification. As in the passage of our text in Acts 8:4-8, 14-17, the Spirit was not given Philip's converts because of their spiritual maturity. Some of them had just been saved; they were babes in Christ a few hours old. Nor was the gift of the Spirit bestowed upon them because of their knowledge of the Word, nor because they had agonized in prayer, nor because of their complete spiritual dedication and separation from the world. The experience was a gift from heaven, sovereignly bestowed.

The gift of the Holy Spirit is for us when we repent, believe, trust and are saved. Jesus bestows the Holy Spirit without measure (John 3:34). The Holy Spirit is a person. He is here, all of Him. His possession of *us* may be partial but our possession of Him is total. He is with His saved always, fully, completely, eternally. But we deny Him ourselves. We refuse Him access to all the compartments of our hearts. We keep Him out of so many areas of our lives. But when we yield our members to Christ, we receive a second blessing. And when we further yield our members, we receive a third blessing. And when we further yield, we receive a fourth blessing.

Do I believe in a second blessing? Yes, indeed! Does the Scripture teach a second blessing? Yes, indeed! And the Holy Bible also teaches a third blessing, and a fourth, and a hundredth, and a thousandth. As we keep on yielding and surrendering, the Holy Spirit keeps on blessing, on and on and on, again and again and again. Oh, for the constant refilling of the Spirit!

Chapter 18

The Gift and the Gifts

Notice the singular use of the word "gift" in Acts 2:38:

> Then Peter said unto them, Repent, and be baptized every one of you in the name of Jesus Christ for the remission of sins, and ye shall receive the gift of the Holy Ghost.

Notice the singular use of the word "gift" in Acts 10:45:

> And they of the circumcision which believed were astonished, as many as came with Peter, because that on the Gentiles also was poured out the gift of the Holy Ghost.

Notice the singular use of the word "gift" in Acts 11:17:

> Forasmuch then as God gave them the like gift as he did unto us, who believed on the Lord Jesus Christ; what was I, that I could withstand God?

Now, notice the plural use of the word "gifts" in I Corinthians 12:1:

> Now concerning spiritual gifts, brethren, I would not have you ignorant.

Notice the plural use of the word "gifts" in I Corinthians 12:4:

> Now there are diversities of gifts, but the same Spirit.

The Scriptures differentiate clearly between "the gift of the Holy Spirit" and "the gifts of the Holy Spirit." The "gift" (singular) is the indwelling of the Holy Spirit whereby He comes to take up residence in the heart of the believer the moment that believer accepts Christ as Saviour. The "gift" is for salvation to the lost. The Paraclete comes at conversion (Acts 2:38). He comes in the new birth (John 3:5). He

145

comes once for all (I Corinthians 12:13), that He may abide
with us forever (John 14:16). The "gifts" (plural) are imparted to the saved by the Holy Spirit for service in the
Church. The child of God is to stir up, to kindle his gift and
not to neglect it (II Timothy 1:6).

The Gift of the Spirit in This Age of Grace

We discuss first the gift of the Holy Spirit. The outpouring of the Spirit of God is the supreme characteristic of this
marvelous, glorious age in which we live. This is the age
of grace, the age of the Holy Spirit, an age of the most
blessed opportunities God has ever laid before man. Jesus
said of John the Baptist that he was the greatest man born
of woman; then the Master added, "notwithstanding he that
is least in the kingdom of heaven is greater than he" (Matthew 11:11). John did not live to see this incomparable age
in which we live. He died before the cross, before the Resurrection, before the Ascension, before the outpouring at Pentecost. He was denied the privilege of becoming a part of
the Church, the body of Christ. But we have that holy privilege, and as great as was the noble Baptist, we are greater
because of our celestial position in Christ. As a disciple of
Christ, the least, humblest Christian can possess the fullness
of the Holy Spirit without measure. In the Old Testament
the Holy Spirit came mightily upon men at different times
and in different places. In the New Testament He dwells
mightily within men through the centuries. In the Old Dispensation He descended upon men for certain purposes. In
this New Age of Grace, since Pentecost, He saturates men,
indwells men, to the praise and glory of God. In the Book
of Judges, "the Spirit of the Lord came upon" Othniel (3:10),
Gideon (6:34), Samson (13:25; 14:19; 15:14). But in the
Book of Acts, all may possess the divine Presence without
hindrance or fear. Men, women, young, old, servants, mas-
ters, boys, girls, all may possess the riches of the gift to the
utmost (Acts 2:16-18).

The resurrected Lord Jesus said to His disciples in John
20:22, "Receive ye the Holy Ghost." The Greek verb is *la-*

bete, second aorist imperative active of *lambano*, and the first meaning of the verb is "take," "seize." Jesus breathed on His disciples and said, "Take ye the Holy Spirit." Sometimes we tremble before the proffered gift. We shrink from taking the priceless possession offered by the hand that was pierced to purchase it. And sometimes, just as we by faith reach forth our hands to grasp it, we shrink back saying, "I am not worthy; it is too much for me." Recently, I looked upon the dazzling riches of the Russian Czars displayed in the armory in the Moscow Kremlin. I thought of a story of the great Emperor Alexander. In the presence of his body guard he turned one time and presented to one of his humblest, most menial servants a magnificent golden cup. The poor vassal drew back and said, "Your Majesty, it is too much for me to take." The Czar hesitated, then thrusting the chalice into the hand of his servant replied, "But it is not too much for me to give!" We also shrink from taking the precious gift of the Holy Presence, saying, "I am not worthy; it is too much for me." But Jesus, with His nail-pierced hands stained with the blood that purchased it for us, presses the gift into our hands saying, "Take it! Take it! It is not too much for *me* to give." Let us look up into the face of our Saviour and say, "O blessed Lord Jesus, unworthy as I am, I take it." The gift is ours forever for the receiving. O wonderful, wonderful Lord! Bless His name, O my soul!

We need but to consent to receive the Holy Spirit *now*. There need be no struggling, no waiting, no agonizing. Just abandon yourself to Him. Let Him fill you, possess you, like breathing deep of celestial air. "And he breathed on them and said, Take ye the Holy Spirit." Did the disciples wait for the gift ten days after the Ascension of our Lord? Yes, because the outpouring of the Spirit is an ascension gift, the beginning of this new age, this new dispensation. But now He is come. Pentecost has happened. The Holy Spirit has already been poured out upon us. We need not wait ten seconds for Him. The soul that consents *now* will be filled *now.* A humble preacher attending a gathering of his denomination spoke to the gifted preacher who had just delivered the message of the hour and said, "I am so glad I consented." The great preacher asked, "To what did you consent?" The humble man replied: "I had agonized for fifteen years, wanting to be filled with the Holy Spirit. Then I heard you say, 'Just consent to be filled and you will be filled.' I abandoned myself to God. I consented and I was filled. Oh, I am so glad I consented." Each time at a convocation of the brethren this humble brother would seek out the great preacher and say, "I am so glad I consented." In telling the story, the great preacher said, "And when I meet my brother in heaven I expect to have him stop me on one of those golden streets and say, 'Oh, I am so glad I consented!'" The gift of the Holy Spirit has been bestowed. We have but to take it. I do not know the author of this poem, but whoever he was, he knew the truth of the Holy Spirit of God.

O Heavenly Father, Thou hast told
Of a gift more precious than silver or gold;
A gift that is free to every one
Through Jesus Christ, Thy only Son.
Thank Thee, Lord, for the gift to me.
Thou hast said, I must believe;
It is only "take" and I shall receive.
If Thou didst say it, it must be true,
And there is nothing else for me to do.
I praise Thee, Lord, for the gift to me.
So I come to take, because my need
Is very great and real indeed.
On the strength of Thy word, I rise and say,
"O thank Thee, Lord, for the promise today,
The Holy Spirit given to me."

The Meaning of the Gifts of the Spirit

We turn now to the "gifts" (plural) of the Holy Spirit. The words used to describe these gifts are most pertinent. In I Corinthians 12:1 the Greek is *ta pneumatika,* literally "the spirituals." Paul literally wrote, "Now concerning the spirituals, brethren, I would not have you ignorant." In I Corinthians 12:7 he defines "the spirituals" as "the manifestation of the Spirit to every man to profit withal." These gifts are impartations of the Holy Spirit and are not to be confused with natural talents. An unbeliever, an atheist, an infidel, the vilest sinner, may have many congenital endowments. They are not *ta pneumatika,* spiritual gifts. The latter are bestowed by the Paraclete upon the believer for service in the Church, the body of Christ.

Paul uses yet another word to describe these gifts of the Holy Spirit to the members of the churches. He calls them, in I Corinthians 12:4, 9, 28, 30, 31, *ta charismata,* literally "grace gifts." The singular form of the word is *to charisma.* The word, *charisma,* is obviously related to *charis,* "grace," "the free, unmerited favor of God." (The beautiful name, Karen, given some of our children, is the accusative form of that Greek word, *charis,* "grace.") In the New Testament the use of the word *charisma* is quite extensive, ranging from the gift of salvation (Romans 6:23) to the gift of God's providential care (II Corinthians 1:11). But usually the word is used of special gifts given to man by God and, with the exception of I Peter 4:10, is used only in the New Testament by the Apostle Paul. Here again we must remember that the word does not refer to a natural talent. It refers to a grace gift, an undeserved favor from God to man. It refers to something bestowed that is neither purchased nor merited; it is given freely of God. Some men are naturally gifted, of high intelligence, possessing natural endowments. These are not *ta charismata.* The *charismata* are supernatural endowments.

In one instance, in Romans 1:11, we find both words, *pneumatika* and *charismata* used together. The King James version reads, "For I long to see you, that I may impart unto you some spiritual gift . . . ." Paul literally wrote, "For I long to see you, that I may impart unto you some 'grace gift of spiritual manifestation.' "

These charismatic gifts are bestowed by Christ upon His

Ascension into heaven. They could be also called "ascension gifts." Paul writes in Ephesians 4:7, 8, 11, 12:

> But unto every one of us is given grace according to the measure of the gift of Christ. Wherefore he saith, When he ascended up on high, he led captivity captive, and gave gifts unto men. And he gave some, apostles; and some, prophets; and some, evangelists; and some, pastors and teachers; For the perfecting of the saints, for the work of the ministry, for the edifying of the body of Christ.

All *pneumatika*, all spiritual gifts are based upon the victory of Christ upon the cross. Jesus entered into contest with Satan, death and the grave, and was victorious over all. Therefore, He has the right to distribute the spoils, to dispense these marvelous presents. The poet so beautifully writes:

> These gifts of grace He gave to His redeemed,
> When He ascended to His throne on high.
> They are His work, His wisdom, and His might;
> The power of His truth and love; indwelling light
> That fills the Church of Christ, the perfect man.

The Gifts of the Spirit Are Sovereignly Bestowed

The gifts of the Holy Spirit are sovereignly bestowed. Look closely at I Corinthians 12:7, "But the manifestation of the Spirit is given to every man . . . ." And look even more closely at I Corinthians 12:11, "But all these worketh that one and the selfsame Spirit, *dividing to every man severally as he will.*" The Greek verb is *bouletai*, as "He chooses," as "He wills." The choice of our gifts is made by the Holy Spirit. We can ask, we can pray, we can covet a gift (I Corinthians 14:39) but the decision lies beyond us. The power of choice is not ours and does not function at our behest. That is why envy, boasting, superiority, contumely are so out of place in the churches of our Lord. Paul wrote of this needed humility so effectively in I Corinthians 4:7: "For who maketh thee to differ from another? and what hast thou that thou didst not receive? now if thou didst receive it, why dost thou glory, as if thou hadst not received it?" All that we have in the kingdom and patience of Jesus is given us by His gracious love. There is no room for personal boasting. The gifts are not even bestowed as rewards. They are not indications of spiritual excellence or superiority. They are meted out to us "as the Spirit will." They are not bestowed because we have sought them. They are not to be vaingloriously sought by men. Although we can ask in prayer, we do not receive them because we prayed for them or coveted them. They are sovereignly bestowed. So many tarry, pray, weep, beg, agonize for some spiritual gift. They are not so obtained. When Paul wrote in I Corinthians 12:31, "But covet earnestly the best gifts," he was writing to a church that was emphasizing the least and the lowest gifts to the loss and deprecation of the most useful and profitable gifts. Paul is admonishing the church that it magnify the greatest gifts among its members (such as prophecy), not the least and last gifts (such as speaking in tongues). The gifts among the members were sovereignly bestowed by the Holy Spirit, but the church, according to Paul, was to magnify and greatly to use the most profitable gifts bestowed.

No one person has all the gifts but each member has at least one or more. Paul further writes in I Corinthians 12: 27-30:

> Now ye are the body of Christ, and members in particular. And God hath set some in the church, first apostles, secondarily prophets, thirdly teachers, after that miracles, then gifts of healing, helps, governments, diversities of tongues. Are all apostles? are all prophets? are all teachers? are all workers of miracles? Have all the gifts of healing? do all speak with tongues? do all interpret?

Each gift is needed and is not to be neglected. Every member is essential to the body. No great church became that way on a one-man ministry. All, each, every one, great, small, rich, poor, old, young, have essential parts. Each one will possess an inner witness of the Spirit concerning the special gift that is his, and that inner witness will be cor-

roborated, recognized, by the assembly of the saints. It was
a surprised George W. Truett who was told by the White-
wright Baptist Church that he was to be ordained to the
gospel ministry. The young man replied, "But I have sought
to be a lawyer." The church answered, "But God has called
you to be a preacher." And they thereupon proceeded to
ordain him! Others will know of your gift.

God has a purpose in bestowing these charismatic gifts.
They are for service. Let us read again I Corinthians 12:7,
"But the manifestation of the Spirit is given to every man
to profit withal." They are "given to every man to profit
withal." Let us read also Acts 1:8, "But ye shall receive
power, after that the Holy Ghost is come upon you: and ye
shall be witnesses unto me both in Jerusalem, and in all
Judaea, and in Samaria, and unto the uttermost part of the
earth." The Lord did not say alone, "Ye shall be witnesses
. . . ." But He did say, "Ye shall receive power . . . and [then]
ye shall be witnesses . . . ." That statement still stands un-
altered. Neither that commission nor the provisions to carry
it out have been withdrawn. These spiritual gifts are the
endowments of God to make us able to do His work in the
earth. Paul was not stressing secondary things when he
wrote I Corinthians 12:1, "Now concerning spiritual gifts,
brethren, I would not have you ignorant." Nor was he ad-
vising a small and meaningless thing when he urged Timothy
to stir up the gift that was in him (II Timothy 1:6). These
gifts are God's enablement for His disciples to evangelize
the world.

Chapter 19

The Wonderful "Charismata"

I Corinthians 12

1 Now concerning spiritual gifts, brethren, I would not
have you ignorant.

Paul writes that he would not have us ignorant of the gifts
of the Spirit. But I do not know any one thing in the realm
of the ecclesiastical world about which we are more ignorant. We need to know, desperately so, the truth God would
reveal to us about these *pneumatika*, these *charismata*,
these "charismatic spirituals."

Four places in the letters of Paul are these gifts of the
Spirit listed; namely, in Romans 12:6-8; I Corinthians 12:8-
10, 28-30; and Ephesians 4:11. In Romans 12:6-8 they are
named as follows:

1. Prophecy
2. Ministering
3. Teaching
4. Exhortation
5. Giving
6. Ruling
7. Showing mercy

In I Corinthians 12:8-10 they are named as follows:

1. Words of wisdom
2. Words of knowledge
3. Faith
4. Healing
5. Working miracles
6. Prophecy
7. Discerning spirits
8. Tongues
9. Interpretation of tongues

In I Corinthians 12:28-30 they are named as follows:

1. Apostles
2. Prophets
3. Teachers
4. Miracles

5. Healings   8. Tongues
6. Helps   9. Interpretation
7. Governments

In Ephesians 4:11 they are named as follows:

1. Apostles   4. Pastors
2. Prophets   5. Teachers
3. Evangelists

The total of all the gifts named comes to thirty. About eleven of these listed are duplicates, leaving something like nineteen differing gifts mentioned by the Apostle Paul.

Typical Groupings of the Gifts of the Spirit

It is interesting to read learned discussions of these *charismata* and to note how each scholar will group them in his own way. Here, for example, is one grouping:

I. Gifts for the Ministering of the Gospel
Those listed in I Corinthians 12:8-10
II. Gifts for the Work of the Church
Those listed in I Corinthians 12:28-30
III. Gifts for the Ministries of the Church
Those listed in Romans 12:6-8
IV. Gifts for the Building Up of the Church
Those listed in Ephesians 4:11

Another scholar has followed a unique outline in I Corinthians 13 and has grouped them as follows:

I. Emotional Gifts
I Corinthians 13:1, "Though I speak with the tongues . . ."
II. Intellectual Gifts
I Corinthians 13:2a, "And though I have the gift of prophecy, . . . and mysteries, . . . and knowledge . . ."
III. Practical Gifts
I Corinthians 13:2b, ". . . though I have all faith, so that I could remove mountains, . . ."

IV. Philanthropic, Sacrificial Gifts
I Corinthians 13:3, "though I bestow all my goods to feed the poor, . . . give my body to be burned, . . ."

Yet another scholar has divided the gifts into two groups as follows:

I. Gifts Connected With the Ministry of the Word
Apostleship, prophecy, discerning of spirits, teaching, etc.
II. Gifts Connected With Practical Uses
Miracles, healings, ruling, helps, governments, etc.

Still another author divides the gifts into three all-inclusive categories:

I. Gifts of Revelation
Word of wisdom
Word of knowledge
Discerning of spirits
II. Gifts of Power
Faith
Working of miracles
Healing
III. Gifts of Inspiration
Prophecy
Tongues
Interpretation of tongues

Another commentator divides the gifts as follows:

I. Basic Ministries, Gifts of Edification
Prophecy, teaching, etc.
II. Sign Gifts for Authentication
Miracles, healings, tongues, etc.

Another astute student of the Bible groups the different gifts into two categories:

I. Natural Gifts
Capacities originally found in human nature, elevated, enlarged by the gifts of the Spirit, such as:

Teaching — capacity to impart knowledge
Healing — the physician's art
Helps — the work of deacons and church officers
Government — natural leadership
II. Supernatural Gifts
Prophecy
Miracles
Tongues

And finally, a seventh scholar categorizes them as either continuing or transitory:

I. Eleven Permanent Gifts
For the building up of the body:
For the edification of the church (Ephesians 4:12-15):
Apostles (in the original sense of one sent on a mission), prophets, evangelists, pastors, teachers, helps, administration, exhortation, giving, mercy, faith.

II. Five Temporary Gifts
Signs to substantiate, corroborate the message:
For unbelievers to authenticate the message (I Corinthians 14:22):
Miracles, healings, tongues, interpretation of tongues, discerning of spirits.

These seven groupings I have chosen as typical of so many others. Every commentator and every scholar will have his own individual approach to these *charismatic* phenomena. Before we begin our own discussion of these heavenly endowments poured out upon the churches, let me make several observations concerning them as they are presented in the Bible.

One striking, salient, yet deplorable fact about the churches to whom the fullest, richest gifts were bestowed is this: the people who possessed these spiritual gifts (even the highest gift of prophecy) were by no means spiritually faultless. The gifts were mixed with human infirmity, and that sometime of the most reprehensible kind. These supernaturally gifted church members were not automatons, even though endowed by the Spirit. They carried with them all their human foibles and weaknesses. Inspiration is one thing, infallibility and sanctification yet another thing. The gifts possessed by the saints were subject to frequent misuse: disorder, vanity, false ambition, exalted self-esteem, overweening egotism, personal superiority. It is hard for the neophyte who is being introduced to the leadership of the church for the first time to understand this. But it is always tragically true and the sooner the initiate learns the hard lesson, the sooner he can continue in the love and admonition of the Lord. Some of the greatest saints have the most glaring faults. They all have feet of clay. None is perfect. Imperfections mar every great life with the exception only of that of the blessed Lord Jesus.

The churches themselves, made up of these imperfect people, also fall into every conceivable kind of error and heresy. False prophets and false spirits lead them astray. Leaders are dominated by personal motives. The entire body is sometimes off on a diverging tangent. Fanaticism often destroys the holiest and purest of the gifts. There must have been something of emotional cynicism that seized the church at Thessalonica to make Paul write to the congregation, "Despise not prophesyings" (I Thessalonians 5:20). Because of these extreme weaknesses, Paul established rules of control over spiritual gifts and declared the need for subjection. In I Corinthians 14:29-32 he writes:

> Let the prophets speak two or three, and let the other judge. If any thing be revealed to another that sitteth by, let the first hold his peace. For ye may all prophesy one by one, that all may learn, and all may be comforted. And the spirits of the prophets are subject to the prophets.

Even the prophet could be misled. His revelation or vision or message must be judged as to its truth by the other prophets. "The spirits of the prophets are subject to the prophets." In fact, so vital was it to the life of the infant church that the truth be unalloyed, that the Holy Spirit bestowed upon some of the members a charismatic gift called "discerning of spirits" (I Corinthians 12:10). John admonished the believers in I John 4:1, "Beloved, believe not every spirit, but try the spirits whether they are of God: because many false prophets are gone out into the world." So prone is the human heart to err and so misguided can be the human spirit, that the divine wisdom set selfguards in the churches to deliver us from the weaknesses of men.

Unity in Diversity

Let us note, also, the make-up of these New Testament churches. They are a unity in a multitudinous diversity. The members of the churches greatly differ, and most especially so in their gifts. Some things of the Spirit we all have in common. All of us have been regenerated by the Spirit. All of us have been baptized by the Spirit into the body of Christ. All of us are temples (in our bodies) of the Holy Spirit. All of us, insofar as we yield ourselves, are comforted, guided and helped by the Holy Spirit. But there the likeness ends. We all have differing gifts and differing degrees of the same gifts. Is this bad? No. It pleases God to make us to differ. We are all needed with our separate gifts to make the Church of Christ glorious.

Paul illustrates in I Corinthians 12:12-17 our unity in diversity by the human body. He writes in verses 14-20:

> For the body is not one member, but many. If the foot shall say, Because I am not of the hand, I am not of the body; is it therefore not of the body? And if the ear shall say, Because I am not the eye, I am not of the body; is it therefore not of the body? If the whole body were an eye, where were the hearing? If the whole were hearing, where were the smelling? But now hath God set the members every one of them in the body, as it hath pleased him. And if they were all one member, where were the body? But now are they many members, yet but one body.

We all are needed. Every member of the church with his separate gift is necessary to the well-being of the whole.

John uses the world of creation to illustrate the manifold diversity of the sovereign will of God. He writes in John 1:

1, 2: "In the beginning was the logos [the creative, activating principle], . . . All things were made by him [the creating Christ]; and without him was not any thing made that was made." Look around you. What kind of a world do you see? The great, living Spirit shows Himself under divers, even opposite, manifestations. But the law is one and the Spirit is one. Lead sinks and wood floats, but they are expressions of the one and the same creative Spirit. The difference between the spiritually-minded man and the materialistically-minded man is this: The materialist sees nothing but an infinite collection of unconnected, unrelated facts, broken, distorted, fragmentary, disordered. He is the existential philosopher. For him, life, the world, existence, creation, have no meaning. It all came from nowhere. It is all going nowhere. It is an accidental concourse of meaningless atoms, signifying nothing. But to the spiritually-minded man, every created thing has a part in the divine purpose of God. All are parts to make up the ultimately perfect whole. As the spiritual man progresses in understanding, he sees the number of basic laws diminish until at last they all are reduced to one; namely, the one that lies beneath the innumerable phenomena of nature — the Spirit of God. All living unity is spiritual not physical; it is inward, not outward. The works of the Spirit of God ever are characterized by diversity, complexity, multifariousness; not sameness.

It is thus with us in the churches. Our unity is not that we are all alike in a dull, wearisome monotony. Our unity is not one of outward uniformity but one of inward motivation. We all are activated by the same living principle, the same quickening Spirit, the same animating vision. We all are moving toward the same holy end. We are like the vision of Ezekiel's first chapter. The prophet saw wheels, faces, rims, eyes, wheels within wheels, and each part differing from the other part. But all the parts moved together, activated by the same living principle, the same quickening Spirit. Ezekiel writes in 1:20, 21:

> Whithersoever the spirit was to go, they went, thither was their spirit to go; and the wheels were lifted up over against

> them: for the spirit of the living creature was in the wheels. When those went, these went; and when those stood, these stood; and when those were lifted up from the earth, the wheels were lifted up over against them: for the spirit of the living creature was in the wheels.

It is thus with the differing members of the church. We possess a unity, not like the pebbles on a beach — a lifeless identity of outward form with no cohesion between the parts, a dead shore on which nothing grows, where even the seaweed dies. Our oneness is like that of the living world, full of infinite diversities which are but expressions of the same living Spirit. The Holy Spirit bestows upon us different gifts. No two of us are alike, as no two leaves are alike, and as no two snowflakes are alike. But however we differ, we are all a part of the testimony of the one saving Spirit.

Each Gift of Each Member Is Vitally Needed

Again Paul emphasizes the contribution each member of the Church can make to the household of faith. All members are needed in the body of Christ. Each one has a special part to play without which the body is broken, enfeebled, destroyed. He writes in I Corinthians 12:21-26:

> And the eye cannot say unto the hand, I have no need of thee; nor again the head to the feet, I have no need of you. Nay, much more those members of the body, which seem to be more feeble, are necessary: And those members of the body, which we think to be less honourable, upon these we bestow more abundant honour; and our uncomely parts have more abundant comeliness. For our comely parts have no need: but God hath tempered the body together, having given more abundant honour to that part which lacked: That there should be no schism in the body; but that the members should have the same care one for another. And whether one member suffer, all the members suffer with it; or one member be honoured, all the members rejoice with it.

When one member is hurt or cut off, all the members are hurt and weakened. This is true even of the smallest member. I hardly know I have a little toe. I rarely think of it; I rarely look at it; I seldom notice it. It is there but I am hardly aware of it. That is, until something happens to it!

Then I do believe I am all little toe! It throbs and aches and is in pain until I cannot sleep, or study, or do any work at all. Yet, what I may come to realize is so important: the health of my little toe, so nearly forgotten throughout the hours of the day, affects the health of the whole body. We all have a worthy contribution to make to the body of Christ, even our feeblest parts. Without these humblest members, the body is not complete.

For forty-eight years our church has conducted noonday, pre-Easter services in a downtown theater. My illustrious predecessor, Dr. George W. Truett, conducted them for twenty-five years and this is now the twenty-third year that I have preached through them. Long ago, when I had just come to be the new pastor of the church, and after I had finished delivering the message at one of those noonday services, I walked through the front lobby of the theater. There I was met by a little, old, stooped lady, dressed in an old-fashioned, black dress. She said to me: "I have been so eager to see my new pastor, but I am too old and sick to go to church. Since today was such a beautiful, warm day, a neighbor brought me downtown to attend this service in order that I might see you. I wish I could help you but I am too old, too sick, and too poor. All I can do is pray for you." I put my arms around that stooped, little, old lady and said: "All you can do is pray! My sweet, little mother in Christ, that means more than anything else in the world. You speak as though it were so small. No. It is the greatest help of all. God hear you as you call my name before the throne of grace and ask His power to fall upon me." One of the gifts in I Corinthians 12:9 is the gift of faith, the ability to claim the promises of God, to lay hold on the horns of the altar and intercede until victory comes. We could never have too many members like that frail, little lady who could only pray. "Nay," as Paul wrote, "much more those members of the body, which seem to be more feeble, are necessary" (I Corinthians 12:22). God has a place for us all, a gift for us all, in the assembly of the faithful.

Chapter 20

Charismatic Gifts for the Great Commission

Ephesians 4

11 And he gave some, apostles; and some, prophets; and some, evangelists; and some, pastors and teachers.

In this passage in Ephesians 4:11 there are named in order of importance five ministering gifts of Christ to His church. The first one, "apostles," is named also in the list of Spirit gifts in I Corinthians 12:28. The second one, "prophets," is named also in the list of Spirit gifts in Romans 12:6 and in I Corinthians 12:10 as well as in I Corinthians 12:28. It is the only one listed in all four places where Spirit gifts are named. The third one, "evangelists," is named only here. The fourth one, "pastors," is also named only here. The fifth one, "teachers," is listed in two other places; namely, in Romans 12:7 and in I Corinthians 12:28.

These five gifts to the churches named in Ephesians 4:11 are basic to the evangelization of the world and to the ministry of the Word. Without them the churches would not be, and the body of Christ would have no existence. They are vital to the carrying out of the Great Commission in Matthew 28:19, 20. There we are told to disciple (*matheteuo*) all nations, to baptize (*baptizo*) our converts, and to teach them (*didasko*) the words and the commandments of the Lord. For that tremendous assignment of conquest and training, the triune God in whose name we are baptized bestows five gifts upon His churches.

The Apostolic Gift

The first and foremost of all the endowments of the Spirit is that of apostleship. The word "apostle" (*apostolos*) was

162

an ordinary, household Greek word meaning "messenger," "one sent forth." In Hebrews 3:1 our Saviour is called "the Apostle and High Priest of our profession" because He was "sent forth" from heaven to make atonement for our sins. From the equivalent Latin word of *missio* we gain our English word "missionary." The word *apostolos* is used in two ways in the New Testament: first, in a limited, technical sense, referring to an office; and second, in a general sense referring to a missionary.

The technical sense of the word *apostolos,* referring to an office, is used as a designation for the twelve apostles of Christ (Matthew 10:2; Luke 6:13; Acts 1:25, 26). We read in Luke 6:13, "And when it was day, he called unto him his disciples: and of them he chose twelve, whom also he named apostles." On special grounds the word was also used as a designation for Paul (Romans 1:1; Galatians 1:1; I Corinthians 9:1, 2; II Corinthians 12:12). The word was probably also used to describe the sacred office held by James, the pastor of the church in Jerusalem and the Lord's brother (I Corinthians 15:7; Galatians 1:19). However the Lord will name them, there are always just twelve apostles, called "The Twelve" (Matthew 26:20; Mark 14:17; Luke 22:14; Matthew 26:47; John 6:71, etc.). I believe that in the first chapter of Acts the disciples chose Matthias to be the apostle to take the place of the fallen Judas, but in the ninth chapter of Acts, God chose Saul of Tarsus. In any event, through time and eternity there are always just twelve apostles. Some day, according to Matthew 19:28 and Luke 22:29, 30, they will sit upon twelve thrones judging the twelve tribes of Israel. The Bride of Christ, the City of God, the New Jerusalem, is built upon twelve foundations, "and in them the names of the twelve apostles of the Lamb" (Revelation 21:14).

Most explicitly do the Scriptures avow that the apostles laid the foundation for the church. "And are built upon the foundation of the apostles and prophets, Jesus Christ himself being the chief corner stone" (Ephesians 2:20). They laid the doctrinal foundation for the body of Christ (Acts 2:42). They laid the structural foundation for the temple of the Lord (Acts 1:15). They used the keys of the kingdom to open the doors to the Jews and to the Gentiles (Acts 2:9-11). They formed the link joining the Old Dispensation with the New. Through them is found unity and continuity in God's purpose of grace. Their roots were in the Old Testament but their ministry was in the New.

The twelve apostles have no successors. For one to be an apostle he had to be baptized by John the Baptist, had to be trained by Christ Himself, and had to be a personal eyewitness of the resurrected and glorified Lord (Acts 1:22). The group did not form a Sanhedrin or a great council. Like the delegates to a constitutional convention, when their work was done the office ceased. In the first chapter of Acts, the Twelve are prominently mentioned; thereafter, they are hardly referred to. After the doctrinal order of the church was committed to writing by inspiration of the Holy Spirit, the Scriptures became the authority for all faith and practice. The carrying out of the work of the Great Commission became the responsibility of all the members of the body of Christ to which the Holy Spirit gave superlative gifts. The last time the twelve apostles were together was in Acts 15 at the Jerusalem Conference. They were assembled there with the elders of the local church. Not Peter but James, the Lord's brother, presided. The whole membership of the church participated in the decision (Acts 15:22). After the Conference the Twelve were widely scattered and with a few exceptions are never heard of again. When they died the office ceased to exist. There are no more twelve apostles.

But there is another use of the word *apostolos* in which sense the Holy Spirit bestows the gift upon His churches today. In a general definition of the word it refers to the missionary who preaches Christ where He is not known, who gathers new converts together, and who organizes them into churches (compare Paul as he writes in Romans 15:20,21, "Yea, so have I strived to preach the gospel, not where Christ was named . . ."). In this general sense, Andronicus and Junia are called "apostles" (Romans 16:7). In this use of the word the messengers who accompany Titus in II Corinthians 8:23 are called "apostles." (The word translated "messengers" in the King James version is in the Greek "apostles.") In this sense Epaphroditus, in Philippians 2:25, is called an "apostle" (translated in the King James version "messenger"). In this sense the Holy Spirit anoints certain of His disciples today. On the mission fields I have seen preachers of the Gospel who were endowed with the unusual gift of winning converts and founding churches in heathen, idolatrous communities. This is the continuing blessing of the Holy Spirit upon those who "preach the gospel where Christ is not named." They are first and foremost in the gift of God to the churches and ought to be thus honored and supported.

The Prophetic Gift

The second gift of the Spirit to the churches is that of "prophet." The Greek verb *propheteo* means to forthtell, to speak out concerning divine things. The noun form, *prophetes,* refers to one who has insight into divine things and who speaks them forth to others. The meaning of "foretelling," "prediction," in the word "prophet" is secondary and incidental. Only in medieval times did the word pass into the English language in the sense of prediction. A "prophet" in the Bible is always one who speaks out for God. The word is used in two ways in the New Testament: first, in a limited, technical sense referring to an office; second, in a general sense referring to a gift of edification and inspiration.

There is a vast difference between the prophetic office and the gift of prophecy. This difference is carefully delineated in the Scriptures. When we think of the prophetic office, we think of Moses, Samuel, David, Elijah, and Isaiah of the Old Testament. In the New Testament we think of Paul, Agabus, Judas and Silas (Acts 11:27,28; 15:32; 21:10,11). Yet, the Scriptures state in Acts 19:6 that these new converts, these raw recruits in Ephesus, did prophesy. Are they to be numbered with Moses, Isaiah and Paul? No. There is a difference between the prophetic office and the gift of prophecy. The difference is again seen in the passage in Acts 21:9, 10. There the four virgin daughters of Philip the Evangelist are described as "prophetesses," but Agabus the prophet is set apart in deliberate contradistinction. Those who prophesy are prophets, but not in the grand, limited, technical sense of Moses, Isaiah and Paul. In the listings of the gifts of God to the churches, the "prophet" is second only to the "apostle" in Ephesians 4:11. But in the list in I Corinthians 12:28 the gift of prophecy comes down in the enumeration in importance. If the prophetic gift qualified for the prophetic office there would have been a correspondence in the two listings. In I Corinthians 14:1 we are admonished to seek not an office (that of a prophet) but a gift (the gift of edification).

Before the writing of the New Testament, the office of "prophet" was a vital one. The prophet told the infant church what it should do, believe and teach. Hence, Ephesians 2:20 reads, "And are built upon the foundation of the apostles and prophets, Jesus Christ himself being the chief corner stone." This necessitated also the gift of discerning of spirits (I Corinthians 12:10), for it was most needed to distinguish between the true revelations from God and false revelations concerning His churches. "The spirits of the prophets are subject to the prophets" (I Corinthians 14:32). "Let the prophets speak two or three, and let the other judge" (I Corinthians 14:29). Prophesyings were not to be despised (I Thessalonians 5:20) but their utterances were to be carefully judged (I John 4:1; Revelation 2:2). When the New Testament was complete, the office of prophet ceased. It was no longer needed. Our appeal now is to the inspired, written Word, not to a man. There are no more revelations to be added to God's Holy Book.

But as with the word *apostolos*, so with the word *prophetes;* there is a general sense in which the gift of the Holy Spirit is poured out upon certain of today's believers. The gift of prophecy is the most prominently witnessed of all the Spirit gifts seen today. It is a gift to be desired by the church (I Corinthians 14:1, 39). In I Corinthians 12 - 14 some form of the word occurs twenty-two times. The purpose of the gift is seen in I Corinthians 14:3: "But he that prophesieth speaketh unto men to edification, and exhortation, and comfort"; in I Corinthians 14:24, 25: "But if all prophesy, and there come in one that believeth not, or one unlearned, he is convicted of all, he is judged of all"; and in I Corinthians 14:31: "For ye may all prophesy one by one, that all may learn, and all may be comforted." The Spirit gift of prophecy is bestowed upon the churches for edification, exhortation, comfort, conversion of the lost, and teaching of the unlearned. It should be the gift most commonly exercised in the assemblies of Christ (I Corinthians 14:3, 24, 31). A preacher who gives forth the message of God in the wisdom and power of the Holy Spirit has the gift of prophecy (I Peter 4:10, 11); I Corinthians 2:1-16). Prophecy is Spirit-inspired utterance. An inspired preacher was the first gift of the Spirit manifested in the church at Pentecost. He is God's man for the delivering of God's message to a lost world. We must never forget Revelation 19:10, "For the testimony of Jesus is the spirit of prophecy."

The Evangelistic Gift

The third gift of the Lord to His people is that of "evangelist." The Greek verb *evaggelizo* means to bring good tidings. The noun form of the word, *evaggelistes,* refers to a messenger of good news. The word "evangelist" is used three times in the New Testament. Philip one of the seven ordained in Acts 6:5, is called "the evangelist" in Acts 21:8. Paul uses the word in II Timothy 4:5 when he admonishes Timothy, the pastor of the church at Ephesus, to "do the work of an evangelist." The third time the word is used is here in Ephesians 4:11 in the gifts of God to His churches.

The word *evaggelistes* involves two ideas. First, it refers to the kind of message preached, the good news of salvation. Second, it refers to the places in which the message is preached, which places are defined in the Scriptures as "scattered abroad." The different "scattered abroad" places can be seen in the itinerate ministry of Philip. The gift of the evangelist is a distinct gift which few men possess in superlative degree, but when it is found, it is the third of all the gifts of the Holy Spirit, preceded only by the gifts of apostleship and prophecy. The famous evangelists through the years have been men so greatly used of God to bless the world. We need them desperately. May God grant that the gift with increased frequency and meaning may fall upon our preachers today.

The Pastoral Gift

Strangely enough, the word "pastor," the fourth gift of the Lord to the churches, is used only once in the entire New Testament, here in Ephesians 4:11. The Greek word is *poimen,* meaning "shepherd." The New Testament uses three titles to describe the same office in the Church: *episcopos,* meaning "overseer," *presbuteros,* meaning "elder," and *poimen,* meaning "shepherd." The word "bishop" (*episcopos*) refers to the work of the pastor. The word "elder" (*presbuteros*) refers to the dignity and rank of his position. The word "shepherd," "pastor," (*poimen*) refers to his relationship to the flock. All three words are referred to in Acts 20:17, 18. The qualifications of a pastor are written in I Timothy 3:1-7; Titus 1:5-9, and in I Peter 5:1-4. Pastors are to be obeyed and to be held in high honor (Hebrews 13:17). Those who are worthy are to be held in double honor (I Timothy 5:17). This is the gift of the Spirit that is most preciously cherished by the people of Christ. A worthy pastor is a true benediction from heaven.

The Teaching Gift

The fifth of the spirit gifts to the assemblies of Christ is that of "teachers," listed in three of the categories named by the Apostle Paul (Romans 12:7; I Corinthians 12:28; Ephesians 4:11). It is the God-given ability to explain the Holy Word, especially to newborn babes in Christ. It is a gift so greatly needed in the churches. The Great Commission is carried out through two main channels of work: preaching, which is directed to the will; and teaching, which is directed to the understanding. With these two gifts in powerful evidence, any people can make an impact for Christ upon a pagan world. Lord, give them to us in increasing meaning and power!

Chapter 21

Precious Ministering Gifts of the Spirit

I Corinthians 12

7 But the manifestation of the Spirit is given to every man to profit withal.

8 For to one is given by the Spirit the word of wisdom; to another the word of knowledge by the same Spirit;

9 To another faith by the same Spirit; to another the gifts of healing by the same Spirit;

10 To another the working of miracles; to another prophecy; to another discerning of spirits; to another divers kinds of tongues; to another the interpretation of tongues.

Romans 12

6 Having then gifts differing according to the grace that is given to us, whether prophecy, let us prophesy according to the proportion of faith;

7 Or ministry, let us wait on our ministering: or he that teacheth, on teaching;

8 Or he that exhorteth, on exhortation; he that giveth, let him do it with simplicity; he that ruleth, with diligence: he that sheweth mercy, with cheerfulness.

There is literally a profusion of rich gifts of the Holy Spirit to make sweet and noble the work of the Church. They are precious endowments that bless the congregations of the Lord and fit us for godly service. We who belong to the household of faith are to be like our Saviour who came, "not to be ministered unto, but to minister" (Matthew 20:28). In spirit and in attitude we are to be like Him who said: "If I then, your Lord and Master, have washed your feet; ye also ought to wash one another's feet. For I have given you an example, that ye should do as I have done unto you" (John 13:14, 15). These precious ministering gifts I have grouped under four headings: first, Enlightenment of Mind; second, Sympathy

of Heart; third, Practical Administration; fourth, Sublimity
of Faith.

The Gifts of Wisdom and of Knowledge

In I Corinthians 12:8 the Apostle Paul names the first two
gifts of the Spirit as "the word of wisdom" and "the word of
knowledge." These have to do with the mind, the understanding, when it is consecrated to God. The first of the nine
endowments listed in the passage is "the word of wisdom,"
(Greek, *logos sophias*). The gift has to do with the making
known, to the people of the Lord, God's plan and purpose
for His Church. It has to do with the spiritual principles
that govern God's elective choices for us. It presents the
deep, spiritual truths that lie back of God's will for our lives.
It reveals to us what to believe and how to do in the wisdom
of God. In I Corinthians 12:32 one of the twelve tribes is
described in these words, "the children of Issachar, which
were men that had understanding of the times, to know what
Israel ought to do." They had the gift of wisdom. In Acts
5:38, 39 the famous Rabbi Gamaliel said, concerning the persecution that rose against the first Christian disciples: "And
now I say unto you, Refrain from these men, and let them
alone; for if this counsel or this work be of men, it will come
to nought: But if it be of God, ye cannot overthrow it; lest
haply ye be found even to fight against God." He had the
gift of wisdom. Elevated, purified, the gift is bestowed in
sublime proportions upon the followers of Christ. The
apostles were led by the spirit of wisdom to create the diac-
onate in order that the Church may be properly cared for
(Acts 6:1-7). Stephen, one of the seven, was so filled with
power that his opponents "were not able to resist the wisdom and the spirit by which he spake" (Acts 6:9, 10). Peter
was wondrously used of God to explain to the Church at
Jerusalem the opening of the door of conversion to the Gentiles (Acts 11:1-18). James, pastor of the Church at Jerusalem, presided over the Jerusalem Conference in Acts 15 and
delivered the final pronouncement concerning the law and
the Gospel. This is the gift of "the word of wisdom," know-

ing and explaining the mind and the purposes of God for
our lives.

Second only to "the word of wisdom" is the gift of "the
word of knowledge," (Greek, *logos gnoseos*). This is the gift
of appraisal and of judgment concerning things as they are.
It is the ability to grasp the truth about a present situation:
seeing, knowing, understanding, as the Holy Spirit sees,
knows and understands. In II Kings 5:20-27 is recounted the
remarkable story of the prophet Elisha and his servant Gehazi. As the prophet recounted the perfidy of the greedy
Gehazi, he said: "Went not mine heart with thee, when the
man turned again from his chariot to meet thee?" (verse 26).
This is the word of knowledge. In the story of the life of
the same prophet, it is written that the king of Syria called
his staff of ministers together to seek out the traitor among
them, for the very thoughts of the monarch were immediately known to his enemies in Israel. The king despairingly
asked: "Will ye not shew me which of us is for the king of
Israel?" The answer came swift and certain: "And one of
his servants said, None, my lord, O king: but Elisha, the
prophet that is in Israel, telleth the king of Israel the words
that thou speakest in thy bedchamber" (II Kings 6:8-12).
This is the word of knowledge. In the New Testament the
gift is most meaningfully and gloriously illustrated. When
Simon Peter said to our Lord Jesus in Matthew 16:16, "Thou
art the Christ, the Son of the living God," the Saviour replied
to His chief apostle, "Blessed art thou, Simon Barjona: for
flesh and blood hath not revealed it unto thee, but my Father
which is in heaven." The word of knowledge is seen in this
heavenly recognition. An earthly recognition is succinctly
illustrated in the conversation of our Lord with the woman
of Samaria. The inter-change of words goes like this:

> Jesus saith unto her, Go, call thy husband, and come hither.
> The woman answered and said, I have no husband. Jesus said
> unto her, Thou hast well said, I have no husband: For thou
> hast had five husbands; and he whom thou now hast is not thy
> husband: in that saidst thou truly (John 4:16-18).

This reminds me of a story I read told by the noble London preacher, F. B. Meyer. Speaking in the Free Assembly Hall in Edinburgh, he said: "There is a man here who owes his employer three pounds and eighteen shillings. Until that sum is repaid, that young man will never have peace with God." The preacher did not know of whom he was speaking. He said the words through "a gift of knowledge." Soon a young man made an appointment to see the preacher. When they were together the youth said, "Do you know me?" The preacher answered, "No, I never saw you before." The young employee answered, "In your sermon you described exactly what I did. My soul has been troubled ever since. Already there* is a letter in the mail with a check returning the money."

It was with this gift of knowledge that Peter revealed the covetous corruption in the Jerusalem church, recorded in Acts 5:3. It was with this gift of knowledge that John wrote of the Seven Churches of Asia in Revelation 2, 3. It is with this gift of knowledge that God's leaders in the churches today come to know in right judgment and appraisal the moral, sound, doctrinal, and organizational situation that blesses the work of our Lord.

The Gift of Sympathy of Heart

The next grouping of these precious gifts of the Spirit I have chosen to call "Sympathy of Heart." Several of the gifts have to do with those precious mysteries that comfort and encourage God's people. Three of them are named in the list in Romans 12:6-8. One is the gift of mercy. Paul writes of it in these words, *ho eleon en hilarotati,* "he that showeth mercy, with cheerfulness." The Greek word *eleos* means "mercy," "pity," especially in the presence of human misery such as is so often seen among the poor, the sad, the afflicted, the widows and the orphans. The New Testament Greek word for alms, *eleemosune,* is built upon the basic word *eleos* and is the origin of our English word "eleemosynary," an adjective to describe charitable institutions and donations. The gift of mercy is the gift to sympathize with and

to suffer alongside those who fall into grievous affliction.
God so sympathizes with us. There is a divine pity in God.
Isaiah 63:9 reads: "In all their affliction he was afflicted, and
the angel of his presence saved them: in his love and in his
pity he redeemed them; and he bare them, and carried them
all the days of old." Psalm 103:13, 14 says: "Like as a father
pitieth his children, so the LORD pitieth them that fear him.
For he knoweth our frame; he remembereth that we are
dust." This is a gift like the heart of our heavenly Father,
the ability to sympathize with another. There was a little
girl who came home from school and told her mother about
her playmate whose mother had died and who was so sad.
The mother asked her child, "And what did you say, dear?"
The child replied: "I did not say anything. I just went over
to her desk, sat down by her side, and cried with her."
Notice that the one possessing the gift is not to feel himself
burdened with it, as though he were weighted with all the
woe of the world. He is, rather, to minister in the assurance
of God's victorious mercies. He is to be "joyous," "cheerful,"
(Greek, *hilaros*) over his deeds of compassion.

Another like gift Paul names in Romans 12:8 with these
words, "he that exhorteth on exhortation," (Greek, *ho para-
kalon en te paraklesei*). The Greek verb *parakaleo* means
"to call alongside," "to comfort," "to encourage." The noun
form, *paraklesis,* means "consolation," "comfort," encouragement." From that Greek word comes the word "paraclete,"
used as a title for the Holy Spirit in John 14:16, 26, and as
a title for Christ in I John 2:1 (translated "advocate" in the
King James version). This is the gift of "encouragement,"
"strengthening" so desperately needed by so many of the
members of Christ's body. God does not forget us in our
human frailty.

Yet another precious ministry that Paul names in Romans
12:8 he describes with these words, "He that giveth, let him
do it with simplicity," (Greek, *ho metadidous en baploteti*).
The Greek verb *metadidomi* means "to share with," "to impart." The Greek noun *baplotes* means "simplicity," "sin-
cerity," "purity." This gift refers to a material ministry

manifesting the love of Christ, a giving, not by sentiment or by emotions, but by the wisdom of the Spirit of God. I sometimes think it could describe the man who is endowed with the ability to make money and who uses his gift to bless the work of God in the churches.

The Gifts of Practical Administration

In another group of gifts Paul describes those of practical administration. In Romans 12:8 he speaks of one in these words, "he that ruleth with diligence," (Greek, *ho proistamenos en spoude*). The Greek verb *proistemi* means "to stand before," "to preside over," "to rule." The Greek word *spoude* means "speed," "haste," "diligence," and finally "earnestness." The man who presides over the congregation of the Lord is to be deeply sensitive to the needs of the group and is to be diligently earnest in his response to them. In I Corinthians 12:28 Paul refers to this gift as one of "government," "administration," (Greek *kubarnesis*). A "kubernetes" is a steersman, a pilot (compare Acts 27:11; Revelation 18:17). The possessor of this gift is one who has the ability to guide the Church through all the fortunes and vicissitudes of daily life, maintaining order and holding the congregation to its heavenly assignment. According to I Timothy 5:17, the gift was entrusted to the pastor (the elder, the bishop) of the Church.

Another ministry gift of administration Paul describes in Romans 12:7 with these words, "ministry, let us wait on our ministering," (Greek, *diakonian en te diakonia*). A servant, in the Greek language, is called a *diakonos*, a "deacon." In I Corinthians 12:28 Paul refers to this gift under the word *antilepseis* (a word used only here in the New Testament). The word comes from the verb *antilambano*, which means "to take hold of," "to share in," to "help." The recipients of that gift are men who are able to assist the pastor in his work of guiding the welfare and destiny of the congregation. Happy is the pastor who has these God-appointed and God-blessed deacons.

The Gift of Faith

As we have spoken of the gifts of the Spirit that pertain to Enlightenment of Mind, Sympathy of Heart, and Practical Administration, we now discuss one that pertains to Sublimity of Faith. In the list of the nine gifts in I Corinthians 12:8-10, Paul names the third one as "faith," (Greek, *pistis*, meaning "trust," "belief," "faith"). There are three uses of the word *pistis*, "faith," in Scripture. One meaning refers to natural faith, mental recognition, and assent. James 2:19 describes the devils as believing the facts of the Gospel and trembling before them. Another meaning of *pistis* refers to saving faith, the committal of our souls to Christ as Paul describes in II Timothy 1:12. A third meaning of the word refers to the gift of faith, power to lay hold on God's promises for results beyond our own ability to achieve. This gift of faith is so wondrously illustrated in the Bible. Hebrews 11:17-19 describes the faithful Abraham who believed that God would raise his son Isaac from the dead if the lad were slain in obedience to the commandment of the Lord.

> By faith Abraham, when he was tried, offered up Isaac: and he that had received the promises offered up his only begotten son, Of whom it was said, That in Isaac shall thy seed be called: Accounting that God was able to raise him up, even from the dead; from whence also he received him in a figure (Hebrews 11:17-19).

Witness the faith of Elijah, in I Kings 17:8-16, who believed that God would take care of both him and the widow's household through the years of the terrible drought. "The barrel of meal shall not waste, neither shall the cruse of oil fail, until the day that the Lord sendeth rain upon the earth." George Muller, by prayer and faith alone, sustained his orphanage in Bristol, England, for a generation. He once said, "It pleased the Lord to give me something like a gift of faith so that unconditionally I could ask and look for an answer." This man of prayer never asked another human being for any need of food, clothing, provisions. He only asked God and God answered abundantly, triumphantly. From paradise in Eden to Patmos in Revelation, this gift of faith marks the trail of the company of the blessed, the heaven-bound saints of God. No wonder the faith chapter, Hebrews 11, sounds like a roll call of God's heroes! The gift of faith was and is their sublimest endowment.

Chapter 22

The Gift of Miracles

I Corinthians 12

7   But the manifestation of the Spirit is given to every man to profit withal.

8   For to one is given by the Spirit the word of wisdom; to another the word of knowledge by the same Spirit;

9   To another faith by the same Spirit; to another the gifts of healing by the same Spirit;

10   To another the working of miracles; to another prophecy; to another discerning of spirits; to another divers kinds of tongues; to another the interpretation of tongues:

11   But all these worketh that one and the self-same Spirit, dividing to every man severally as he will.

Three times the charismatic gift of miracles is named in the twelfth chapter of I Corinthians; namely, in verses 10, 28, and 29. Three Greek words are used in the New Testament for "miracle"; namely, *semeion, tera,* and *dunamis. Semeion* is a miracle as a sign authenticating the divine mission of the doer. It is translated "sign." *Tera* is a miracle as a wonderful thing, named for the effect of astonishment it has on the beholder. It is translated "wonder." *Dunamis* is a miracle as an exhibition of divine power. It is translated "miracle" (as here in I Corinthians 12:10, 28, 29), as a "mighty deed" (II Corinthians 12:12). All three words are used in such passages as Acts 2:22; II Corinthians 12:12; Hebrews 2:4.

A miracle is an interruption, an intervention, in the system of nature as we know it. It is a temporary suspension of the laws that govern this world as we commonly observe them. A miracle is "supernatural," above the "natural." The virgin birth of our Lord Jesus Christ is a "miracle." There

178

is no other way to explain the birth of Christ as one without a human father except as a sovereign act of God suspending the laws of nature. Sometimes we use the word "miracle" in a figurative sense. We say "a sunset is a miracle of beauty and loveliness," or, "a Christian is a miracle of grace," or, "a mother is a miracle of patience and self-sacrifice." But this use of the word is not in the same sense as turning common dust into insects (Moses), or dividing a stream by the sweep of a mantle (Elijah and Elisha), or feeding five thousand with a few loaves and fishes (Jesus). To turn water into wine through the processes of nature is one thing; to turn water into wine by fiat, as a sovereign act apart from the processes of nature, is another thing. The latter is truly a "miracle."

The Astonishing Gift of Miracles

The gift of miracles is an astonishing gift. In the list of *charismata* in I Corinthians 12:8-10, of the nine gifts named, that of "healing" is fourth and that of "miracles" is fifth. The gift of healing is a specific category within the larger gift of miracles. Miracles that are not bodily healings are illustrated in the fish with the shekel in its mouth, caught by Simon Peter at the direction of the Lord Jesus (Matthew 17:24-27), Jesus walking on the water (Matthew 14:25-33), Peter being liberated from Herod's prison with the iron gate opening of itself (Acts 9:36-42), and Paul calling down blindness on Elymas, the sorcerer in the court of Sergius Paulus (Acts 13:8-11).

The gift of miracles was not for show or for entertainment. Miracles in the Bible were never performed to be spectacular. They were never presented in a Circus Maximus to attract attention to the doer. In the second temptation (Matthew 4:5-7) Jesus pointedly refused to hurl Himself down from the pinnacle of the temple in order to be lavishly applauded by the people for His deliverance in so great a feat. When the Jews required of the Saviour a sign (Matthew 12:38-40), He refused to accommodate their empty curiosity with anything but a verbal denunciation of their hard hearts (Matthew 12:41,42). The same reaction was witnessed in our Lord when He was brought to trial before Herod Antipas (Luke 23:5-11). The Scriptures state that "when Herod saw Jesus, he was exceeding glad . . . because he hoped to have seen some miracle done by him" (verse 8). When the Lord not only refused to work a cheap miracle for the monarch's entertainment but also refused even to answer him a word, Herod mocked Him and returned Him in contempt to Pontius Pilate. Never for ostentation was any miracle wrought, and for the most part the miracles of our Lord and of the apostles were works of compassion and mercy.

It is most noticeable that very few converts were won by "signs and wonders and miracles." After the feeding of the five thousand on the eastern side of the Galilean sea, Jesus left and made His way in a boat to Capernaum. The multitudes followed Him, walking to the city around the north end of the lake. When they found Him in Capernaum they were greeted with the announcement that they sought the Saviour not because they had seen in Him the presence of God but because "they did eat of the loaves and were filled" (John 6:26). When Jesus proceeded to preach to them a sermon on the bread of life, beginning with the words, "labor not for the meat which perisheth, but for that meat which endureth unto everlasting life" (verse 27), they were offended in Him and walked no more with Him (verse 66). The miracle of the feeding of the five thousand did not convert one life, not one. The same effect of the wonder-working life of our Lord can be seen in the reaction of the Jewish rulers to Jesus. They finally, in desperation, attributed His astonishing power to Satan and furthermore set about to have Him removed from the earth. His restoration of life to the four-day dead Lazarus in Bethany was the climax that sealed His fate. Instead of the leaders' obdurate spirits softening and their hard hearts repenting, they gathered together the Sanhedrin to find formal means of putting Him to death (John 11:47-53).

The sterile fruitlessness of conversion by miracles is dramatically emphasized by Jesus in His teaching. The story of Dives and Lazarus in the life beyond the grave is unforgettable. In torment Dives pleaded with father Abraham to send back to this earth Lazarus that the rich man's five brothers may be warned of hell and may thereby repent and be saved (Luke 16:19-31). Abraham replied, "They have the Bible (Moses and the prophets); let them hear them." To this the rich man responded, "Nay, father Abraham: but if the miracle of one raised from the dead could be seen by them and if that dead man's pleas for repentance and faith could be heard by them, they would turn and be saved." Abraham from heaven closed the conversation with these words: "If they heed not the appeal of the Word of God, neither will they be persuaded though one rose from the dead." Miracles do not bring conversion, even the astonishing wonder of one raised from the grave. Thus said and thus taught the Lord Jesus.

The teaching and example of the Master concerning the effect of miracles on the unrepentant is corroborated in the experience of the apostles. In Acts 14:8-18 the story is recounted of the reception of Paul and Barnabas as gods by the city of Lystra when the citizens saw Paul heal a man crippled all the days of his life. The narrative seemingly is about to present a glorious revival of salvation wrought by the convicting effect of one wondrous healing. But the story continues in verse 19 with these succinct words, "having stoned Paul, [they] drew him out of the city, supposing he had been dead." How empty and barren of results is conversion by miracle! When Paul healed the demented, spirit-possessed girl of Philippi (Acts 16:12-24), we would have thought the whole populace would have rejoiced in so great a deliverance and that the Apostle would have received his greatest ovation. Instead, he and his companion, Silas, were brutally beaten because of the miracle and, furthermore, were placed in stocks and chains in the deepest part of the dungeon. The simple truth is that no saving faith is achieved by the miraculous. Nor did the apostles ever seek to evangelize through signs and wonders. They relied entirely upon the convicting, regenerating power of the Holy Spirit for their converts, the same as do we and the same as God instructed from the beginning. No, miracles are recorded in the Book of Acts as Luke recounts the founding of the churches in Pisidian Antioch, Derbe, Thessalonica, Berea, Athens, Corinth, and other places. We are saved by God not by miracle.

The Purpose of Miracles

What, then, is the purpose of the miraculous? Miracles are for introduction, for authentication, for corroboration, for substantiation. There have been times in the economy of God when they were mightily needed to introduce a new life, a new dispensation. They bore a special testimony at the beginning of each new age. The creation story (Genesis 1 - 3) is filled with miracles. The introduction of the law through Moses is filled with miracles. The revival under Elijah and Elisha, in the dark days of apostasy when it seemed that worship of the true God would die from the earth, is filled with miracles. The introduction of the Christian era, under Jesus and the apostles, is filled with miracles. The consummation of the age recounted in the Apocalypse is filled with miracles. But outside of these introductory eras they are rarely seen and hardly found. For example, they are much in evidence in the first part of the Book of Acts (cf. Acts 2:43). Then they become less and less common until in the latter part of the Book of Acts they are rarely mentioned.

No one could read Hebrews 2:3, 4 without astonishment. Look at the passage closely and carefully: "How shall we escape, if we neglect so great salvation; which at the first began to be spoken by the Lord, and was confirmed unto us by them that heard him; God also bearing them witness, both with signs and wonders, and with divers miracles, and gifts of the Holy Ghost, according to his own will?" (Hebrews 2:3, 4). Whoever wrote the Book of Hebrews (and I think it was written by the eloquent Alexandrian orator, Apollos) belonged to the second generation of Christians. The author had not seen the Lord nor had he heard the message of the Gospel from the lips of the Saviour. He had heard it from those who had seen the Lord, second hand, second generation. But most important for us in our understanding of the gift of miracles, he had not seen the confirmation of "signs and wonders and divers miracles." Even in his second generation these had died out. The message was not confirmed to *him* by these miraculous signs; rather, the message was confirmed to *them* (the Apostles and the personal witnesses) by those miraculous authentications. He had heard the report of the miracles; he had not seen them himself.

The dying out of the gift of miracles is most reasonable and obvious. When they served their purpose, they ceased to be. They were needed no longer. Moses, going down into Egypt's land, was armed with three wondrous miracles for introduction: the rod into a serpent, the leprous hand cleansed, the water turned into blood (Exodus 4:1-9). Jesus authenticated His claim to forgive sins (the prerogative of deity alone) by the miracle of raising the palsied man to strength and health (Mark 2:7-12). Paul confirmed his apostleship with "the signs of an apostle" (II Corinthians 12:12, "Truly the signs of an apostle were wrought among you in all patience, in signs and wonders, and mighty deeds," cf. Romans 15:18, 19; Acts 19:11, 12). The two witnesses from heaven are fortified in the tragic days of the Great Tribulation with the power to do miracles.

> And I will give power unto my two witnesses, and they shall prophesy a thousand two hundred and threescore days, clothed in sackcloth. These are the two olive trees, and the two candlesticks standing before the God of the earth. And if any man will hurt them, fire proceedeth out of their mouth, and devoureth their enemies: and if any man will hurt them, he must in this manner be killed. These have power to shut heaven, that it rain not in the days of their prophecy: and have power over

waters to turn them to blood, and to smite the earth with all plagues, as often as they will. And when they shall have finished their testimony, the beast that ascendeth out of the bottomless pit shall make war against them, and shall overcome them, and kill them (Revelation 11:3-7).

When the need for the sign ceased, the sign was no longer given.

The Church is built upon the foundation of the apostles and the prophets (New Testament inspired men who told the infant church what to do and what to believe). These apostles and prophets were accredited by signs and wonders and mighty works. After the foundation was laid, the office ceased. There were no more prophetic offices upon which the church is built. The prophets' utterances of wisdom and revelation are written down forever in the pages of the New Testament. There are no more apostolic *offices* upon which the church is founded. The apostles' message from heaven is forever contained in the inspired books of the New Testament. Look at the number of foundations undergirding the Bride of Christ (the church) in the New Jerusalem. They number twelve and twelve alone. The *office* of apostle is held by twelve men and twelve only. (As I have suggested already, the disciples at Jerusalem chose Matthias to take the office vacated by Judas Iscariot; I believe God chose Saul of Tarsus, Paul, to fill it.) In the foundation of the city are written the name of the twelve apostles of the Lamb. Upon them the church is built (Ephesians 2:20). To these apostles in their sacred *office* (as to the infant church in its beginning) the gift of miracles was bestowed. The gift was for introduction and authentication. Paul writes to the church at Corinth: "for in nothing am I behind the very chiefest apostles, though I be nothing. Truly the signs of an apostle were wrought among you in all patience, in signs, and wonders, and mighty deeds" (II Corinthians 12:11, 12). Here plainly is seen the purpose of the *semeion*, the *tera*, and the *dunamis*. The miracle confirmed the calling of the apostle to his holy office. After the foundation of the church was laid, the apostolic office ceased, *and the sign ceased.* There was no more need for authentication. The Bible is complete and our appeal now is not to an apostle in his God-appointed office but to the infallible, inspired Word. The infant church, blessed with the gift of miracles, confirmed in its doctrine and practice by signs of approval from heaven, is now firmly founded and the need for the sign has ceased to exist. We have the Bible and that is enough.

As no one person has all the gifts of the Spirit, so it is possible that no one age has all the gifts. If every Christian does not possess every charismatic endowment, then it could be that every generation does not possess all the gifts. This is certainly true with regard to the sign gift of miracles.

The Gift of Miracles and Our Miracle-Working God

There is a vast difference between the miracles of God sovereignly wrought and the *gift* of miracles sovereignly bestowed. God can, has, does work miracles throughout history; yesterday, today and forever. The sign of the presence of God is always the miraculous, whether in heaven above or on earth beneath. If it is of God, it is wondrously miraculous. But the *gift* of miracles is always temporary. There are times in the history of God's elective grace bestowed upon men when the period is filled with intense activity and the gift of miracles is the wonder of the age (cf. the days of Moses, of Elijah, of Peter and Paul). But there are also times when the program of God enters a great calm, such as the four hundred years of silence between the days of Malachi and the days of Matthew. The gift of miracles appears, then enters a state of quiescence, then reappears more startling than ever. We shall witness a mighty return of the gift of miracles during the last days described in the Book of the Revelation.

Miracles of God are on every hand. They are recorded every day. The *gift* of miracles possessed by the saints may be temporary but miracles and the miracle-working God are with us forever. God does not change or evolve. His power and wisdom are this day what they were before the morning stars sang together.

> Thou, Lord, in the beginning hast laid the foundation of the earth; and the heavens are the works of thine hands: They shall perish; but thou remainest; and they all shall wax old as doth a garment; And as a vesture shalt thou fold them up, and they shall be changed: but thou art the same, and thy years shall not fail (Hebrews 1:10-12).

The fires that forged the strong bands of Orion are the same as those that were seen by Moses in the burning bush of Horeb; that Israel looked upon in the Shekinah glory above the tabernacle and the temple; that smote Abihu in the day of judgment; that consumed the sacrifice and the altar and the very dirt of the ground upon the appeal of Elijah; that rose in amber flames before the rapt attention of Ezekiel; that sat in cloven tongues upon Peter and the apostles; that blinded the eyes of Saul of Tarsus on the road to Damascus; and the same as shall someday clothe our glorious returning Lord when He descends through the clouds of heaven. God does not change nor does His power to work miracles among men cease.

The Book of Acts has no formal conclusion. The story stops in the middle of the most interesting part. This is because the writing of the Book of Acts has not concluded. The story does not cease with the present chapter 28. It is plainly an unfinished volume. Other chapters are being added, chapters 29, 30, 31 and on and on until the consummation of the age and the intervention of the Lord Christ in human history. On mission fields and in a thousand places the wondrous, miraculous works of God are seen. But the *gift* of miracles is not bestowed upon the servants of the Lord with great frequency, and when it is, it is for a special purpose. It is not a permanent but a special, temporary gift. Our faith and our assurance are not dependent upon a sign or a wonder or a miracle, but upon the promise of the Word of God and the witness of the Holy Spirit in our hearts (Romans

8:14-17). This is enough. If God gave me a vision of an angel or a light from heaven or a flaming bush that burned unconsumed, I would be ever so grateful. If I could work miracles by the gift of God, I would praise His name forever. But these gifts lie in His sovereign will. I do not need their authenticating, confirming testimony. I have the word of the Lord and that is enough. I ask for no sign beside.

Chapter 23

The Gifts of Healing

I Corinthians 12
9 To another faith by the same Spirit; to another the gifts
of healing by the same Spirit.

Three times Paul names this sign gift of healing (one of
the four sign gifts: miracles, healing, tongues, and interpretation of tongues) in the twelfth chapter of I Corinthians.
It is mentioned in verses 9, 28 and 30. In all three instances
the plural is used, *charismata iamaton,* "gifts of healings."
As there are different kinds of sicknesses (we can be sick
in our bodies, we can be sick in our minds, we can be sick
in our souls), so there are different kinds of healings.

The discussion of illness and healing touches all our lives,
both in ourselves and in the circle of our family and friends.
There is no one but who knows the heartache of illness, and
illness can be so tragic. In my first pastorate a young deacon and his wife called me to their home to pray for their
little two-year-old baby girl stricken with diphtheria. "Tell
the Lord," they desperately said to me, "that we will do anything for Him, give Him all we have and are, if only He will
spare our precious child." I earnestly sought for an answer.
I did so with all my heart. But the child died. That pitiful
story has been repeated throughout these many years of my
ministry and continues to this present day. Last week I received this letter from the wife of a preacher who is pastor
of one of our finest churches:

Dear Dr. Criswell:
    My husband is sick here in a Shreveport hospital. There are
no medical answers and the time is urgent. You have great
faith and have seen physical and spiritual miracles. Please pray
in Jesus' name for my husband's healing.

188

We are expecting this healing not because my husband is a preacher. He would say that he is the least of His children. We trust God for a miracle because of His love, mercy, power, and willingness to heal.

Thank you for praying. Any promise that you claim for his healing or any suggestions on prayer will be helpful. We want God to get glory to His name.

Very gratefully yours,

But within a few days the pastor died.

It Is Right to Turn to God for Healing

What of the appeal to God in the hours of illness? It is right, it is pre-eminently correct and Scriptural to turn to God for healing. Only God can heal. All healing is divine healing. There is no other kind. Man can operate, cut, saw, sew, prescribe, diagnose, but only God can heal. We have every Scriptural right to look to heaven for healing. We have the right because of who and what God is. His very name is "Jehovah Ropheca," "I am the Lord that healeth thee" (Exodus 15:26). We have the right because of the example and the ministry of our Saviour. "When the even was come, they brought unto him many that were possessed with devils: and he cast out the spirits with his word, and healed all that were sick: That it might be fulfilled which was spoken by Esaias the prophet, saying, Himself took our infirmities, and bare our sicknesses" (Matthew 8:16, 17). We have this right because of the Spirit's indwelling. "But if the Spirit of him that raised up Jesus from the dead dwell in you, he that raised up Christ from the dead shall also quicken your mortal bodies by his Spirit that dwelleth in you" (Romans 8:11). All three Persons of the Godhead are pledged to this remembrance of our infirmities in saving, healing grace.

God has healed in days past in answer to prayer. God healed Abimelech when Abraham prayed for him (Genesis 20:7). God healed Miriam when Moses prayed for her (Numbers 12:14). God healed Hezekiah when the king turned his face to the wall and with bitter weeping asked God for length of days. "Then came the word of the LORD to Isaiah, saying, Go, and say to Hezekiah, Thus saith the LORD, the God of David thy father, I have heard thy prayer, I have seen thy tears: behold, I will add unto thy days fifteen years" (Isaiah 38:4, 5). Jesus healed the leper who in faith prayed to Him, "Lord, if thou wilt, thou canst make me clean" (Matthew 8:2). Recently, at a men's and boys' dinner in the church I heard the testimony of "the strongest man in the world," a man who had won the title at a world Olympic meet. To my amazement he began his talk with a divine healing experience. When he was a little boy, four years of age, the doctors said he could not live. In keeping with the customs of the times, arrangements were made in the home for his casket to be brought to the house. But a godly grandfather brought his sorrow to a pastor who prayed to God for the life of the child. The lad was miraculously delivered. The next day he was well. Could this be so? Yes. A thousand times yes. God heals! His name is "Jehovah Ropheca." "I am the LORD that healeth thee."

Professional Divine Healers and Their Gifts of Healing

But professional divine healers, with their purported "gifts of healing" for money, are something else. As there is an all-significant distinction between the miracles of God and "the gift of miracles," so there is an all-significant distinction between God's healings and "the gifts of healing." The gift is a sign gift for the purpose of corroboration, authentication, substantiation, and introduction while the gospel message was in its formative state, before the New Testament was written. The sign gift authenticated the messages as from God. This is seen in the life of Jesus.

> Ye men of Israel, hear these words; Jesus of Nazareth, a man approved of God among you by miracles and wonders and signs, which God did by him in the midst of you, as ye yourselves also know (Acts 2:22).
>
> How God anointed Jesus of Nazareth with the Holy Ghost and with power: who went about doing good, and healing all that were oppressed of the devil; for God was with him (Acts 10:38).

This is seen in the life of the apostles.

> By stretching forth thine hand to heal; and that signs and wonders may be done by the name of thy holy child Jesus (Acts 4:30).

It is seen in the life of Paul.

> Truly the signs of an apostle were wrought among you in all patience, in signs, and wonders, and mighty deeds (II Corinthians 12:12).

It is emphatically seen in the letter to the Hebrews.

> How shall we escape, if we neglect so great salvation; which at the first began to be spoken by the Lord, and was confirmed unto us by them that heard him; God also bearing them witness, both with signs and wonders, and with divers miracles, and gifts of the Holy Ghost, according to his own will? (Hebrews 2:3, 4).

When the Word with its authority was written, the appeal no longer is to the "signs of an apostle" as Paul presented in II Corinthians 12:12, but to the holy verses of the Holy Book. The sign is no longer needed nor is it necessary. In Joshua 5:11, 12, we are told:

> And they did eat of the old corn of the land on the morrow after the passover, unleavened cakes, and parched corn in the selfsame day. And the manna ceased on the morrow after they had eaten of the old corn of the land; neither had the children of Israel manna any more; but they did eat of the fruit of the land of Canaan that year.

The miracle of the manna in the wilderness was no longer needed. They ate of the fruit of the land. So with us. The miraculous sign-gift is no longer needed. We have the living Word.

The modern increase of professional money-making divine healers is a phenomenal development in itself. From an article in a current magazine I copy these words: "In Britain alone the number of spirit healers belonging to the National Federation of Spiritual Healers is in the region of four thousand, and the number of people who claim to be spirit healers is increasing all over the world. Hundreds of thousands claim to have been cured by them. One of the healers, all his life, has been guided by a voice. He claims his healing power comes from God. He smokes cigars and does not go to church. He believes that God does not need the trappings of religion, and goes down to the pub [liquor bar] after a day's work. Yet, his reported healings are numerous and remarkable." Through the wee hours of the morning I stood in Father Divine's central "heaven" in Harlem, New York City, and heard dozens of adorations addressed to the little "God" by people who had in answer to prayers poured out to him been miraculously healed. Until he died, this "God" kept on healing by miracle and kept up the lavish estate in which he and his "wife" and angels lived.

Yesterday I received this letter: "Send a snapshot of yourself or of any loved one who is in need of prayer. We will lay our hands upon the picture and ask God to meet every need. Your generous gifts and faithful pledges are needed. Read God's Bible promises for your healing. As you vow, pay your vows to the Lord. Surely every Bible believing Christian can vow to give a hundred dollars. Some can give a thousand. I will be looking for your letter [and I might add, for your money]. Yours in God's Miracle." What do you think of that? If a man had the gifts of healing, I doubt that he should use it for money. But how do these professional miracle workers succeed and continue? For the simple reason that eighty-five per cent of all the sick will get well anyway, and to the other fifteen per cent the divine healers can blandly and piously say, "You do not have the faith." It is a sure-fire racket, far more certain than betting on horses at the race tracks or playing the game tables at Las Vegas. If the odds are eighty-five per cent in your favor, how can you lose? Anyone can announce himself as a divine healer and make big money if he knows how to go about it, with personality, publicity, showmanship, and all the other accoutrements and embellishments of the trade. But oh, thus to prey upon the miseries of people! If there are gifts of divine healing they ought to be employed in a hospital, up and down the corridors; not in a tent, up and down the aisles.

The Distressing Doctrines of Professional Divine Healers

Remembering our sick and sorrowing, I hear and read so many hurtful fallacies that bring grief and distress to the soul. Let me recount some of the things professional divine healers avow. They say that God wills that we never be sick; that we all be well; that all the sick be healed; that none ever be sick. But *you* are sick. Why? The doctrine brings anguish to the sensitive soul. Why was Timothy, Paul's son in the ministry, continuously sick? Why did not God heal him? Paul refers in I Timothy 5:23 to Timothy's "often infirmities." He was such a teetotaler that he would not take even a small amount of medicine spirits for his sick stomach. Paul had to plead with him to do so. Yet Paul had the miraculous "gift of healing." In II Timothy 4:20 Paul writes to Timothy, the pastor of the church at Ephesus, that he left Trophimus at Miletum sick. This is Paul's last letter. He is writing from the Mamertime dungeon in Rome from which imprisonment he was delivered to the heads-man or block on the Ostian Way. Paul would never be in Asia again. He would never see Trophimus again. Why did not Paul heal him or leave a miracle-working handkerchief or apron? Is it truly God's will that we never be sick? Plainly, the gifts of the Spirit are sovereignly bestowed (I Corinthians 12:7, 11). They do not work indiscriminately. Even the apostles were not able to heal promiscuously. Not when men desire to employ them are the gifts of the Spirit seen, but when the Holy Spirit Himself desires to further some work of God.

Professional faith healers say that Christ healed *all* who were sick. But *you* are sick. Why does He not heal you? Apparently, God does not love you. He has forgotten you. No. Not at all. The fault lies in the false doctrine. Christ no more healed all the sick than He raised all the dead. He raised three from the dead (the widow's son from Nain, the daughter of Jairus, and the brother of Mary and Martha) and possibly others (Matthew 11:5), but the vast host of the bodies of the saints He left in their graves awaiting the final resurrection day. It is most preciously true that as Jesus entered the villages and cities of Galilee and the countryside round about, He healed all the sick who were brought to Him (Matthew 9:35; 10:1; 12:15; 14:14; Luke 6:17-19). This very ministry with its gifts of healing set Him apart, for such a mercy is not usually given unto man. The sign designated Him as the Son of God; it was the prerogative of deity. But this is not the whole story. Read John 5:1-9. Bethesda's porches were filled with the sick, all of them believing in divine healing, and all of them waiting for the heavenly miracle. But how many did Jesus heal? One. Read Luke 5:15, 16. The Saviour whose endearing name is "the Lord moved with compassion" withdrew from the multitudes who were sick, and went into the wilderness to pray. Think of the sick in the world whom He did not heal! The miracles of Christ were not for the purpose of contravening the judgment of God upon this world, a sentence solemnly pronounced in Genesis 3:14-19. Our deliverance from that awesome sentence of death was wrought through the atonement on Calvary, but the full effects will be seen only at the end of the world. (For example, I Corinthians 15:26 says, "The last enemy that shall be destroyed is death.") The miracles of Christ were for the purpose of identifying Him as Saviour of the world; they bore evidence of His deity, they proclaimed Him to be the Son of God, they formed the credentials of His Messiahship (Mark 2:7-12; Acts 2:22; 10:38; Isaiah 53:4; Matthew 8:17). The miracles of Christ were not for ostentation or notoriety, but that we could know the heart of God, "moved with compassion and touched with the feeling of our infirmity" (Hebrews 4:15; Matthew 9:36; Mark 1:4; 6:34; Luke 7:12, 13).

The professional divine leader preaches that the atonement of Christ included not only all our sins but also all our illnesses. Our sins are carried away in the death of Christ and also our infirmities (Isaiah 53). They say since disease entered by sin, its true remedy must be found in the redemptive work of Christ. This is true, of course, and the whole system of sin, disease, and the works of the devil are to be destroyed by the manifestation of Christ (I John 3:8). But *you* are a Christian and you still sin, living sometimes in the agony of Paul in Romans 7:24, "O wretched man that I am! who shall deliver me from the body of this death?" Why? For the simple reason that all the benefits of the atonement are not immediately realized. The curse is still upon creation (Romans 8:22). The woman is still in travail in childbirth. The man still must live by the toil and sweat of hard labor. The body still falls into age and senility. The drag of sin and human weakness is still the despair of our better hopes (Romans 7:15-24). Accepting Christ does not change that. We are saved but we still groan within ourselves waiting for the redemption of our bodies (Romans 8:23). Forgiven, the spirit regenerated, we must still wait for the resurrection of the whole purchased possession at the final day of the Lord. Though saved and sanctified, we still are not glorified. We still know sin and weakness in this life.

Illness Not a Sign of Disobedience to God

The faith-healer-for-hire yet avows another thing. He says that illness is a sign of disobedience to God. "Get right with God, do God's will," he proclaims, "and you will be well." I read a tract the other day which concludes with these words: "I don't care how many times you have been prayed for, it is God's will that you have a well body. Friend of mine, will you obey God? When you make up your mind to obey God you will be healed." But *you* are sick. It must be, therefore, that you have sinned in disobedience to God. So you live through the agony of soul-searching to ascertain what sin of disobedience has brought on such a heavy illness. This whole interpretation is inhuman and unsupported by Scripture. Job's comforters (divine healers) steadfastly avowed that Job's terrible sickness was due to his terrible sins. Yet God said he was the best man in all the earth (Job 1:8; 4:7, 8). Daniel became ill because of the abundance of the revelations given to him (Daniel 8:26, 27; 10:15-17). Look at this passage in John 9:1-3:

> And as Jesus passed by, he saw a man which was blind from his birth. And his disciples asked him, saying, Master, who did sin, this man, or his parents, that he was born blind? Jesus answered, Neither hath this man sinned, nor his parents: but that the works of God should be made manifest in him.

A like sentiment is expressed by our Lord concerning the terminal illness of Lazarus: "When Jesus heard that, he said, This sickness is not unto death, but for the glory of God, that the Son of God might be glorified thereby" (John 11:4).

Paul wrote in II Corinthians 4:16, "For which cause we faint not; but though our outward man perish, yet the inward man is renewed day by day." Though the body weakens and finally loses all its strength, yet the inward spirit is daily renewed by the mercies of God, a situation that would not be true if the weakness were due to the sinful disobedience. Epaphroditus became ill unto death "for the work of Christ" (Philippians 2:27-30). Whatever Paul's "thorn in the flesh" may have been, when he writes of it he uses the word "infirmities" (sicknesses). He says:

> And lest I should be exalted above measure through the abundance of the revelations, there was given to me a thorn in the flesh, the messenger of Satan to buffet me, lest I should be exalted above measure. For this thing I besought the Lord thrice, that it might depart from me. And he said unto me, My grace is sufficient for thee: for my strength is made perfect in weakness. Most gladly therefore will I rather glory in my infirmities, that the power of Christ may rest in me. Therefore I take pleasure in infirmities, in reproaches, in necessities, in persecutions, in distresses for Christ's sake: for when I am weak, then am I strong (II Corinthians 12:7-10).

He had just written in the first part of the letter (II Corinthians 1:8-11) that in Asia he had been sick unto death, "we had the sentence of death in ourselves." Paul knew what it was to be repeatedly ill, desperately so, even unto death. Were these tragic bodily weaknesses and illnesses due to his sinful disobedience? No, no, no! God answered Paul's inquiry and prayer with these sublime words: "My grace is sufficient for thee: for my strength is made perfect in weakness." And Paul answered God's will with these incomparable words of dedication: "Most gladly therefore will I rather glory in my infirmities, that the power of Christ may rest upon me" (II Corinthians 12:9). And this may be God's will for us. If it is, may we answer as fully as did His servant, the Apostle Paul.

Chapter 24

Faith and Healing

James 5

14 Is any sick among you? let him call for the elders of the church; and let them pray over him, anointing him with oil in the name of the Lord:

15 And the prayer of faith shall save the sick, and the Lord shall raise him up; and if he have committed sins, they shall be forgiven him.

There is a Christian attitude toward illness. First, let us admit its reality. Let us be honest if we are Christians! There is a large cult in Christendom that denies the existence of disease. They avow that its presence is only in the mind. Ignore it in the mind, overcome it in thought, and it will cease to be. I was pastor one time in a college town. A professor of music in the institution belonged to that cult. Her devoted mother was a faithful member of our church. The mother fell down the steps in her home to the concrete basement floor. She hurt herself terribly. The daughter ran down to her mother, helped her up, saying: "Mother, you are not hurt! You are not hurt!" I went out to the house to see the dear mother. She was very heavy and the fall had broken her up. She was black and blue all over. But no doctor could be called. No ointments or medicines could be used. Her hurt was only in her mind! The cult pursues that same denial of reality even unto death. A couple I knew belonged to the group. The husband died and the poor, lonely wife was in deepest grief. But after a representative of the cult called upon her, she acted as if she were getting ready for a birthday party, not a funeral. She was all smiles, gaiety and laughter. "For," she said, "my husband is not

198

dead; death is only in the mind." But that casket and that grave looked grimly real to me.

Why We Become Sick

Admitting the presence of illness as we honestly ought to do, and confessing the reality of death as any sane person should, we, therefore, who are followers of the dear Lord, have a responsibility to search the mind and will of God to ask for a reason. Why are we sick? What are the causes of illness? The Holy Scriptures are ready to answer fully and explicitly. The Bible reveals that some sickness is of Satanic origin. In some way that we cannot understand, God permits it. When the Saviour healed the woman who had an infirmity eighteen years, "and was bowed together and could in no wise lift herself," He said in defense of His healing her on the Sabbath Day, "And ought not this woman, being a daughter of Abraham, whom Satan hath bound, lo, these eighteen years, be loosed from this bond on the sabbath day?" Her grievous affliction was a work of Satan (Luke 13: 11-16). In Peter's sermon to the household of Cornelius at Caesarea he recounted, "How God anointed Jesus of Nazareth with the Holy Ghost and with power: who went about doing good, and healing all that were oppressed of the devil" (Acts 10:38). It is undeniable that sickness in large measure is a part of the evil work of Satan. One time, at least, God has given us an inward glimpse of the divine permission for that oppression. It is seen in the story of the old patriarch, Job. He was tried and he was afflicted that it might be proved he served God for love and not for personal gain.

Sometimes we are ill because of the chastening of the Lord. God not only permits but sometimes directs bodily affliction. If there is divine healing, there is also divine sickness. This is plainly seen in the life of God's people, Israel (Exodus 15:26; Numbers 11:33; Deuteronomy 28:20-22, 27, 35, 60, 61; II Corinthians 7:13). God's judgment through disease is seen in the leprosy of Miriam (Numbers 12:9, 10), in the illness of David (Psalm 38:3-8), in the leprous curse upon Gehazi and his family (II Kings 5:27), and in the smiting of Herod Agrippa I by the angel of the Lord (Acts 12:23). It is most interesting to read Josephus' account of the reason for the death of Herod Agrippa and compare it with the record in Acts (Ant. 19, 8, 2). Undeniably, some sicknesses are judgments from the hand of the Lord. Paul's solemn admonitions concerning the reverence by which we should partake of the Lord's Supper are fortified by the heavy reminder that because of the Corinthians' irreverence "many are weak and sickly among you, and many sleep." Some have even died under this judgment of God. The Apostle continued: "For if we would judge ourselves, we should not be judged . . . we are chastened of the Lord" (I Corinthians 11:30-32). This chastening of God is minutely discussed by the author of the Hebrews in his famous passage 12:5-13. If we are true sons and not illegitimates, then we can expect to be corrected from the hand of the Lord. Our illnesses may be because of heaven's discipline of us that we become better children of the Great King.

Without doubt, sometimes we are sick for the glory of God. Job was. Most emphatically Jesus said the man born blind was. Let us read again John 9:1-3: "And as Jesus passed by, he saw a man which was blind from his birth. And his disciples asked him, saying, Master, who did sin, this man, or his parents, that he was born blind? Jesus answered, Neither hath this man sinned, nor his parents: but that the works of God should be made manifest in him." Jesus said a like word regarding the terminal illness of Lazarus of Bethany, "This sickness is not unto death, but for the glory of God, that the Son of God might be glorified thereby" (John 11:4).

Violating God's Laws of Health

Many times, yes, so very many times, are we sick because we have violated God's laws of health. We do not eat right, we do not drink right, we do not breathe right, we do not sleep right, we do not exercise right; then we wonder why we are sick. We do not eat right. The medical profession looked through the records of over a million deaths in the

United States and discovered that seventy per cent of these deaths were caused by diseases associated with overweight. We dig our graves with our teeth. We do not drink right. The human system was not built for the consumption of alcohol. It is a damaging drug when drunk as a beverage. The alarming increase in alcoholism in the United States harbingers the dissolution of the very fabric of our national strength. This week I clipped out of our daily newspaper a report from a nationally famous doctor. I quote from the article: "A recent survey shows some eighty-five per cent of our present teenagers drink. What starts teenagers on alcohol? There are two causes: One is their desire to belong, to be one of the group. The second cause is the most serious — it is home environment where parents drink. Abstaining families have the greatest number of abstaining children. The seriousness of adolescent drinking is shown in one statistic: that we are producing five hundred thousand new alcoholics every year, a new crop under way every twelve months. We are producing far more alcoholics than college graduates."

We do not breathe right. The respiratory system was not made to inhale through incessant days the smoke of burning material. Because of our breathing-smoking habits, over fifty thousand Americans die every year of lung cancer alone. *Reader's Digest* entitled an article on cigarette use "Cancer by the Carton." Sometimes I hear cigarettes referred to as "coffin nails" and "cancer sticks." Heart attacks are twenty-five per cent more frequent among smokers. Because money is involved in both alcohol and tobacco, it is well nigh impossible to control their use, but death rides in the profit nonetheless. We do not jump off a building without paying the consequences of violating God's ordinances. What is true of the laws of gravity is also true of the laws of health. God is the author of them both.

We do not rest right, relax right, sleep right. We are tormented with anxieties, distractions and fears. We worry ourselves into sickness through lack of confidence in God. We cross a thousand bridges before we reach them; live under the pressure of a thousand possible confrontations that never materialize. We try to live, not one day at a time, but a dozen days or a whole year at a time. In the Sermon on the Mount, five times in the passage on trusting God does Jesus use the word *merimnao*. What does the word mean? Its use is clearly demonstrated in Paul's injunction to the Christians at Philippi when he said, "Be careful for nothing [*merimnao*]; but in every thing by prayer and supplication with thanksgiving let your requests be made known unto God" (Philippians 4:6). The Greek word *merimnao* refers to fretful distraction, worrisome anxiety, cankering care. Jesus says we are not to be like that, worried by fears of any tomorrow. We are to rest in the goodness and in the love of God (Matthew 6:25-34). In all of these ways by which God can bless us and bestow health upon us, Daniel is an abounding illustration. He was taken captive by the Babylonians in 605 B.C. He lived through the seventy years of the captivity. He was thrown into the den of lions when an old man. He was still sound in body three years after Israel had returned to their land under the decree of Cyrus (Daniel 10:1). His temperate life was surpassed only by his trust in God (Daniel 1:8, 14-16). This is the way of strength and health.

Why are we sick? Sometimes we fall ill because of the burdens of service. Even Daniel fell into sickness because of the revelations given him (Daniel 8:26, 27). The godly friend of Paul and servant of the church at Philippi, Epaphroditus, came nigh unto death because of his disregard for health in his dedication to the work of the Lord (Philippians 2:25-30). We need to rest. This injunction was enforced upon the children of Israel when they sought to gather manna on the Sabbath day. The story in Exodus 16:27-30 reads:

And it came to pass, that there went out some of the people on the seventh day for to gather, and they found none. And the LORD said unto Moses, How long refuse ye to keep my commandments and my laws? See, for that the LORD hath given you the sabbath, therefore he giveth you on the sixth day the

bread of two days; abide ye every man in his place, let no man
go out of his place on the seventh day. So the people rested
on the seventh day.

There was no manna on the seventh day. One day in seven
is to be a day of cessation from all labor. Even Jesus said to
His disciples when they were so busy preaching, healing,
and casting out demons that they had "no leisure so much
as to eat," "Come ye yourselves apart into a desert place,
and rest a while" (Mark 6:31). No man can ever do all the
work. The discipline of self-limitation is difficult to achieve
but it must be exercised by every servant of God.

Why are we sick? Sometimes it is for our spiritual deepening. Paul thus looked upon his "infirmities," his sicknesses (II Corinthians 12:7-10). The psalmist humbly writes
in Psalm 119:67, "Before I was afflicted I went astray." Then
he writes in Psalm 119:71, "It is good for me that I have
been afflicted." Pain, sorrow and sickness usually have one
of two effects upon those who are forced to face the dark
night in the deep valley; they either embitter the sufferer
or they draw him closer to God.

What the Christian Should Do in Illness

What should the Christian do in illness? How are we to
meet sickness? We are to meet the heavy day of our infirmity with faith in God. We are to take it to God in prayer.
The Apostle John wrote to his friend, the well-beloved
Gaius, that he prayed for him that he be in health (III John
2). James, the pastor of the church at Jerusalem, wrote, "The
prayer of faith shall save the sick" (James 5:15). When
King Hezekiah was told by the prophet Isaiah that his sickness was unto death, Hezekiah took it to the Lord in prayer.
So much of healing is bound up with faith. Turn to Matthew,
chapter nine, and look at the marvelous healings in that narrative. Faith is offered unto God by four different people
and groups of people in that one chapter alone. Matthew
9:1-8 recounts the healing of the palsied man through the
faith of the four men who carried him (even through the
roof) to Jesus. "Jesus seeing *their* faith said . . . ." Matthew

9:22 records the faith of the one who is healed, "Thy faith hath made thee whole." Matthew 9:25 describes the faith of the Healer, Himself. Matthew 9:27-30 recounts the faith of both the Healer and the ones who were healed. "And Jesus saith unto them, Believe ye that I am able to do this? They said unto him, Yea, Lord. Then touched he their eyes, saying, According to your faith be it unto you." The faith of the recipient is vital (Mark 10:52; Acts 14:9). The faith of the healer is no less needed (Matthew 17:19, 20; Acts 3:1-7).

Unbelief utterly destroys hope in the healing of a sufferer (Matthew 13:58). Encouragement to faith is seen in the methods Jesus used to heal. Twice Jesus made clay of spittle to anoint the eyes of the blind (John 9:6; Mark 8:23). Once He did it for the deaf (Mark 7:32). Spittle was believed to be efficacious in the healing art. Jesus used it as a visible means to help the man in himself. Somehow it is easier to believe when visible means are used. Human beings living in this natural world seem to grope for visible signs to stimulate their faith. Thus did Gideon with his fleece of wool in Judges 6:36-40. Thus did Hezekiah with his request for the shadow to return on the sundial of Ahaz in II Kings 20:8-11. Thus anointing oil was used in Mark 6:13 and James 5:14, 15. Medical science would be the first to recognize the dependence of the physical upon the spiritual. There is control of bodily functions by the subconscious self. One's mental, spiritual, emotional attitude has much to do with one's healing. A mighty faith in God is in itself a mighty adjunct to triumphant therapeutics. Psychosomatic diseases are those illnesses caused by aberrations of the mind. To be well in the inner man contributes to our being well in the outward man. The two so often go together.

How shall the Christian meet illness? He shall meet it with God's means for healing. Look at Isaiah 38:21. Even though God had said to the praying king, "I have heard thy prayer, I have seen thy tears: behold I will add unto thy days fifteen years," yet the prophet said, "Let them take a lump of figs, and lay it for a plaister upon the boil, and he shall recover." God healed Hezekiah according to His miraculous word, but God did not disdain to use means in doing it. Jesus referred to the gracious ministries of the physicians: "But when Jesus heard that, he said unto them, They that be whole need not a physician, but they that are sick" (Matthew 9:12). In recounting the story of the Good Samaritan, the Lord said the kindness of the Samaritan prompted him to pour into the wounds of the beaten pilgrim "oil and wine" (Luke 10:34). The resurrected, glorified Saviour counseled the worldly church at Laodicea to "anoint thine eyes with eye-salve, that thou mayest see" (Revelation 3:18). Both the Apostle Paul and the beloved physician, Dr. Luke, healed the sick on the island of Melita (Malta). Paul laid hands on the sick and *iaomai*, "healed them." Luke practiced medicine on other of those who had diseases and *therapeuo*, "healed them." So reads Acts 28:8, 9. For verse ten continues, "Who also honoured *us* [plural] with many honours; and when *we* [plural] departed, they laded *us* [plural] with such things as were necessary." The preacher and the doctor are here working together, the preacher praying to God and *iaomai*, "healing"; the doctor practicing medicine and *therapeuo*, "healing." The two different Greek verbs used and the plural pronouns used have tremendous significance. Modern movements of hostility to medicine are mistakes and unscriptural. To disregard means of healing is like a farmer who prays for a harvest but who sits down to see God do it alone. God has given to us means of healing as well as the desire to be healed. Medicines come from Him. Without His creative work they would not be in existence in this earth. Penicillin has been here from the dawn of time. It is just now that we have discovered it (not invented it). God made it. If you are sick in eye, or tooth, or ear, or body, trust in the Lord and call for "the beloved physician," a Dr. Luke to prescribe and a Preacher Paul to pray. That is the way to get well.

Glorifying God in Our Illnesses

How shall the Christian meet sickness? With committal to the sovereign purposes of God. The Lord can heal. The

Lord has healed. The Lord does heal. The Lord may not heal. The Lord may take His servant home. Surely, surely, there is no more pitiful, pathetic appeal in all literature than the prayer of Moses to God that the Lord let him live to go over "this Jordan." The story reads:

> And I besought the LORD at that time, saying, O LORD GOD, thou hast begun to shew thy servant thy greatness, and thy mighty hand: for what God is there in heaven or in earth, that can do according to thy works, and according to thy might? I pray thee, let me go over, and see the good land that is beyond Jordan, that goodly mountain, and Lebanon. But the LORD was wroth with me for your sakes, and would not hear me: and the LORD said unto me, Let it suffice thee; speak no more unto me of this matter, Get thee up into the top of Pisgah, and lift up thine eyes westward, and northward, and southward, and eastward, and behold it with thine eyes: for thou shalt not go over this Jordan (Deuteronomy 3:23-27).

I turn the pages to Deuteronomy 34:4-6. There, before the Lord, Moses died on the east side of Jordan. We all shall die in the will of God. It is just a question of when and how. None of us can escape. We shall grow old (if we outlive our youth) and die. The sentence of death has never been cancelled. The *last* enemy that is to be destroyed is death (I Corinthians 15:26; Revelation 20:14). To pray exception from this sentence is not faith but presumption. In God's sovereign purpose we shall die, but we shall not die until *He* wills our decease. When we die, it will be *His* gracious hands that open the door into the upper and better world. *He* has the keys of life and of death.

When that day comes, the hour of our heavenly translation and coronation, we are to glorify God in our yielded surrender. Jesus prayed in dark Gethsemane, "O my Father, if this cup may not pass away from me, except I drink it, thy will be done" (Matthew 26:42). He suffered and died upon the cruel tree in the sovereign purpose of God. Out of His death came life; out of His sufferings, salvation; out of His weakness, strength. He glorified God and redeemed us in His agony and death. The risen Saviour in turn said to His chief apostle, Simon Peter, "Verily, verily, I say unto

thee, When thou was young, thou girdest thyself, and walk-
edst whither thou wouldst: but when thou shalt be old, thou
shalt stretch forth thy hands, and another shall gird thee, and
carry thee whither thou would not. This spake he, signifying by what death he should glorify God. And, when he had
spoken this, he said unto him, Follow me" (John 21:18, 19).
Simon Peter is to die by outstretched hands; that is, by crucifixion.

This is the most cruel, agonizing form of execution ever
devised by the depraved mind of man. But what is God's
choice for Peter? Is it that he suffer and die in the most
horrible way possible? Yes. But there is more. "This spake
[Jesus], signifying by what death he should glorify God."
We glorify God not in our songs sung when all goes well,
when we are healthy and happy and affluent, when everything is going our way. An infidel can sing then. We glorify
God in our songs sung in the night, when the dark day
comes, when evil assails us, when we are afflicted, tormented, cast down to the ground. To praise God thus is to
be triumphant in the faith, to win the crown of glory. This
is the Christian way to meet sickness and death.

Chapter 25

The Gift of Speaking in Tongues

I Corinthians 14

6 Now, brethren, if I come unto you speaking with tongues, what shall I profit you, except I shall speak to you either by revelation, or by knowledge, or by prophesying, or by doctrine?

7 And even things without life giving sound, whether pipe or harp, except they give a distinction in the sounds, how shall it be known what is piped or harped?

8 For if the trumpet give an uncertain sound, who shall prepare himself to the battle?

9 So likewise ye, except ye utter by the tongue words easy to be understood, how shall it be known what is spoken? for ye shall speak into the air.

At one time there was a weekly, nation-wide television program featuring a crime buster. The series was immensely popular. In every story a situation was developed in which the star detective would say to a witness he was questioning: "Just the facts, Mister. Just state the facts." This is pre-eminently what is needed in a Scriptural discussion of the gift of speaking in tongues. "Just give us the facts, preacher. Just tell us the facts." With God's help, we shall do just this.

In three places in the Book of Acts, speaking in tongues is mentioned; namely, at Pentecost (Acts 2:1-11), in Caesarea (Acts 10:44-46), and in Ephesus (Acts 19:1-6). In Jerusalem, on the day of Pentecost, the outpouring of the Holy Spirit was attended by three miracles: one, the sound of a rushing, mighty wind; two, the sight of a great flame of fire that, descending, divided into tongues which burned above the heads of the apostolic witnesses; three, the hearing on the part of men from the nations of the civilized world, each in his own tongue, the wondrous words of God. The

208

gift of tongues at Pentecost was one in which the language spoken was understood by the different nationals. No interpreter was necessary. The languages spoken were *not* unknown tongues. They were the native languages of the hearing people.

This unusual phenomenon was repeated at Caesarea in the household of the Roman centurion, Cornelius. Simon Peter described the outpouring as "the like gift" as the apostles had experienced at Pentecost (Acts 11:17). Could it have been that in the household of the centurion there were soldiers, slaves, servants, and governmental officials from many of the nations of the Roman world? Could it have been that in their superlative, heavenly ecstasy they reverted each to his mother tongue in praising God for so great a salvation? It is a most commonplace psychological truth that in moments of extreme peril or delight a foreigner will exclaim in his native language "in which he was born," rather than in the later language he has more recently acquired.

Similar expressions of ecstasy were poured out before the Lord in the case of the twelve disciples of John the Baptist at Ephesus. When Paul met these twelve men, he immediately sensed that something was tragically wrong with their faith. He asked, therefore, the simple question, "Did you receive the Holy Spirit *when* you believed" (Greek, *pisteusantes,* not "since ye believed" as the King James version, but *"when* ye believed.") These men replied that they had never heard of the Holy Spirit. Now, John the Baptist preached the Holy Spirit (cf. Matthew 3:11). Why do these followers of John, then avow that they never heard of the Third Person of the Deity? For the simple reason that the true message of John had been lost as it was passed down from disciple to disciple to disciple. The John the Baptist movement continued alongside the Christian movement for many, many years. When these misled men, who were converts of the converts of the converts of John the Baptist, heard the saving message of the Son of God they received the mercy of the Lord Jesus, they were baptized; and when

Paul in prayer and consecration laid his hands upon their heads, they broke forth in marvelous praises to God. As at Caesarea, did each speak in his own native tongue? Ephesus was a polyglot city and each man could have come from a different part of the Roman world. In their celestial joy the dozen men spoke in languages (plural) and prophesied (exhorted in the faith unto edification, spoke by holy inspiration).

The Unknown Tongues of Corinth

Aside from these three instances in the Book of Acts, one other place in the New Testament mentions the phenomenon of speaking in tongues. It is in Paul's long discussion of the gifts of the Spirit in I Corinthians 12:1-14. In I Corinthians 12:10 Paul names one of the *charismata* as being "divers kinds of tongues." In I Corinthians 14:1-40 the Apostle discusses this gift. Apparently, the speaking in tongues that characterized the assembly of the Corinthian Church was totally unlike the miraculous gift at Pentecost. At Pentecost the disciples spoke in known, understood languages. No interpreter was needed. At Corinth the language was unknown. Paul writes in I Corinthians 14:2: "He that speaketh in an unknown tongue speaketh not unto men, but unto God; for no man understandeth him." Again, Paul says in I Corinthians 14:14: "For if I pray in an unknown tongue, my spirit prayeth, but my understanding is unfruitful." For this reason the speaker in an unknown tongue had to have by his side one who had the gift of interpretation (I Corinthians 14:27, 28), or else he had to be given the gift of interpretation himself (I Corinthians 14:5, 13).

This outbreak of speaking in unknown tongues at Corinth is an amazing development. It is utterly unlike anything we have ever witnessed before in the kingdom of God. The phenomenon is not in the Old Testament. At times and in places the saints of the Old Testament were filled with the Holy Spirit as well as the saints of the New Testament, but never in their lives is seen anything like this. All the other gifts of the Spirit are seen in their lives, but not this. The phenomenon is not seen in the life and experience of our Lord Jesus. He was filled with the Holy Spirit (Luke 3:21, 22; 4:1, 14, 18, etc.). All the other gifts of the Spirit can be found in Him beautifully, gloriously. But not this. Nor can I imagine, in my wildest imagination, the blessed Saviour speaking in unknown tongues. It does not fit. It does not become Him. He never did it. Never. Nor is such a phenomenon mentioned in any of the gospels. The most spiritual book of the New Testament, the gospel of John, never refers to it, nor even approaches such a thing.

The gift of speaking in tongues is not found in the charismatic lists in Romans 12:6-8; Ephesians 4:11. With the exception of this passage in I Corinthians, the gift is never referred to in any of the epistles of Paul. It is not mentioned in the pastoral letters (I, II Timothy, Titus), it is not mentioned in the Book of Hebrews, it is not mentioned in the General Epistles (James, I, II Peter, I, II, III John, Jude), and it is never mentioned in the Revelation. With the exception of Corinth, the phenomenon is never seen in any of the churches of the New Testament; it is not in the churches of Macedonia, Achia, Judaea, Samaria, Asia, Rome, or any other place. It is seen only in the church at Corinth, a congregation that Paul called "carnal" (I Corinthians 3:1-3), and a people whom Paul described as "babes in Christ" (I Corinthians 3:1). The gift of tongues was not nearly so prominent in the early churches as those who advocate it would have us believe. At the most, it was a rare phenomenon found only in a few places, and, as far as we know, in only one church, and that not a spiritual church but a carnal one filled with every problem and disorder.

A Problem to the Apostle Paul

"Just the facts, preacher. Just give us the facts." Let us look at I Corinthians 14:1-40 and write down the plain facts. As we read the discussion, one fact stands out above all others. It is this: speaking in tongues is plainly a problem. The church is having serious trouble with it and Paul is wrestling with it (cf. I Corinthians 14:23, 39). If the church at Corinth had been giving itself to prayer, to praise, to love, to soul-winning, to intercession, to sacrifice, to giving, or to any one of a thousand other Christian virtues, the Apostle would have written them words of deepest, sincerest commendation. But *this!* This is a problem and a heavy one. The discussion of Paul is not a list of exhortations to speak in tongues, but a long enumeration of restrictions against the practice. The Apostle is not encouraging the Corinthians to exercise the gift but to refrain from its use. He is not presenting a set of rules to glorify the congregation in tongue-speaking, but he is rather laying down stringent regulations to restrain this thing that has broken out in the church. Paul is hedging the gift on every side.

Let us cite here every sympathetic word of toleration that Paul writes concerning the exercise of tongue-speaking and see if he does not qualify the use with an appeal for something else. In I Corinthians 14:4 the Apostle writes, "He that speaketh in an unknown tongue edifieth himself." Then, he writes the better alternative, "But he that prophesieth edifieth the church." In I Corinthians 14:5 he writes, "I would that ye all spake with tongues." Then he qualifies the sentence with this addendum: "But rather that ye prophesied: for greater is he that prophesieth than he that speaketh with tongues." In I Corinthians 14:18 the Apostle says, "I thank my God, I speak with tongues more than ye all." (There is no record that he ever used the gift. Could he be referring to his messages to the different nations to which God sent him as an apostle to the Gentiles?) Then, he qualifies this startling statement with the most stringent avowal of all: "Yet in the church I had rather speak five words with my understanding, that by my voice I might teach others also, than ten thousand words in an unknown tongue." There is one other passage of toleration in this Corinthian discussion. It is I Corinthians 14:39, where the Apostle says: "Forbid not to speak with tongues." But in the same sentence he again qualifies the permission with an earnest alternative, "Wherefore, brethren, covet to prophesy [not to speak in tongues]."

Having written down every word of toleration on the part of the Apostle Paul concerning speaking in unknown tongues, now we shall look at some of the vigorous statements he uses against the practice. The first is I Corinthians 14:19: "Yet in the church I had rather speak five words with my understanding, that by my voice I might teach others also, than ten thousand words in an unknown tongue." These are tremendous odds — five to ten thousand! This would be enough to allay the practice forever in the judgment of any ordinary, fair-minded person. The practice has no place in the church.

Another heavy, uncompromising mandate of the Apostle is I Corinthians 14:34, 35. Under no conditions is a woman to speak in an unknown tongue in the church. In this passage on tongue-speaking, Paul says: "Let your women keep silence in the churches: for it is not permitted unto them to speak; but they are commanded to be under obedience, as also saith the law. And if they will learn any thing, let them ask their husbands at home: for it is a shame for women to speak in the church." What does the Apostle mean, "It is a shame for women to speak in the church"? In I Corinthians 11:3-10 he had just given instructions how the women were to dress when they prayed or when they prophesied in the church. Now, here in I Corinthians 14: 34, 35, he excludes their speaking in no uncertain terms. Has he lost his mind? Is he stupid? Has he already forgotten what he has just written? No, not at all. What the Apostle is saying is most plain and most pertinent. These verses on women not speaking in the church are imbedded in the middle of this chapter on speaking in tongues. He is not interdicting women's praying or prophesying in public worship (he had already given directions permitting that in I Corinthians 11:3-10); he is interdicting their speaking in *tongues* in public worship. The woman is not to do it. But why is the Apostle so severe about women exercising the gift of tongue-speaking. Here again the answer is plain.

In front of the ancient city of Corinth was the deep blue sea. Behind the city of Corinth was the steep, high Acro-

Corinthus, an Acropolis far more prominent than that in Athens on which was built the Parthenon. Crowning the imposing Acropolis at Corinth was a magnificent temple to Aphrodite (Latin, "Venus"). The Greek goddess of love and beauty was worshiped with sexual orgies. The temple prostitutes who were used in these orgies of worship worked themselves up into ecstatic frenzies as they followed their heathen, immoral rituals. The sight of frenzied women speaking in unknown tongues in their dedication to immorality was a common one in the days of Graeco-Roman culture. Paul's abhorrence of such speaking is explicable and obvious. Paul assumes that even strangers walking by an assembly of God's people, seeing and hearing the women talking in unknown tongues, would immediately say: "What have we here; a little colony of Aphrodite? Let us go in and enjoy the sensual pleasure." "No," said the Apostle, "a thousand times no! When it comes to speaking in tongues, let your women keep silence in the churches. It is a shame [mark this word 'shame'] for women to speak in unknown tongues in the church." That interdiction still stands, unremoved. The hysterical, unseemly excess of tongue-speaking women in public worship is a reproach to the name of the Lord.

A Sign to the Jewish Nation

In I Corinthians 14:21, 22 Paul discusses the purpose of the gift of speaking in tongues. He says that it is a sign to the unbelieving Jewish nation. From the Old Testament (from "the law" as Paul here calls the entire Hebrew Scriptures) he quotes Isaiah 28:11, 12 regarding the refusal of Israel to hearken to Jehovah when He spoke to them in plain, understandable language. "Therefore," said the Lord God to the people of Israel, "since you will not hear me when I speak to you in clearness and simplicity in your own tongue, I shall now speak to you in languages which you cannot understand." (In the historical situation in which Isaiah is delivering the prophecy, God says He will speak in the foreign, strange languages of the Assyrians and the

Babylonians, who were used by the Lord to chasten His disobedient people, Israel.) Paul takes this passage from Isaiah to show that speaking in tongues was a *sign* to the lost, Christ-rejecting nation of Israel. This can be easily seen in the signs at Pentecost given to the men of Jerusalem and Judaea (Acts 2:14). Of the three miraculous attestations of God to the reality of the heavenly outpouring of the Holy Spirit, one was the gift of speaking in "other" tongues. We see this attestation of heaven's will in the marvelous miracle of tongues that confirmed the inclusion of the Gentiles into the body of Christ at Caesarea. The proof to the Jewish brethren at Jerusalem that the Gentiles were to be also a part of the salvation of our Lord was seen in the sign of tongues. So writes Luke in Acts 10:44-48. So said Simon Peter in his report to the Jewish church at Jerusalem in Acts 11:15-17. The marvelous gift of speaking in these languages was a *sign* to the disbelieving nation of Israel.

But to the heathen, pagan, unbelieving Gentiles the phenomenon is anything but a sign. To the Gentile world it was plain idiocy. Paul continues in I Corinthians 14:23-25: "If therefore the whole church be come together into one place, and all speak with tongues, and there come in those that are unlearned, or unbelievers, will they not say that ye are mad? But if all prophesy, and there come in one that believeth not, or one unlearned, he is convinced of all, he is judged of all: And thus are the secrets of his heart made manifest; and so falling down on his face he will worship God, and report that God is in you of a truth." Look at this passage carefully. The Apostle avows that if a pagan unbeliever walking down the streets of Corinth passed by an assembly of the Church and, stopping by, saw and heard them speaking in tongues, that pagan would certainly say, "Ye are mad." The Greek word translated "mad" is *mainomai,* which means, "to be insane," "to rave as a madman." Is not this obvious? Could you imagine Paul on Mars' Hill, speaking before the Areopagus (the Supreme Court of the Athenians) in an unknown tongue, and Silas by his side doing the interpreting? Would they not have said that those two Jews were insane? The same effect is produced upon the pagan world today by those who would do such a thing. According to Paul, in I Corinthians 14:23, the effect produced upon the unbeliever is that we who name the name of Christ are raving madmen.

The Demand for a Sign

There were four sign gifts bestowed upon the witness of Christ during the transitional days of the Apostolic Age, while the New Testament Scriptures were being written. One of these sign gifts was speaking in tongues. When the authenticating necessity for the sign gift ceased, the phenomenon ceased. It was needed no longer. It had served its purpose. For us to seek to re-create the sign is not faith but presumption. In the days of Moses, God authenticated the law-giver with signs and miracles. With his rod, for example, he parted the Red Sea. What would you think of a people who said to Jehovah: "God, you did it one time; now let's see you do it again"? Elijah was taken up into heaven in a whirlwind. What would you think about a people who would demand of every prophet a like sign, that he be taken up into glory in a chariot of fire? "You did it one time, Lord; now do it again!" When Jesus was born, the angelic hosts praised God and a star led the Magi to the manger in Bethlehem. What would you think of a people who demanded that the signs be repeated for us to see? "Let us see that star and let us hear those angels praise God." At Pentecost and at Caesarea, and in a few other places, a sign was given to attest the marvelous outpouring of the Spirit. What about the demand that the authenticating sign be repeated and repeated and repeated? "Do it again, Lord. Do it again." The need for the sign ceased (and that most early) and the phenomenon ceased. It is now useless, just as useless as if someone went down to the Red Sea and divided it again with a miraculous rod. As Paul emphatically concluded in I Corinthians 13:8, "Tongues shall cease."

We have the complete Bible. We have the open Book before us, God's Holy Scriptures. The need now is for plain language, understandable language, simple language. Paul so exhorted in I Corinthians 14:6-12. Listen to the Apostle as he makes the most sensible appeal a man ever made: "Now, brethren, if I come unto you speaking with tongues, what shall I profit you, except I shall speak to you either by revelation, or by knowledge, or by prophesying, or by doctrine? And even things without life giving sound, whether pipe or harp, except they give distinction in the sounds, how shall it be known what is piped or harped? For if the trumpet give an uncertain sound, who shall prepare himself to the battle? So likewise ye, except ye utter by the tongue words easy to be understood, how shall it be known what is spoken? for ye shall speak into the air. There are, it may be, so many kinds of voices in the world, and none of them is without significance. Therefore if I know not the meaning of the voice, I shall be unto him that speaketh a barbarian, and he that speaketh shall be a barbarian unto me. Even so ye, forasmuch as ye are zealous of spiritual gifts, seek that ye may excel to the edifying of the church" (I Corinthians 14:6-12). This "sounding of the trumpet" reminds me of God's watchman in Ezekiel 33:1-11.

If you are an unbeliever, God calls you to faith, but not by signs, wonders or miracles. He will not use the parting of the Red Sea or the fire on Elijah's altar to speak to you. He will not use strange sounds or unearthly voices to speak to you. He will speak clearly, intelligently, understandably, by the Word. He will appeal to you in the Spirit of Isaiah 1:18: "Come now, and let us reason together, saith the LORD: though your sins be as scarlet, they shall be as white as snow; though they be red like crimson, they shall be as wool." He will call you minus tongues, minus signs, minus miracles. He will call you by your simply trusting Jesus.

Chapter 26

The Interpretation of Tongues

I Corinthians 14

13 Wherefore let him that speaketh in an unknown tongue pray that he may interpret.

27 If any man speak in an unknown tongue, let it be by two, or at the most by three, and that by course; and let one interpret.

28 But if there be no interpreter, let him keep silence in the church; and let him speak to himself, and to God.

Of the four charismatic sign gifts introducing the new Christian era, listed by Paul in I Corinthians 12:9 and 10 (the gift of healing, the gift of miracles, the gift of divers kinds of tongues), one is the gift of the interpretation of tongues. What is this "interpretation of tongues"?

If the "tongue" be a true foreign language, then to interpret it by one who knew the language would be no charisma, no grace-gift. Anyone, even an infidel familiar with the language, could do it. If the "tongue" be a true foreign language not understood by the speaker, and the interpreter does not understand it either, then we are witnessing a double miracle: to speak it and to interpret it. This is certainly a round about way to edify the Church, by means of a double-action miracle, a miracle of foreign speech followed by a miracle of interpretation. If the "tongue" be a series of ejaculations, broken and disjointed syllables, abrupt and exclamatory utterances (and the phenomenon in Corinth was this, I Corinthians 14:2, 4, 14) then the gift of interpretation consisted of turning what seemed to be meaningless utterances into words easy to be understood (I Corinthians 14:9). The interpretation could be made by the speaker himself if he had the gift (I Corinthians 14:5, 13), or, if he lacked the gift, by one who possessed it (I Corinthians 14:27, 28).

Trouble With Different Interpreters

Three things about the gift of interpretation are most noticeable in this discussion of Paul in I Corinthians 14:1-40. The first is this: Those who possessed the gift were well-known in the Church. No exercise of tongues was to be permitted in public if no interpreter was present (I Corinthians 14:28). The second obvious observation is this: One interpreter was looked upon as being capable and competent to interpret any tongue (I Corinthians 14:27). Whatever the number of tongue-speakers allowed to speak (Paul permitted three at the most), the interpretation was to be made by only one person. This leads to a third serious but painful conclusion: It is all too apparent that interpreters did not agree. When Paul appeals in all this outbreak that "all things be done decently and in order" (I Corinthians 14:40), and that "all things be done unto edifying" (I Corinthians 14:26), he names the sources of turmoil and dissension. He says the trouble is caused by the brethren who stand up in church with differing doctrines, revelations, tongues and interpretations (I Corinthians 14:26). It does not take much imagination to see what was happening in this disorderly church. When more than one interpreter was allowed to exercise his gift, those other interpreters did not always agree and trouble ensued. Therefore, the limitation Paul makes to *one* interpreter lest the church fall into a wrangle.

It would be most easy to choose sides in an altercation over whose interpretation of an unknown tongue was correct. Not understanding anything that was being said, anything could pass for the truth. But who would know? "For no man understandeth him," as Paul says in I Corinthians 14:2. A seminary graduate who had majored in Hebrew attended a tongues meeting in California. In the midst of the meeting he stood up and quoted by memory the first Psalm in the original language. After he had finished, the interpreter arose and solemnly, piously made known in plain

English what the brother had spoken in an unknown tongue. The interpreter made it an utterance, Spirit-inspired, about women prophesying in church. When the seminarian made known what he had done and what he had said, pandemonium broke loose. In such a Corinthian situation there is no limit to the possibilities of trouble. One sister might receive an utterance about the personal life of another saint in the sisterhood. There is no end to it, as Paul sorrowfully found in the troubled church at Corinth.

Paul's Interpretation of the Sign Gift

What is Paul's interpretation of tongues? In I Corinthians 14:19 he writes in no uncertain terms: "Yet in the church I had rather speak five words with my understanding, that by my voice I might teach others also, than ten thousand words in an unknown tongue." In I Corinthians 13:8-11 he writes of the cessation of the movement: "Charity never faileth: but whether there be prophecies, they shall fail; whether there be tongues, they shall cease; whether there be knowledge, it shall vanish away. For we know in part, and we prophesy in part. But when that which is perfect is come, then that which is in part shall be done away. When I was a child, I spake as a child, I thought as a child: but when I became a man, I put away childish things." Paul's use of verbs in I Corinthians 13:8 is most instructive and decisive. Of love, he says that it will never *ekpipto*, it will never "fall," "fail," (Greek, *pipto,* "to fall," *ek,* "from"). Of the gifts of prophecy, he says that they will be rendered useless (Greek, *katargethesontai,* future passive of *katargeo,* "to render useless," "to make inoperative"). After the writing of the New Testament Scriptures, the gift of the prophet to tell the Church what to do and what to believe will be no longer needed. Our appeal now is not to a man with the charismatic gift of prophecy but to the written Word of God. Of the gift of knowledge, Paul uses the same word, *katargethesontai.* The gift no longer will be needed to direct the Church in the knowledge of the Lord. We have the full, all-sufficient rule for faith and practice in the Holy Scriptures.

Prophecies will "fail" (the word used in the King James translation), not in the sense that they will break down but rather in the sense that they will become unnecessary, useless. Knowledge will "vanish away" (the translation of the King James version), not in the sense that it has no contribution to make but in the sense of the fragment being swallowed up in the whole. When we have the complete Word (written now in the Bible, or personally present at His coming), we no longer need a small, incomplete, unfinished portion.

When Paul comes to speak of tongues in I Corinthians 13:8, he not only changes the verb but he also changes the voice of the verb he uses. As with "prophecies" and as with "knowledge" we would have expected him to use the future passive *katargethesontai*. *Not so.* He uses a different verb, *pauo*, "to cause to cease," and he changes the voice from passive to middle, *pausontai*, which literally translated means "tongues shall make themselves to cease," or "tongues shall automatically cease of themselves." Phillip's translation of the verse goes like this: "If there are prophecies they will be fulfilled and done with, if there are 'tongues' the need for them will disappear, if there be knowledge it will be swallowed up in truth."

Most emphatically Paul avows that "tongues will automatically cease of themselves." In the next verse, I Corinthians 13:9, they have already ceased in his thinking, for he mentions the gift of prophecy and he names the gift of knowledge but he pointedly omits the gift of tongues. Tongues are needed no longer. This is not only seen as Paul writes in I Corinthians 13:9 but it is also vividly illustrated in his epistles written during the remaining years of his ministry. I Corinthians is one of Paul's earliest letters. It is preceded only by the two epistles to the church at Thessalonica. After Paul wrote I Corinthians, he wrote II Corinthians, but in this latter epistle he never refers to speaking in tongues. After Paul wrote I Corinthians, he wrote a letter to the churches of Galatia, but he never refers to tongues. After Paul wrote I Corinthians, he wrote the letter to the church at Rome, but he never refers to speaking in tongues. After Paul wrote I Corinthians, he wrote Philippians, and Colossians, and Philemon, and Ephesians, and the Pastoral Epistles of I Timothy and Titus and II Timothy, but in none of them does he ever mention speaking in tongues. Tongues is the first sign-gift that ceased. It ceased almost immediately. The sign belonged to the infancy of the Church. "When I was a child, I spake as a child, . . . but when I became a man, I put away childish things" (I Corinthians 13: 11). The Church grew up and no longer needed the sign. To re-create the useless gift is to seek to return to the babyhood of the assemblies of Christ. To the grown man, the rattle and the teething ring have no purpose. They have been rendered useless.

Facts Concerning Modern Glossolalia

Since Paul wrote his interpretation of speaking in tongues, almost two thousand years have passed. In reviewing that long history and in observing the phenomenon of modern-day glossolalia, I have a definite interpretation that comes from the depth of my own soul. These observations will be made in factual presentations. "Just the facts, Mister. Just give us the facts." There are five of these plain, clearly recognized facts to be seen in ecclesiastical chronology and in contemporary Christendom.

First fact. The basic doctrine that lies back of glossolalian practice is wrong. That doctrine is this: that speaking in tongues is the necessary evidence of the filling [they use the word "baptism"] of the Holy Spirit. This doctrine is in direct opposition to the distinct and emphasized teaching of the Word of God. In I Corinthians 12:13 Paul says that *all* the Christians at Corinth had been baptized by the Holy Spirit, had been added to the body of Christ. But in I Corinthians 12:28-30 Paul avows that all do not speak with tongues. If you have been saved, you have been made a member by Spirit baptism of the precious body of our Lord. "By one Spirit are we all baptized into one body" (I Corinthians 12:13). But whether you speak with tongues or not has nothing to do with that holy, heavenly baptism. The two are in nowise connected; neither is one the evidence of the other.

Again in Ephesians 5:18 we are emphatically enjoined to be filled with the Spirit. It is God's will that *all* be filled with the Spirit. But here, also, it must be observed in contradistinction to this injunction that we all be filled with the Spirit. The Apostle writes that we are *not* all given the gift of tongues. "Are all apostles? [No.] Are all prophets? [No.] Are all workers of miracles? [No.] Have all the gifts of healing? [No.] Do all speak with tongues? [No.]" (I Corinthians 12:29, 30). There is no such Scriptural teaching as that speaking in tongues is the sign of the filling ("baptism") of the Holy Spirit. It is a man-made doctrine and does not come from the Bible.

Second fact. In the years of my reading through Christian history and of my studying the lives of great men of God, I have never once found an instance where a mighty hero of the faith spoke in unknown tongues. Preachers, missionaries, theologians, pioneers, translators, evangelists, all have come under review, but glossolalia is never a part of their lives. John Wesley will describe his Aldersgate experience, but never will he approach such a thing as speaking in tongues. Charles G. Finney will write in his famous *Autobiography* the fillings of the Holy Spirit that came in waves over his soul, but never will he intimate that he spoke in tongues. Dwight L. Moody will describe his marvelous infilling of love that swept his very being, but never does he suggest that he spoke in tongues. R. A. Torrey will write in a book on the baptism of the Holy Spirit, but his words of experience are pointedly directed against glossolalia. There is no exception to this witness, whether the great man of God lived in the ancient or the medieval or the modern world. John Chrysostom (John the Golden-mouth), possibly the most eloquent preacher of all time and one of the most gifted commentators on the Scriptures, born in A.D. 345, pastor of the churches at Antioch and Constantinople, expressed even in his day puzzlement at Paul's account of the tongue-speaking situation at Corinth. He said: "The whole passage (I Corinthians 14:1-40) is exceedingly obscure and the obscurity is occasioned by our ignorance of the facts and the cessation of happenings which were common in those days but unexampled in our own." Glossolalia is always outside the circle of the life and experience of the great men of God who lived in Christian history.

Third fact. In the long story of the Church, after the days of the apostles, wherever the phenomenon of glossolalia has appeared it has been looked upon as heresy. Glossolalia mostly has been confined to the nineteenth and twentieth centuries. But wherever and however its appearance, it has never been accepted by the historical churches of Christendom. It has been universally repudiated by these churches as a doctrinal and emotional aberration.

The Amazing Way We Are Supposed to Receive the Baptism of the Holy Ghost

Fourth fact. Modern glossolalia is a bewildering development. In the last century (after a silence in tongue-speaking for hundreds of years) there appeared in England a man by the name of Edward Irving who presented himself as a prophet of God. He dressed like one (with long, uncut hair) and he looked like one (with a towering stature). He and his "Irvingites" began the tongue-speaking movement that has reached down to us today. Of him, rugged old Thomas Carlyle said, "God is evidently working miracles by hysterics."

The program of the glossolaliasts to teach us how to speak in tongues is something new for the books. A few days ago I received through the mail a tract concerning how to receive the "baptism" of the Holy Ghost and how to speak in unknown tongues. I quote from the tract: "How can I receive the Holy Ghost? All you have to do to be saved is to raise your hands up toward Heaven and turn your head up toward Heaven and begin praising God just as fast as you can and let your tongue go and let the Holy Ghost come in. Thousands of people receive the Holy Ghost this way. You can receive it too, if you will just let the Holy Ghost speak through your tongue." A book that I read, from a famous glossolaliast, gave specific instructions how anyone could receive the "baptism" of the Holy Ghost. "Raise up your hands and your eyes to heaven," he said, "and begin speaking words, sounds, syllables, and keep it up, faster, faster, faster, louder, louder words, more words, faster, faster, and it has happened! You have received the baptism of the Holy Ghost!" Seekers after the "baptism" are encouraged to remain in "tarrying meetings" in which they are taught to loosen the tongue by imitation of the leader in saying "ah-bah, ah-bah, beta, beta," etc. The leader will shake the lower jaw of a seeker to loosen it so that the gift will come. What am I to think about all of this? Is the Holy Third Person of the Trinity, the moving, mighty Spirit of God, thus controlled and directed by the loosening of the joints of the jaw? By the gibberish of senseless sounds? I am bewildered by the suggestion.

Fifth fact. As far as I have been able to learn, no real language is ever spoken by the glossolaliast. He truly speaks in an unknown and unknowable tongue. Tape recordings of those speaking in unknown tongues were played before the Toronto Institute of linguistics. After these learned men in the scieice of phonetics had studied the recordings, they said, "This is no human language." At another time, other tape recordings were played before a group of governmental linguists at our nation's capitol. These gifted men found the sounds unrecognizable. "What they speak is meaningless to the human ear," was their verdict.

Sixth fact. Wherever and whenever glossolalia appears, it is always hurtful and divisive. There is no exception to this. It is but another instrument for the tragic torture of the body of Christ. I have seen some of our finest churches torn apart by the practice. I have seen some of our churches that were lighthouses for Christ in a pioneer and pagan land destroyed by the doctrine. In a revival situation that promised many souls for Jesus and a true outpouring of the Holy Spirit, the leader decimated it all by beginning to speak in

tongues. He came to see me in Dallas. I said to him: "Had
you driven these many miles to come and see me to say, 'I
have been filled with the Holy Spirit, I have been led of the
Lord to give to the work of the Kingdom ninety per cent of
all I make and to live on the remaining ten per cent,' I would
have said, 'Praise God, Hallelujah!' Had you driven all the
way to Dallas to say to me, 'I have been filled with the Holy
Spirit, I have resolved to pray six hours every day,' I would
have said, 'Glory to God for such a commitment!' Had you
come these many miles to my study to say to me, 'I have the
visitation from heaven in my soul; I will win at least one
person to Jesus every day,' I would have said, 'Bless the
name of God for so meaningful a dedication!' But when you
come over these many miles to see me and you say, 'I have
received the baptism of the Holy Ghost, I am speaking in
tongues,' I reply, 'Oh, oh, oh! What a tragedy! The work
of the revival is ruined.' " And it was. No revival came.
Only trouble, disorder, and confusion, as at Corinth.

I close with the avowal of the Apostle Paul: "Yet in the
church I had rather speak five words with my understanding, that by my voice I might teach others also, than ten
thousand words in an unknown tongue" (I Corinthians 14:
19).

Chapter 27

The More Excellent Way
(Love and the Gifts of the Spirit)

I Corinthians 12

31 But covet earnestly the best gifts: and yet shew I unto you a more excellent way.

I Corinthians 13

1 Though I speak with the tongues of men and of angels, and have not charity, I am become as sounding brass, or a tinkling cymbal.

2 And though I have the gift of prophecy, and understand all mysteries, and all knowledge; and though I have all faith, so that I could remove mountains, and have not charity, I am nothing.

3 And though I bestow all my goods to feed the poor, and though I give my body to be burned, and have not charity, it profiteth me nothing.

13 And now abideth faith, hope, charity, these three, but the greatest of these is charity.

The location of the greatest "love chapter" in the Bible is most amazing. It is placed in the middle of Paul's long discussion on spiritual gifts. Herein is a special message in itself. A large part of the importance of the thirteenth chapter of I Corinthians lies in its contextual placement. It is not as though the author set out to write a hymn on love. That would have been worthy, but it has nothing to do with this passage. The chapter is an integral part of the Apostle's presentation of the meaning and use of the gifts of the Spirit. Chapter twelve is a discussion of the purpose of the gifts. Chapter fourteen is a discussion of the perversion of the gifts (particularly tongues). Chapter thirteen, the in-between chapter, is a discussion of the sublimest, highest uses of the gifts.

Chapter twelve of I Corinthians introduces the long dissertation on the *pneumataka* (literally, "the spirituals"), the *charismata* (literally, "the grace gifts"). Paul, in this chapter, describes the gifts and their relationship to the church as a whole. He begins in 12:1 by saying that we all should have clear knowledge concerning spiritual gifts. Paul faced the same problem in his day that we face in our day; namely, ignorance concerning spiritual gifts. I would suppose the subject is the least understood by Christian people of any of the significant doctrines of the Bible. There are two extremes: one is abuse, excess and fanaticism. The other is the opposite pendulum reaction of neglect and cold formalism. Satan, also, is most eager and delighted to counterfeit the true gifts of the Spirit, even as Jannes and Jambres (II Timothy 3:8) counterfeited the miracles of Moses and Aaron; as the false prophet Zedekiah opposed God's true prophet Micah, and as Simon Magus sought to use for money the marvelous outpouring of the Spirit.

Chapter thirteen of I Corinthians continues the discussion of the *pneumataka* begun in chapter twelve. In this passage Paul presents that love which alone gives the ministry of the gifts any value. Love in the use of the gifts of the Spirit is the fulfillment of every heavenly purpose, the remedy for every excess, and the protection against every error. Without love the gifts fail of their purpose.

Chapter fourteen of I Corinthians continues the discussion of the *pneumataka* begun in chapter thirteen. In this portion of the long section, the Apostle seeks to regulate the ministry of the gifts as they are exercised in the open assembly of the church, especially giving attention to the abuse of tongues.

The three chapters (I Corinthians 12, 13, 14) are inseparably linked. Chapter thirteen is not an interlude, as though the Apostle had burst into a song on love. It is an interlink between chapters twelve and fourteen in this discussion on the gifts of the Spirit. Chapter thirteen is not a digression or a change of direction regarding the subject. It is rather an intensification of the theme followed in chapters twelve and fourteen. Chapter thirteen is not a dissertation on love as such. The subject of chapter thirteen concerns the true motive for the use of spiritual gifts. The last verse of chapter twelve makes a plea for the more excellent "way" of blessedness in the use of the gifts. Every gift is to be baptized in love. The first verse of chapter fourteen follows almost the same Greek wording as is found in the last verse of chapter twelve. The gifts are to be subservient to the motive of love The chapter between twelve and fourteen, chapter thirteen, deals with the gifts in the hands of love, the gifts controlled by love, the gifts motivated by love. Without love the gifts are willful and wayward, inevitably and eventually ministering to selfish pride. Without gifts, love becomes cheaply sentimental and unoccupied. With both love and gifts, the Lord glorifies His Word through His servants.

Love the Motive for the Use of Spiritual Gifts

The great theme of I Corinthians 13 is that love must be the actuating principle back of any employment of spiritual gifts. It is love that renders the *charismata* blessed and profitable. Verse one avows that the gift of tongues, whether of men or of angels, however eloquent or fervent, will not profit or bless the speaker without love. "I [not the gift] am become as sounding brass [metal castanets] or a tinkling cymbal." Without compassionate sympathy for those listening, eloquence in speaking only accentuates the emptiness of the heart of the speaker. He sounds, and he is, hollow. There are those with no greatness but in forensic speech. There are those whose whole genius expires in a fray of words and in forms of easily forgotten rhetoric. Only love can give any real power to eloquence. The dead heart and the selfish soul need the live coals from off the altar of God's compassion to touch their lips. Otherwise, their speaking gift is empty vanity.

Verse two of I Corinthians 13 avows that the sublimest gifts of prophecy, knowledge, and faith are profitless to the possessor of the gifts without love. "I [not the gifts] am nothing." These greatest of all the gifts fail of their blessing unless love sets the possessor afire with a passion for help-fulness. "I am nothing," if I possess the gifts without love. We cannot get below or behind nothing.

Verse three of I Corinthians 13 speaks of the gift of phil-anthropy. Paul does not say that philanthropy in itself profits nothing, even though it is unaccompanied with love. A bequest of a million dollars will profit an institution whether bequeathed in anger to rob a hated son, or given in vainglory or ostentation. Philanthropy that blesses a good cause can be used as a selfish instrument to minister to one's hope to be known as a generous soul, or to advertise one's affluence, or to buy one's way into heaven, or to uphold one's image in a business community. But without love, the phil-anthropy profits *the giver* nothing. Andrew Fuller once asked an English nobleman for a donation to William Carey's mission endeavor. The nobleman flung in contempt a gold crown on the table in response to the appeal. Andrew Fuller returned it to the rich man, saying: "My Lord demands the heart. Without the heart, I cannot take it." The nobleman felt the rebuke. He accepted the returned gold coin, sat down at his desk and wrote out a generous check for the mission enterprise. "There," he said, "take this; this comes from the heart." James Russell Lowell well wrote:

> Not what we give, but what we share,
> For the gift without the giver is bare.

Paul even avows that the gift of the body in a flaming mar-tyrdom can be profitless to the sufferer unless the sacrifice is bestowed in love. Even martyrdom can be but an example of vainglorious (and empty) fanaticism. So many of the early Christian martyrs thus died, seeking for selfish pur-poses the martyr's crown.

The emphasis Paul makes on the necessity of love in the use of the gifts is presented with dramatic forcefulness. The Apostle holds before our gaze the image of a man whose gifts, graces, and endowments would combine in one person the eloquence of an Apollos (and of a John Chrysostom), the wisdom of a Solomon (and of a Plato), the vision and poetic insight of an Isaiah (and of a Shakespeare), the faith of an Abraham (and of a Martin Luther), the self-sacrifice of a Stephen (and of a Savonarola). Such an incomparably gifted personality! Yet Paul says that if he himself were that man, gathering into his own life all the gifts and graces of these men, it would profit him nothing without the motivation of love. (In his humility Paul arrogates to himself the image of the vain and profitless person. He says not, "*You* are nothing," but "*I* am nothing.")

The Characteristics of True Christian Love

The great Apostle now writes in I Corinthians 13:4-7 about the characteristics of true Christian love. He defines what this love is. In our English New Testament the word "love" is translated from a number of different Greek words. *Philagathos* is the Greek word for the good (Titus 1:8). *Philadelphia* is the Greek word for love for the brethren (Romans 12:10; Hebrews 13:1). *Philanthropia* is the Greek word for love for mankind (Titus 3:4). *Philotheos* is the Greek word for a lover of God. *Philosophia* is the Greek word for love of wisdom. *Phileo* is love for a friend. *Agape* (John 3:16; I John 4:8) is the Greek word for the highest, purest, Godliest love. There is yet another word in the Greek language that was commonly, currently used for love in those ancient times by the philosopher, the poet, the mythologist, and the man on the street. It is the Greek word *eros*. Eros was also the name of the god of love (Latin "Cupid"), the son of Aphrodite (Latin "Venus"). But the word is never found in the Bible. Its use in that ancient world was carnal, sensual, degrading.

The love Paul speaks of here in I Corinthians 13 is in a different world from sexual excitement and amorous affection. The word Paul uses is *agape,* the word used to describe God Himself (I John 4:8). The devoted, consecrated linguist, Jerome, in translating Greek Scriptures into the Latin Vulgate, refused to use the Latin *amor* as an equivalent for the Greek *agape*. The word amor had too many voluptuous overtures. Jerome, therefore, chose the Latin word *caritas* to convey the fulsome meaning. *Caritas* has the connotation of "dearness" in the sense of costliness, esteem, regard, preciousness. Jerome's choice then came into our King James English translation in the word "charity." It refers to the highest love known to God or man, like the love of Jesus for us on the cross (John 3:16).

In I Corinthians 13:4-7 Paul describes the holy and heavenly devotion meant by the word *agape* (love). Love, in Paul's definition, is not a weakness but a commitment that bestows strength and character. It is an affection that can sit up all night and say in the morning, "I am not tired." It is the kind of personal joy in service and sacrifice that made the fourteen years Jacob worked for Rachel "seem but a few days, for the love he had to her" (Genesis 29:20). It is the kind of forgiving compassion that causes Ananias in Damascus to come to the persecuting Saul of Tarsus with the loving words, *"Brother Saul . . ."* (Acts 22:12, 13). It is the kind of triumphant spirit that graced the dying testimony of Stephen when he prayed with his last breath for those who took his life, a martyrdom that shook Saul to the depths of his soul (Acts 22:20). This love is the very might and strength of God. It is the *agape,* the *caritas,* the "charity" of I Corinthians 13.

The Impermanence of Spiritual Gifts

In I Corinthians 13:8-13 Paul writes of the impermanence of spiritual gifts and the imperishable nature of love. In verse nine he describes the gifts as being fragments, pieces, portions of a greater whole. In verse ten he says that when the *teleios* is come, when the perfect, the mature, the complete, the full-grown is realized, the fragments of the immature will be no longer necessary. They have become useless. To make an acorn permanent would be to extinguish oak trees forever. To sacrifice an acorn is to get a forest full of them, trees with boughs hanging thick with them. So the gifts are ephemeral, transitional, transitory. They have a use in immaturity, but when maturity is achieved, they are un-necessary.

In verse eleven Paul avows that gifts cease in the sense that they are assimilated into the whole of which they are a part, as the child is done away in the man. The speech of the child (the gift of tongues) is no longer needed in the mature man (the church beyond its infant stage). The un-derstanding of the child (the gift of prophecy) is no longer needed in the full-orbed revelation of God (the church with the completed, written Word). The thinking of the child (the gift of knowledge) is useless in the maturity that ac-companies God's final, revealed will (the church with the fullness of inspired revelation). These gifts belong to the infancy, the babyhood of the church. In maturity they are no longer needed.

In verse twelve the Apostle looks forward to the final con-summation when all our stumblings and immaturities and incomprehensions are resolved in the perfect clarity of our Lord's full revelation, the Presence of the Saviour Himself. We see now as in an *esoptron,* a polished piece of bronze metal that reflects the image so imperfectly. The ancients had no splendid mirrors of silver-lined glass as we possess today. Their looking glasses were wavy, indistinct, shadowy. Thus they say "as in an *ainigma,*" as in an enigma," "as in an obscure thing." But someday, some glorious day, we shall see and know and understand fully and completely, even as God knows all things.

In verse thirteen Paul triumphantly declares that the three graces of faith, hope, and love shall endure forever, long after all the gifts have ceased and been lost in the full-ness of the revelation of God. Faith will be forever the basis for our enjoyment of our Lord. Hope will be forever the forward projection of our expectations and persuasions in God. Love will be forever and unchangeably that in which all things subsist, even faith and hope. Verily, God is love. Love is the greatest of the graces, abiding, imperishable, world without end. With the grace of love in our hearts, every gift of God is a blessing. Giving is a joy, service is a delight, and church is a bit of heaven. We shall not win souls nor mediate the preciousness (*caritas*) of Christ without love. A successful doctor may not love his patients. A clever lawyer may not love his clients. A rich merchant may not love his customers. A brilliant professor may not love his students. A professional preacher may not love his parishioners. But without love we can never win souls to Jesus nor worthily, beautifully exalt our Lord. Isaac Watts has placed in verse the dramatic words of the Apostle Paul.

> Had I the tongues of Greeks and Jews,
> And nobler speech than angels use;
> If love be absent, I am found
> Like tinkling brass, an empty sound.

> Were I inspired to preach and tell
> All that is done in heaven and hell;
> Or could my faith the world remove,
> Still I am nothing without love.

> Should I distribute all my store
> To feed the hungry, clothe the poor,
> Or give my body to the flame
> To gain a martyr's glorious name.

> If love to God and love to man
> Be absent, all my hopes are vain.
> Nor tongues, nor gifts, nor fiery zeal
> The work of love can e'er fulfill.

"And now abideth faith, hope, charity, these three: but the greatest of these is charity."

Chapter 28

The Fruit of the Spirit

Galatians 5

16 This I say then, Walk in the Spirit, and ye shall not fulfill the lust of the flesh.

17 For the flesh lusteth against the Spirit, and the Spirit against the flesh: and these are contrary the one to the other: so that ye cannot do the things that ye would.

18 But if ye be led of the Spirit, ye are not under the law.

19 Now the works of the flesh are manifest, which are these; Adultery, fornication, uncleanness, lasciviousness,

20 Idolatry, witchcraft, hatred, variance, emulations, wrath, strife, seditions, heresies,

21 Envyings, murders, drunkenness, revellings, and such like: of the which I tell you before, as I have also told you in time past, that they which do such things shall not inherit the kingdom of God.

22 But the fruit of the Spirit is love, joy, peace, longsuffering, gentleness, goodness, faith,

23 Meekness, temperance: against such there is no law.

24 And they that are Christ's have crucified the flesh with the affections and lusts.

25 If we live in the Spirit, let us also walk in the Spirit.

26 Let us not be desirous of vain glory, provoking one another, envying one another.

Seven times the Holy Spirit is named in this brief passage of Galatians 5:16-26. Among these instances Paul speaks of walking in the Spirit (5:16), being led by the Spirit (5:18), bearing fruit of the Spirit (5:22), and living in the Spirit (5:25). The text is written against the background of a struggle in our souls. The Apostle writes in 5:17, "For the flesh lusteth [Greek, *epithumeo*, "to desire," "to long for"] against the Spirit and the Spirit against the flesh: and these are contrary the one to the other." The human personality is not of one nature but two. Every man is both good and bad, both light and dark, both of flesh and spirit. This quality of life is greatly heightened in the child of God. Paul describes the torment of the conflict between the old nature of the flesh and the new nature of regeneration in Romans 7: 14-24, a passage ending with the agonizing cry, "O wretched man that I am! who shall deliver me from the body of this death?"

The Conflict Between the Old and the New Natures

Paul calls the old nature "the flesh" (Greek, *sarx*). He includes in the word the totality of our depraved, Adamic inheritance. The deep, disturbing depravity of man is tragically portrayed in every page of history and in the daily experience of every human life. We all know the drag of our fleshly passions. The new nature Paul calls the life of the Spirit. When we are born again, we have a new heart, a new love, a new commitment. But the old heart of sin and the old nature of depravity are still with us. Because we are saved does not mean that we are delivered from the passions of the flesh. As long as we live in these mortal bodies, we shall know the trials and temptations that come from the black drops of sin in our blood. Between our two natures there is constant warfare, the flesh against the Spirit and the Spirit against the flesh. Every man is a civil war in his own self. Yea, at the very heart of the universe there is conflict and strife. John writes most vividly in Revelation 12:7, "And there was war in heaven: Michael and his angels fought against the dragon; and the dragon fought and his angels." Nor will this dreadful conflict that involves us all be resolved until Satan is cast into hell at the consummation of the age.

For us to live in these mortal bodies is to know nothing but the agony of sinful conflict. Our worst enemy is ourselves. Augustine frequently prayed, "Lord, deliver me from that evil man, myself." All the fire the devil could bring from Gehenna could do us little harm had we not so much combustible fuel in our hearts. It is the powder in the magazine of our old natures that threatens our spiritual lives with daily disaster. Our perpetual foe is ourselves. Our worst sins are those that arise out of the depravity of our souls. Cain killed his brother Abel because God made a difference between the sacrifices of the two. The brothers of Joseph hated him because they had no coat of many colors. Saul the king sulked in his tent, eaten up of jealousy, as he heard the women of Israel sing, "Saul hath slain his thousands but David his tens of thousands." Judas, coveting for his mercenary life all he could retrieve out of a lost cause, sold his Lord for thirty pieces of silver. The elder brother, in the parable told by Jesus, refused to come into the house because the younger, prodigal son had been welcomed back home. It is a sorry picture, this picture of depraved human nature, this life of the flesh.

Look at Galatians 5:22. "But," Paul says in effect, "there is something more, there is something besides, there is something better." How meaningful that little word "but" can sometimes be, that distinctive conjunction, that dividing monosyllable! "But the fruit of the Spirit is love, joy, peace . . . ." Our evil natures may be capable of the worst and the darkest of sins, but the Holy Spirit of God within us is the power of heaven to make us fruitful unto righteousness. We who are saved can know also the glorious fruit of the Spirit.

Notice that in Galatians 5:19 Paul uses a plural word to describe the life of the flesh. "Now the works [plural] of the flesh are manifest." But in Galatians 5:22 the Apostle uses the singular to describe the life of the Spirit. "But the fruit [singular] of the Spirit . . . ." The works of the flesh are many, dark and devious. Paul names seventeen of them in this list recorded in Galatians 5:19-21, and after he has named the monstrous brood, he adds the words "and such like," as if to say he could have added five hundred more even more repulsive. The works of the flesh are a ferment of confused, contradictory, conflicting depredations. Each one but contends against another for an evil mastery. It is not so with the fruit of the Spirit. The fruit of the Spirit is one, singular. All throughout is consistent. One grace does not take away from another grace, but rather each one contributes to the richness and beauty of the whole. Whether known by the name of love or joy or meekness, yet all are one because of the Holy Spirit in our hearts.

The life that produces these marvelous graces is not of us but of God. They are not the product (Moffatt calls them the "harvest") of natural generation but of supernatural regeneration. In our natural, human strength we sometimes try to exhibit these graces. We obey laws, make resolutions, observe rules, enter periods of reformation, seek to make ourselves over. All these attempts at goodness only emphasize our ultimate failure. We are like the prisoner pardoned out of the penitentiary but back again after three months for the same offense. We in ourselves cannot change ourselves. If the tree is evil, the fruit is evil. But what we cannot do in ourselves, the Holy Spirit does for us. *He* is in the sanctifying business and He is the One who can remake our lives, giving us strength for weakness, victory for defeat, and enriching us with the nine graces of holy blessedness. But the life that exhibits this fruit must be rooted in the Spirit, quickened by the Spirit, alive in the Spirit. There is never fruit out of a dead tree. Dead posts produce no fruit. These beautiful graces cannot be outwardly hung upon a life like toys and ornaments upon a Christmas tree. Fruitage in the Spirit requires rootage in the Spirit.

The normal life of the child of God ensues in this heavenly fruit. We are not surprised to find apples on an apple tree or grapes hanging down from a grapevine. We would be surprised and disappointed if there were no apples on the apple tree and no grapes hanging down from the vine. In the parable told by our Lord in Luke 13:6-9, the husbandman who found no figs on his fig tree for three years demanded that it be cut down, "for why cumbereth it the ground?" In Matthew 21:18-20 Jesus cursed the fig tree that bare nothing but leaves. In John 15:8 our Lord said, "Herein is my Father glorified, that ye bear much fruit: so shall ye be my disciples." If we have been born again and if we love

God, we shall exhibit those nine graces, the loving fruit of the Spirit.

The Nine Gifts of the Spirit and the Nine Graces of the Spirit

There are nine gifts of the Spirit listed in I Corinthians 12:8-10. There are nine graces of the Spirit listed in Galatians 5:22, 23. What are the differences between the gifts of the Spirit and the graces of the Spirit? The differences are most apparent. The ninefold gifts of the Spirit are for power, service and ministry. The ninefold graces are for Christian character, for what the child of God is in himself. The nine gifts are distributed among the members of the congregation, one here, two there, three yonder. The nine graces are to be represented in every Christian. They are but facets of the same glorious gem. The nine gifts are sovereignly bestowed. We may ask for a gift, but the Holy Spirit chooses as to whether our request is accepted or denied. The nine graces crown all who walk in the Spirit. The Spirit does not choose among them. They all are ours — fully, richly, everlastingly.

A gift may enjoy perfect expression even though it is a solitary one bestowed upon the individual. But no grace can enjoy perfect expression if it is not accompanied by every other member in the list. Love, for example, is not complete if it is not accompanied by the grace of long-suffering. ("Love suffereth long," I Corinthians 13:4). Love is not complete if it is not accompanied by the grace of gentleness, kindness ("Love is kind," I Corinthians 13:4). Love is not complete if it is not accompanied by the grace of meekness ("Love vaunteth not itself, is not puffed up," I Corinthians 13:4). Love is not complete if it is not accompanied by the grace of temperance ("Love doth not behave itself unseemly," I Corinthians 13:5). Love is not complete if it is not accompanied by the grace of peace ("Love is not easily provoked," I Corinthians 13:5). Love is not complete if it is not accompanied by the grace of goodness ("Love thinketh no evil," I Corinthians 13:5). Love is not complete if it is not accompanied by the grace of joy ("Love rejoiceth not in iniquity, but rejoiceth in the truth," I Corinthians 13:6). Love is not complete if it is not accompanied by the grace of faith ("Love believeth all things," I Corinthians 13:7). The nine graces are inseparable. To possess one, we must surely possess all. They are the fruit (singular) of the Spirit.

When we look at these nine graces closely we notice that they easily fall into three groups of three. The first triad pertains to our relation to God: love, joy, peace. The second triad depicts our relation to others: longsuffering, gentleness, goodness. The third triad presents our relation to ourselves: faith, meekness, temperance. These three trilogies are both Godward and manward. They are both perpendicular and horizontal. They come down from God and flow toward man.

The Fruit of the Spirit Described in the Nine Graces

The first of the nine graces is love (Greek, *agape*). Love heads the list, as we know after reading I Corinthians 13: 1-13. This is in perfect keeping with the teaching of our Lord in Matthew 22:35-40: "Then one of them, which was a lawyer, asked him a question, tempting him, and saying, Master, which is the great commandment in the law? Jesus said unto him, Thou shalt love the Lord thy God with all thy heart, and with all thy soul, and with all thy mind. This is the first and great commandment. And the second is like unto it, Thou shalt love thy neighbour as thyself. On these two commandments hang all the law and the prophets." Paul later added, "Love worketh no ill to his neighbour: therefore love is the fulfilling of the law" (Romans 13:10). Our Saviour said to His disciples, "By this shall all men know that ye are my disciples, if ye have love one to another" (John 13:35). Love is of God for verily "God is love" (I John 4:8). Love makes us want to do what once we felt we had to do.

The second grace is joy (Greek, *chara*). In the light of the New Testament this is an amazing virtue. Look at Paul's letter to the Thessalonians in I Thessalonians 1:6, where he speaks of that faithful congregation as "having received the word in much affliction, with joy of the Holy Ghost." Do those two words go together? *Affliction* and *joy*? The world would not think so. Late on a Thursday night, before He was to be crucified at 9:00 the next morning, Jesus spoke to His disciples about His "joy" (John 15:11; 16:22). What "joy" could there be in the agony of crucifixion? Hebrews 12:2 describes that amazing and heavenly phenomenon, "joy" in the presence of shame and suffering and death. When Paul and Silas were beaten until their backs were crimsoned in blood, when they were placed in stocks and in chains and thrown into the innermost part of a dungeon, at midnight they prayed and sang praises to God. What kind of "joy" was that? No wonder "the prisoners heard them" (Acts 16:25). The pastor of the church at Jerusalem, James, the Lord's brother, wrote in his epistle, "My brethren, count it all joy when ye fall into divers temptations [trials]" (James 1:2). It is the first thing that he said in his letter. What kind of a "joy" is this? Only the Christian knows. The world has merriment, laughter, entertainment, revelry, but only the Christian knows "joy." Bars and stone walls and fagots and persecution cannot take it from him. It is the joy of the presence of God in the soul.

The third grace is peace (Greek, *eirene*). Thus Paul writes in Romans 5:1, "Therefore being justified by faith, we have peace with God through our Lord Jesus Christ." This is "the peace of God which passeth all understanding," which keeps our hearts and minds through Christ Jesus (Philippians 4:7).

The fourth grace is long-suffering (Greek, *makrothumia*). In the presence of wrong and persecution, we are to be patient and full of forbearance. We are to wait on God for *His* justification (Romans 12:19). In a world of speed, we are to be slow to take offense and we are to leave vengeance in the hands of the Lord.

The fifth grace is gentleness (Greek, *chrestotes*). It is the kindness so beautifully spoken of in Ephesians 4:32, "Be ye kind one to another, tenderhearted, forgiving one another even as God for Christ's sake hath forgiven you."

The sixth grace is goodness (Greek, *agathosune*). Thus Barnabas is described in Acts 11:24, "For he was a good man, and full of the Holy Ghost and of faith." That would be a worthy epitaph upon the tombstone of any man.

The seventh grace is faith (Greek, *pistis*). This is the only one found in both the lists of gifts in I Corinthians 12:9 and the list of graces in Galatians 5:22. Faith, the gift, is for power, for doing great things in the name of the Lord (Mark 11:23; James 5:16-18). Faith, the grace, is for character, the gift of resting in God, free from cankering care and corroding anxiety. We exercise the gift of faith when we accept the promises of God and attempt to do great things for Him. We exhibit the grace of faith when we quiet our hearts before the Lord and trust in Him who is able to keep us forever.

The eighth grace is meekness (Greek, *praiotes*). In our bearing toward others, we are to exhibit mildness, gentleness. Thus Moses is described as being the meekest man in all the world (Numbers 12:3). Thus Jesus said the meek shall inherit the earth (Matthew 5:5).

The last and the ninth grace is temperance (Greek, *egkrateia*). The word means self-control. It is the victory of the Spirit over the flesh.

Someone has said these graces are a portrait of Christ. That is so true. But Paul was painting a portrait of us who name the name of Jesus. May God grant that the beauty of this life of the Spirit may shine forth in all of our ways to the glory of our blessed Saviour. Amen.